JESUITS AND RACE

JESUITS *and* RACE

A Global
History of
Continuity
and Change,
1530–2020

Edited by Nathaniel Millett *and*
Charles H. Parker

University of New Mexico Press | Albuquerque

© 2022 by the University of New Mexico Press
All rights reserved. Published 2022
Printed in the United States of America

ISBN 978-0-8263-6367-1 (cloth)
ISBN 978-0-8263-6368-8 (electronic)

Library of Congress Control Number: 2022933149

Founded in 1889, the University of New Mexico sits on the traditional homelands of the Pueblo of Sandia. The original peoples of New Mexico—Pueblo, Navajo, and Apache—since time immemorial have deep connections to the land and have made significant contributions to the broader community statewide. We honor the land itself and those who remain stewards of this land throughout the generations and also acknowledge our committed relationship to Indigenous peoples. We gratefully recognize our history.

Cover illustration: *Kunyu Wanguo Quantu* map of 1602 by Matteo Ricci
Designed by Felicia Cedillos
Composed in Minion Pro 10.25/14.25

Dedicated to our friend and colleague Phil Gavitt (1950–2020)

Contents

Illustrations

Acknowledgments

We would like to thank each of the authors who have contributed an essay to this volume. They have been unfailingly patient, professional, and committed to this important undertaking. Thank you to Routledge for allowing us to reprint Nathaniel Millett, "The Memory of Slavery at Saint Louis University," *American Nineteenth Century History* (Winter 2016): 329–50. The History Department at Saint Louis University kindly paid for the reprint and indexing for which we are grateful.

Introduction

Jesuits and Race from the
Sixteenth to the Twenty-First
Centuries

NATHANIEL MILLETT AND CHARLES H. PARKER

IN THE FALL OF 2015, students at Georgetown University began to pressure the administration to address the ugly history of enslavement and trafficking by the Jesuits who ran the school since its inception. The most notorious episode occurred in 1838, when university presidents Thomas F. Mulledy, S.J., and William McSherry, S.J., sold 272 slaves from the Maryland province to plantation owners in Louisiana to keep the university financially solvent. Though a number of universities had already acknowledged their complicity in the slavery regime of the United States, the fact that a Jesuit institution— and a highly prestigious one at that—sold slaves, including children, to the killing fields of the Deep South exposed the contradictions between the core Jesuit value of charity and the inhumanity of financial expediency. At roughly the same time, faculty and administrators at Saint Louis University, also a Jesuit institution, began to delve into the story of slaveholding and trafficking in the Missouri (Jesuit) Province and the school. Subsequently, traces of Jesuit slave-trafficking networks from Maryland through Saint Louis down to New Orleans and Mobile have begun to emerge. Both universities have launched memory and reconciliation projects dedicated to recovering material about enslaved peoples at their campuses and locating descendants. Both institutions have promised restitution. Thus far, precious little fragments of information have come to light beyond names, dates, and mercantile data. The historical record, it seems, often conspires with history writers to conceal, forget, or misremember.[1]

Growing out of these revelatory moments, *Jesuits and Race: A Global History of Continuity and Change, 1530–2020* seeks to contribute to our understanding about the tensions between Christian universalism, hierarchy, and exploitation in relation to conceptions about race that produced such profound misery and death. This volume does not seek to trace back in time the attitudes that gave rise to slaveholding at these Jesuit universities. But the conditions at Georgetown and Saint Louis do provide a point of departure for an investigation into a historical legacy. Neither is the intent to show that Jesuits were more prejudicial or less so than their contemporaries. In fact, these essays show that Jesuits fell along a spectrum, from promoting universal human equality on one end, to embracing the hierarchies sanctioned by notions of racial difference on the other, to coming down somewhere in the murky middle. For example, Emanuele Colombo's treatment of disagreements among Jesuits about the status of New Christians (Christians of Jewish and Muslim ancestry) in Iberia and the Americas highlights the distinct racial attitudes that animated these debates. In a similar vein, Erin Rowe calls attention to the remarkable discussion of the afterlife by the Spanish Jesuit Martín de Roa, who argued in the early seventeenth century that the resurrected bodies of Africans would remain black in heaven. Yet, the remarkability of Roa's contention derived from its rarity, including among Jesuits.

By virtue of their global presence in missions, imperial expansion, and education, Jesuits offer a useful portal to examine the oscillating attitudes about race and difference in patterns of estrangement and assimilation, enfranchisement, and coercion with people from Africa, Asia, and the Americas. As John McGreevy notes in his epilogue, the Society's long history enables a team of scholars to examine patterns and trajectories over an extended period of time. The essays in this collection bring together case studies from around the world as a first step toward a comparative analysis of Jesuit engagement with racialized difference.

The authors drill down into labor practices, social structures, and religious agendas at salient moments during the long span of Jesuit history. Founded in 1534, the Society of Jesus quickly developed into the most extensive and prodigious missionary order in the early modern period. Jesuit missions flourished on every inhabited continent and played a prominent role in the globalization of Catholic Christianity. Jesuits came into their own from a small band of pilgrims to a vast corporation with an international reach. At the same time, peoples around the world were engaging with one another more directly and at an unprecedented level in world history. Colombo and Rowe illustrate how various Jesuit intellectuals sought to reconcile a growing sense of racial complexity with traditional theoretical understandings of the human body and the human soul. Situating his research within this age of proselytization, Liam Brockey charts Jesuit acquiescence to enslaved labor in China; Susan Deeds tracks the growing racialization of genealogy in northwest Mexico; Andrew Redden puzzles out categories of human difference in Chile; and Michelle Molina explores the racial hierarchies that were folded into the sacramental order upheld on Jesuit haciendas. Through the twentieth century, Jesuits continued to direct thousands of schools, universities, and parishes across the world. In doing so, Jesuits interacted in complex ways with millions of Indigenous and disenfranchised peoples. In these contexts, Nathaniel Millett, Sean Dempsey, S.J., and James O'Toole examine Jesuit entanglements with race, civil rights, education, and equal rights in the United States during the Cold War. Millett in particular shows how some Jesuits in the twentieth century were only too eager to reimagine the Order's involvement with African Americans.

The global presence of the Society meant that Jesuits had a virtually unrivaled view into questions of race across the early modern and modern worlds. Functioning as cross-cultural brokers in an increasingly interconnected world, Jesuits represented alien European values to local societies and in turn deciphered unfamiliar overseas cultures to Western audiences. Jesuits were also agents of empire and colonization and often aligned themselves with the heavy-handed repression that imperialism entailed. In the nineteenth and twentieth centuries, Jesuits have remained deeply embedded in communities around the world as pastors, teachers, intellectuals, and spiritual directors. Over this long period, Jesuits ran the gamut from slave traffickers on one end to ardent advocates of social justice for Indigenous peoples marginalized in the processes of imperialism, colonialism, and Jim Crow on the other.

Within the immense scholarship on the Society of Jesus over this vast period, the attention to race appears rather localized and largely related to studies of enslavement and discrimination. Academic study pertaining to Jesuits and race thus far falls into two large subfields: imperial expansion from the sixteenth to the twentieth centuries and civil rights struggles in the twentieth century. Jesuit missionaries rode the imperial wave of the Catholic colonial powers, establishing missions across the Americas, Africa, South and Southeast Asia and Japan (to 1613). Ming and Qing emperors welcomed Jesuits at the imperial court, which enabled them to make inroads throughout China until the mid-eighteenth century. Many books, such as John M. Monteiro's *Blacks of the Land* (1994) and Bronwen McShea's *Apostles of Empire* (2019), have attested to the central roles that Jesuits played in the development of colonial policy and administration. The raison d'être for Jesuit engagement in colonialism, of course, was the pursuit of conversion, which pulled them into complex webs and often compromising circumstances that included warfare with Indigenous societies and enslavement of non-European peoples. Despite a few dissenting voices, Jesuits for the most part embraced, in principle, all dimensions of European cultural, economic, and political expansion with little quandary over what modern observers understand as their essential contradictions. Namely, the universal reach of Christian charity and spiritual equality stood at odds with enslavement and exploitation. These contradictions did not end with the early modern era. Through the nineteenth and first half of the twentieth century, most Jesuits and the larger Order usually sided with the Catholic Church, national and local governments, and white, mainstream opinion on questions of race and racial justice while simultaneously working closely with nonwhite peoples across the globe. This time, however, the backdrop was not slavery, Indigenous displacement, and empire, but rather world wars, the Cold War, the Civil Rights Movement, and decolonization. While there were exceptions, by the second half of the twentieth century, especially after Vatican II, Jesuits came to be reliable champions of racial justice, particularly in the United States and Latin America.

Several trends have come to the fore in scholarship on these interactions and entanglements. One is the well-known Jesuit penchant for assimilating Christian teachings with established cultural traditions in order to make headway among Indigenous peoples. Matteo Ricci and Ferdinand Verbiest allowed Chinese converts to practice Confucian rites; Robert de Nobili dressed as a Brahmin and accommodated the caste structure in South Asia. Jesuits not only wished to appear on equal footing with Native elites, but they also worked to conflate Christian saints, notably the Virgin with the Mexican lunar goddess Tonantzin and Saint Anne with Toci, an Aztec deity. The Christianization of Native symbols, rites, and sacred figures allowed for varying degrees of Indigenous influence in the expressions of Catholic Christianity in Jesuit theaters of mission. Openness to Native spiritual potential was nowhere more evident than in the beatification of the Mohawk convert Kateri Tekakwitha, championed by Claude Chauchetière in the 1680s. Karin Vélez even shows how Jesuits promoted the Catholic cult, the Holy House of Loretto, to foster a transatlantic Catholic community that brought together Italians, Canadians, and Bolivians through "mythohistory."[2]

Jesuit writers from José de Acosta in Peru to Alonso de Sandoval in Cartagenas, to Martín de Roa in Seville emphasized the humanity of all peoples and their ability to experience salvation and live as Christians. In *De instauranda Aethiopum salute* (*On restoring Ethiopian salvation*; 1627), Sandoval argued for the dignity of Africans shipped through Cartagenas into the haciendas and mines of Spanish America. Influenced by Acosta and other Jesuit observers in South America, Sandoval attempted to distinguish ethnic characteristics of "Ethiopians" and to describe their deprivations. He gave primary attention to the spiritual dignity of Africans and Native Americans and pointed out abuses they suffered at the hands of slave traffickers. Sandoval called on fellow Jesuits to see Christ's presence in African slaves and to work at saving the white souls embodied in black bodies. Martín de Roa, as Erin Rowe illustrates in her essay, went a step beyond Sandoval in characterizing blackness, arguing that black Christians would retain their skin color, albeit without any "defections," in their resurrected bodies. Black bodies in heaven would show forth the glory of God in the diversity of redeemed humanity.

Yet these and other Jesuit writers stopped short of applying the tenets of spiritual dignity and equality affirmed by the Gospel to the material concerns of this life. The eighteenth-century Jesuit manual on hacienda management (*Instrucción que han de guardar los hermanos administradores de haciendas del campo*) analyzed by Michelle Molina assumed that coerced servitude harmonized quite well with pastoral care for the enslaved. Sandoval might have criticized the slave trade and its brutality, but he tempered his disdain so that he might give attention to the spiritual care of the enslaved. As many other theorists, he believed in the legitimacy of turning prisoners in a just war into slaves, as an act of mercy, rather than executing them. A colonial judge in Quito in 1592 also justified the trade "to save them [these wretches] from Guinea's fire and tyranny & barbarism and brutality, where without law or God, they live like savage beasts."[3] Sandoval and other Jesuits were somewhat skeptical about the African wars that produced so many enslaved prisoners, but the most daring were quite tepid in their disapproval of the transatlantic enslavement system.[4] Likewise, Roa accepted contemporary ways of thinking that gave meaning to difference and that manifested themselves in corporal disposition. He understood it as self-evident and indisputable that whiteness connoted perfection and goodness, whereas blackness signified defection and evil. As Liam Brockey demonstrates, Jesuits in East Asia, such as Francis Xavier, Luís de Almeida, Alessandro Valignano, and André Palmeiro, also accommodated themselves quite readily to enslavement based on local cultures of servitude. Manuel de Nóbriega, first Provincial of the Society in Brazil (1553–1559), defended basic human rights for most Native Americans against the depredations of colonialists and slave traffickers. Yet in particular circumstances, he showed no reticence in advocating enslavement for Native Americans and Africans if colonial needs dictated it. Conversely, Andrew Redden shows that Luis de Valdivia, rector of the Jesuit college in San Miguel (Chile), fought against the interests of the colonial establishment by opposing the enslavement of the Mapuche people in the early seventeenth century. For his part, Nóbriega followed the well-worn trope, also evident in the *Instrucción* at the center of Molina's essay, that enslavement would benefit these peoples, since they could be Christianized in servitude.[5] Jesuits followed through on this commitment, as the Order developed into the largest corporate slave holder in the Americas by the time of its suppression in 1773.[6]

Between 1773 and 1814 the Society of Jesus was suppressed within most European states and their empires, including Portugal, France, and Spain. During these years, which roughly overlap with the Age of Revolution, Jesuits were limited primarily to Prussia and Russia while maintaining a small presence in places like the United States and a shadowy one in regions where the priests had been officially outlawed. In 1814 Pope Pius VII restored the Society of Jesus. The Restoration occurred at a tumultuous time in world history: post-Napoleonic Europe lay in tatters, independence movements and slave rebellions swept the Atlantic World, nationalism was emerging as a new and intoxicating ideology, and the Industrial Revolution had begun in Great Britain, ushering in a radical departure in economic, social, and political life. Within a milieu that was defined by change and the upending of ancient hierarchies, early modern ideas about human difference were giving way to new and more insidious theories and beliefs. While postsuppression Jesuit numbers in Europe were less than they were previously, many of the priests returned to academic, educational, and scientific life. Others again became missionaries, this time accompanying an acutely racialized wave of European imperialism in Asia, the Middle East, and Africa. As had been the case during the early modern era, Jesuit scholars and missionaries in the century or so after the Restoration again grappled with contradictions that emerged from their role in these new imperial projects.

Across the postsuppression Atlantic World, Jesuits debated slavery and the Order's historical involvement with the institution. In the United States, the Order eventually sold all its slaves for moral and financial reasons. North American Jesuits now turned their attention from the rural South to Indigenous missions in the West, urban centers that were home to growing immigrant populations, and the creation of schools. Jesuits, who were frequently the targets of anti-Catholic and xenophobic bigotry, were also deeply conservative on matters of politics, social questions, and race—siding with Rome and secular officials on most matters. Thus, nineteenth-century American Jesuits sought to thread a needle in which they simultaneously missionized Indigenous people, ministered to some nonwhites including formerly enslaved men and women and many immigrants, created an empire of largely segregated schools, and strove, above all else, to maintain the devotion of white Catholics. As James O'Toole and Sean Dempsey illustrate in their essays, the Order would not confront this racist legacy until the second half of the twentieth century.

In nineteenth-century Latin America—both newly independent Spanish-speaking nations and Royalist Brazil—Jesuit fortunes and influence were greatly reduced from presuppression days. Across Latin America, Jesuit Reductions were now gone, as were plantation holdings. Many architects of post-Independence nation-building treated Jesuits with suspicion regarding the priests as conservative relics whose loyalties could not be trusted. Under this cloud and with far less financial and institutional support than earlier, Jesuits in Latin America resumed mission activity with Indigenous people, tended to the spiritual needs of many nonwhites, and expanded their involvement with education. In twentieth-century Latin America, like in the United States, racialized structures of power teetered, collapsed, and were reconstituted under the weight of economic transformations, world wars, the Cold War, expansion of education, generational change, and shifting political winds. From missions, lecture halls, pulpits, and schools, Jesuits were intimate witnesses to these transformations, sometimes disapprovingly, but at other times as advocates for racial justice. As is evidenced by this brief outline of Jesuit history, constructions of race in both the early modern and modern periods were inseparable from forms of exploitation and deprivation.

As a category of human differentiation, race has typically served to justify mistreatment and prejudice, coexisting with other types of hierarchical classifications and rationales for expropriation. The literary scholar and writer Margo Hendricks has challenged specialists to view racism within their own subfields as a "structural process" taking different shapes, codes, and expressions at different times.[7] Indeed, understandings of race have evolved significantly during the almost five-hundred-year history of the Society of Jesus. Consequently, it is worthwhile here to characterize some of those changes and the scholarly approaches to race across quite distinct historical periods of study.

The longstanding view identifies racial thinking as a modern phenomenon with its origins in the emergence of pseudoscientific theories about human anatomy from the late eighteenth and early nineteenth centuries. The rise of the biological sciences, the creation of universalizing human taxonomies, and the persistence of black slavery in European colonies and North America fostered a pseudoscientific construction of race that endured in mainstream thinking into the post-World War II era. Abolitionism regenerated discussions of Aristotle's human category of the "natural slave" that had influenced European imperialists in the sixteenth century. This discourse converged with the classification of humans into typologies that produced a comparative anatomy for a science of humankind. Nancy Stepan has described the consequences for race aptly: "The moral claim of the black and other so-called 'inferior' races, slave and free to equality of treatment [became] a matter not of ethical theory but of anatomy. . . . The appeal to nature in deciding what was in reality a moral issue was fatal. . . . Nature was now the arbiter of morality."[8] The so-called scientific basis for race studies was nothing more than biological racism that essentialized human differences based on physical markers, chief among them being skin color. Biological racism proved murderous on a monstrous level, leading to the eugenics movement, medical experimentation on African Americans (without their knowledge or consent), and the Nazi program of racial purity. Only in the 1950s did geneticists begin to show that race does not exist as a biological phenomenon.

Medieval and early modern scholars have generally exhibited caution on the topic of race in order to avoid shoehorning fixed modern conceptions into modes of interactions that varied considerably according to a wide range of factors. Henry Louis Gates contended in 1985 that race was a modern creation.[9] This view played itself out in Colin Kidd's transatlantic study on Protestant engagements with the Bible and race. Kidd posited that "race was not a central organizing concept of intellectual life or political culture during the early modern era . . . white domination did not rest on articulate theories of white racial superiority." Yet he did note the existence of racism and confirmed that Europeans deployed other rationales to exploit and deprive peoples from theories of land use to just war theory to the supremacy of the Christian faith.[10] Historians sought to avoid somehow reifying race as "an underlying physiological reality," but rather, stressed ethnicity as a "social and cultural artifact." Similarly, biologists even abstained from using the term "race" because its amorphousness made it ripe for misuse.[11]

In the last twenty years, a variety of historians and literary scholars working in premodern eras have devoted renewed attention to race and its application before the rise of biological racism. Their work has yielded important insights despite ongoing disagreements over the degree of continuity from the distant past into modernity. Among American and European scholars, the Jim Crow laws of the American south, the apartheid structures of South Africa, and the pograms of Nazi-occupied Europe remain a troika that overshadows work on race in much earlier periods. Many historians have resisted the temptation to interpret racial constructions as the "inevitable outcome of a long history."[12] Kathryn Burns cogently argued against "upstreaming contemporary notions of race to interpret" exploitation in previous eras, "which can lead us to gloss over the very dynamics of difference and discrimination we want to understand."[13] While many scholars take care not to draw too straight a line between race and racism from the premodern to the modern period, others have come to regard narratives of discontinuity with suspicion. David Nirenberg contended that "we pre-modernists too often rely on the questionable axiom that modern racial theories depend upon evolutionary biology and genetics, in order to leap to the demonstrably false conclusion that there exists a truly modern biological racism against which other forms of discrimination could be measured and judged innocent."[14]

Influenced by critical race theory, a cadre of literary scholars, social scientists, and historians has challenged basic assumptions of premodernists who skew toward discontinuity. Critical race theory emerged in the mid-1980s and sought to draw attention to and combat what practitioners recognized as the deeply embedded racism in modern society. Premodern critical race theorists, such as Margo Hendricks, advocate an activist study of race, which can "affect a transformation of the academy and its relationship to our world."[15] Critical race practitioners disparage traditional historical and literary scholarship around race as failing to see the embodied character of race in the premodern period and its continuities to the injustices of the present day; accordingly, scholars have succumbed to white supremacist assumptions and methodologies. The stakes are tangible and dangerous in the contemporary world as neo-Nazis and other white supremacist groups in the United States and Europe claim the Middle Ages as a utopia of Aryan purity and hail the Crusades as a glorious race war.[16] The frustration of critical race theorists is palpable, evidenced by the penetrating, uncompromising, and polemical criticism they heap on scholars they regard as ignorant or recalcitrant about these issues.

During the last two decades, a growing number of medievalists and early modernists—some as critical race theorists, but some not—have elucidated corporal features of human differentiation that presage modern biological racism. Suzanne Akbari has shown that Western theologians developed images of "Saracens" and Jews not just as religious opponents of Christendom, but also in "racial or ethnic terms." European intellectuals utilized humoral physiology, supposedly influenced by diet, climate, and internal disposition, to create body types of Muslims and Jews.[17] Cord J. Whitaker built on this analysis by drawing attention to the porous boundaries between internal constitution and external temperament in humoral pathology. Thus, blackness, taken since the fourteenth century as a signifier of sinfulness and evil, came to epitomize an essential and permanent marker of moral defection.[18] Craig Kolofsky contends that the polarity in the humoral body between the whiteness of Europeans and the blackness of others became much more pronounced at the beginning of the sixteenth century.[19] Geraldine Heng in a sweeping examination of "race-making" across the Middle Ages also captures the embodied character of ethnicity, yet she warns against an over reliance on skin color as the litmus test for race. She writes that "multiple locations of race [emerge] over a simple epidural focus: fanning out attention to how religion, the state, economic interests, colonization . . . have configured racial attitudes, behavior, and phenomena across the centuries."[20]

Rooted in humoral physiology, religious antagonism, and material opportunity, the medieval heritage around race underwent important alterations during the early modern age of empire building. Historians tracing this evolution and its seepage into the Atlantic have focused on late medieval and early modern Spain. It represented the most active theater of religious and racial antagonism, owing to the royal obsession with the conversion of Jews and Muslims in the fifteenth and sixteenth centuries. Authorities established blood purity laws (*limpieza de sangre*) that conflated religious belief and morality with embodiment. When Jews and Muslims did capitulate to the compulsion to convert, their "contaminated" blood rendered them constitutionally susceptible to heresy, apostasy, and immorality. It perhaps should not be surprising, as Nirenberg points out, that "race," "caste," and "lineage," intermingled in discourse about the intractable religious enemies of Christendom.[21] As the European colonial project got underway, theologians expanded the "curse of Ham" described in Genesis chapter 9, enabling propagandists in the seventeenth century to apply it to black Africans. As a cursed lineage, symbolized by blackness, Africans were marked to suffer enslavement. The darkness of blackness thus acquired biblical legitimacy and lineage in the Ham mythology.[22]

As the Spanish and other European powers colonized in the Atlantic world, new ethnic categories intersected with questions of blood purity and religious conversion: mestizo/a, criollo/a, mulatto/a, zambo/a. Many scholars, such as Kathryn Burns and Ruth Hill, have stressed that notions of race in the early modern colonial contexts were by no means fixed, but subject to very specific and local circumstances.[23] Race often functioned as an ancillary or subsidiary element in colonial subjugation. Patricia Seed, in her comparative study of European colonization in the Americas, argued that racism, as "the physical method of identification," became an imperial instrument when colonizers required units of labor in their domains. Colonial authorities, she shows, also employed other criteria, such as improper conduct or ineffectual possession, in the preemption of natural resources, to legitimize the implementation of European colonial designs.[24]

Early modern understandings of race appear as incongruous and perplexing in the sources and among the actors scrutinized in this volume as they have in other studies. Following Colin Kidd, Andrew Redden argues that any biological notion of race was negligible in Luis de Valdivia's letters. Race was absorbed into the conceits of civilizational hierarchy that for the Spanish justified the colonial subjugation of the Mapuche people. Yet Erin Rowe's treatment of Martín de Roa clearly affirms the "essential embodied nature of race," derived from humoral physiology and the centrality of the body in Christian salvation. Susan Deeds and Michelle Molina reconstruct race in colonial Mexico as an evolving, fluid concept that Jesuits used to essentialize differences for colonial and missionary purposes. Focusing on debates over whether New Christians could join the Order as priests or brothers, Emanuele Colombo points to the frustratingly amorphous links between corporality, moral capacity, and social ostracism. Jesuits excluded *conversos* and *moriscos* because of a preoccupied loathing of "blood impurity," which seems at the very least to approach a biological basis for racial exclusion.

Western ideas about race underwent a dramatic transformation in the nineteenth century with consequences that were profound. While eighteenth century writers such as Johann Friedrich Blumenbach had sought to divide humanity into distinct races based on things such as cranial measurements, and various Enlightenment thinkers had created racial taxonomies while debating monogenism versus polygenism, it was not until the nineteenth century that science—increasingly professionalized and university-based—came to exert great influence over the perception of human difference. Based on the claims of men such as Samuel Morton and Louis Agassiz, many academics, policy makers, and members of the public came to believe in a "scientific" definition of race that was rooted in biology. Believers held that race and racial differences between groups of people were natural phenomena that were manifested in varying levels of group-wide talent and ability. From this perspective, race represented an inescapable destiny for individuals and societies. Despite pushback from people as renowned as Charles Darwin, what has been remembered as "scientific racism" was a powerfully alluring ideology to defenders of slavery and then Jim Crow, advocates of empire, nationalists, antiimmigrant advocates, and anti-Semites.

By the early twentieth century, some of the earliest anthropologists such as Franz Boas began to argue that mainstream beliefs about race mistakenly linked biology with cultural and behavioral traits. Boas criticized the race-baiting, pseudoscientific arguments that scarcely concealed a white supremacist anxiety about uncivilized immigrants overrunning the United States and replacing the master race.[25] Boas's criticism remained a minority view in the United States where the racialized legal theory of separate but equal served as the foundation for segregation across a continent from which Indigenous people had been ethnically cleansed from ancestral homelands and was dotted with cities that teemed with recently arrived immigrants. Elsewhere in the West, scientific racism proved equally resilient to countervailing claims, in part explaining the tenacity with which Europeans clung to outdated empires and the ease by which Adolph Hitler coaxed the German people into a genocidal fury. The Holocaust, American Civil Rights Movement, and expansion of universities and academic professions drew increasing scrutiny to the notion of race as a biological category of human difference. By the second half of the twentieth century, academic consensus held that this earlier idea was a dangerous fiction with no basis in science.

Instead, what had been called race by previous generations was in fact a social construction. Despite this heartening reversal, racism still thrives in today's world while the structural legacy of earlier policies and actions has resulted in continuing economic and social inequality between whites and people of color in much of the West while the legacy of racialized European imperialism is still intensely felt in parts of Africa, Asia, and the Americas.

These historical contexts engulfed Jesuits, as missionaries, pastors, teachers, healers, scientists, and intellectuals, in the early modern and modern periods. Because of the Order's vast reach, countless numbers of men, women, and children had their lives, societies, and cultures altered irrevocably by exposure to the forces of colonization and imperialism that Jesuits accompanied and, frequently, aided. Thus, on one hand Jesuits provide modern observers with a powerful lens through which to view evolving ideas about human difference on immense spatial and temporal scales. In the hands of intellectual and cultural historians, the writings of individual Jesuits and the dictates of the larger Order yield valuable insights into the interconnected process through which elite Westerners theorized human difference, rationalized slavery, legitimized dispossession of Indigenous people, and explained empire. This research by intellectual and cultural historians has produced important lines of inquiry. On the other hand, the presence of Jesuits on the ground outside of Western Europe and their involvement with slavery, Indigenous missions, local economic life, education, hospitals, and colonial and national bureaucracies meant that the priests not only theorized human difference from the comfort of Rome, but they also influenced greatly the lived experience of people across the globe.

Furthermore, Jesuit actions, conscious or not, helped to create and then reinforce hierarchies of human difference when, for example, Jesuit slaveholders sought to rationalize their ownership and exploitation of non-Europeans, missionaries commented on Indigenous bodies, priests helped colonial officials craft color-based legal codes, or Jesuit schools in the early twentieth-century South supported segregation by refusing to educate African Americans. Jesuits themselves began to acknowledge systemically the Order's shortcomings in the 1960s in the context of the Civil Rights Movement. For example, in his examination of desegregation in Jesuit schools and colleges, James O'Toole shows that until Pedro Arrupe, superior general of the Order, pressed Jesuit educators in 1967 to address structural racism, Jesuits largely fell in line with segregationist attitudes. Focusing on the activity of George Dunne, Sean Dempsey reminds us that there were exceptional Jesuits—also including John and William Markoe and Claude Heithaus—who challenged racialized injustice. Yet outside the rare moments when the broader Order did so, most Jesuits reflected the values and attitudes of the Western societies from which the priests originated. Nevertheless, after Vatican II most Jesuits in the United States adopted antiracist attitudes modeled by Dunne, Heithaus, and the Markoe brothers. Perhaps it was the painful racist legacy of the past that led the Jesuit historians that Nathaniel Millett analyzes to write slavery out of the history of Saint Louis University.

The essays in this volume utilize three approaches to the subject of Jesuits and race. First, the essays examine Jesuits as privileged witnesses to shifting ideas about human difference, creators and cultivators of arising hierarchies, and agents who helped to impose these hierarchies on people across the globe. Second, the essays analyze the impact of Jesuit actions and ideas on various societies and people that the priests encountered. In both cases, space is devoted to discussing Jesuits who challenged prevailing norms. Third, the authors seek to recreate the perspective of non-Europeans and analyze their experience. This multifaceted approach captures the richness and complexity of Jesuits and race across a near five-century period.

Chronologically, the combined essays cover a period that spans from the mid-sixteenth-century founding of the Society of Jesus to the first quarter of the twenty-first century. Geographically, *Jesuits and Race* is a true work of world history, with essays that focus on the Americas, Europe, and Asia. The collection does not, however, seek to provide exhaustive coverage of every topic relating to Jesuits and race. This undertaking would be impossible. Instead, the essays focus on key moments, texts, and methods to represent current scholarship and promote future research. Accordingly, and by way of example, readers will learn about the still understudied topic of Jesuit involvement with slavery in early modern Asia, but less about the Order's plantations in Brazil; an important subject, but one that has received much attention from scholars.

Organized chronologically, the collection begins in Europe during the era of the founding of the Society of Jesus. First is Emanuele Colombo's "'The Society of the World': Jesuits and the Purity of Blood," an essay that zooms in on the intense debates that erupted within the Order about the incorporation of New Christians. Despite powerful memories of the Reconquest and limpieza de sangre statutes, which codified deep-seated Iberian beliefs about those of non-Christian ancestry, Ignatius of Loyola adopted a flexible policy of incorporating conversos into the Society of Jesus. One result of this unique "nondiscrimination policy" was that many New Christians joined the early Jesuits. In the decades after the death of Ignatius in 1556, the Order lurched between continuing his policy of tolerance and rejecting it, along with New Christian members. Colombo traces and analyzes these debates, using them as a lens through which to view racialized thought, policy making, and the influence of people of diverse origins within the early Order.

Erin Rowe, in "Eternal Blackness: Body and Soul in Jesuit Martín de Roa's Afterlife," closely examines the writings of de Roa, an early seventeenth-century Jesuit scholar from Spain. Writing in Seville, which was home to a growing population of free and enslaved Africans, Roa became an active participant in Jesuit debates about the "spiritual capacity of black Africans." While his involvement is far from surprising, Roa's claim that Africans would be resurrected into black bodies in heaven was, in Rowe's words, "astonishing." Equally so was the priest's assertion that in the afterlife blackness would no longer be a defect but would, as was the case with whiteness, serve as a reflection of the beauty and diversity of humanity in heaven. Rowe provides a brilliant analysis of Roa's ideas, which she skillfully situates within scholarly conversations about early modern Atlantic racial thought.

Liam Brockey, in "Jesuits and Unfree Labor in Early Modern Asia," shifts the volume's focus to seventeenth-century Asia. While much excellent scholarship exists about Jesuits and unfree labor in the Atlantic World, less is known about the topic in the region that Brockey studies. It becomes quickly evident in his essay that Jesuits involved themselves in many forms of unfree labor in East Asia, from enslavement to indentured servitude, to other variants that were not easily classified. Unlike enslavement in the Atlantic world, bondage in Indian Ocean networks was not directly and explicitly related to ethnicity. Most frequently, Jesuits participated and, by extension, perpetuated preexisting systems by buying and selling people who were already enslaved or unfree. Brockey argues that Jesuits in early modern East Asia possessed a certain ambivalence about unfree labor, but, at the same time, sought to regulate these practices in order to constrain the most egregious forms of exploitation.

The next two essays pivot to Jesuit missionary efforts in Latin America. Andrew Redden, in "Jesuits and 'Race' in Early Modern Chile: Valdivia's Letters to the King, 1604–1618," examines thirteen letters that were written by Luis de Valdivia, S.J. (1561–1642)—a political broker between Spanish authorities in Lima and local actors on the Chilean frontier. Valdivia's letters, set against the backdrop of a Mapuche uprising against forced labor conscription, invoke an incredible 203 categories of human difference. Redden utilizes a quantitative-based methodology to analyze the letters before turning to the work of the prominent Jesuit scholar José de Acosta (1540–1600) to provide context. What follows is a thoughtful meditation on the limitations of race as a tool for understanding categories of human difference in colonial Latin America.

J. Michelle Molina, in "How to Run a Jesuit Hacienda—Practices of Continence, Care, and Containment in a Racializing Religiosity," turns the reader's attention northward to Jesuit haciendas in eighteenth-century New Spain. Molina provides a close reading of the *Instrucción*, which was designed to guide a Jesuit who was charged with overseeing a hacienda. Molina argues that the *Instrucción* and its recommendations for hacienda management show that Jesuits conceived of a sacramental order intertwined with economic control based on the themes of self-restraint and spatial containment. Within this framework, the *Instrucción* racialized the paternal care of Indigenous servants and slaves. Molina provides much context that strengthens her close analysis of the still-underutilized *Instrucción*.

Keeping the spotlight on New Spain, "'The Most Barbarous and Fierce Peoples in the World': Decoding the Jesuit Missionary Project in Colonial North Mexico" by Susan Deeds skillfully pairs elite Jesuit writings about Indigenous people with the experience of missionaries on the ground in northwest Mexico during the seventeenth and eighteenth centuries. Through her reading of archival and printed sources, Deeds argues that the various phases of Jesuit mission activity in northern Mexico (optimism, sense of martyrdom, obstruction, and despondency) shaped how priests viewed Indigenous peoples. More specifically, Jesuits began to replace culture with genealogy when explaining differences between Indigenous societies and those of Europe. With subtlety, Deeds explores the racialized dimensions and implications of this process of difference-making.

From the founding of the Society of Jesus to the present day, Jesuits and Jesuit schools and colleges have educated millions of people. Two essays, by James O'Toole and Nathaniel Millett, call attention to the troubled history of race in Jesuit educational institutions. O'Toole addresses the entanglements of Jesuit education with race in "A Challenge to our Sincerity: American Jesuits Discover 'The Negro.'" Using a 1967 directive by the General Pedro Arrupe to frame his study, O'Toole focuses on the Society of Jesus's efforts to integrate schools from the 1940s to the early 1970s. In O'Toole's analysis, initially most Jesuits possessed traditional segregationist views. However, inspired by the Civil Rights Movement, a few priests developed a moral conscience about segregation by the 1940s and 1950s. Slowly Jesuits began to take measures to integrate their schools. This activism hastened by the late 1960s with Jesuits becoming more assertive about recruiting African American students and integrating facilities on campus. O'Toole uses the priests' attitudes about segregation, integration, and education to chart the shifting nature of racialized thought in the minds of twentieth-century Jesuits.

In "The Memory of Slavery at Saint Louis University," Nathaniel Millett recounts the significant roles that enslaved African Americans performed in the construction and maintenance of SLU and the Jesuit Missouri Province from the early nineteenth century to Emancipation in January 1865. Yet histories of the university beginning in the 1870s ignored the presence of slavery, which spawned a narrative that enslavement had no place at SLU. Over the course of the twentieth century, a handful of Jesuits wrote historical accounts of the university—at least two of whom worked energetically to desegregate Catholic schools—yet neither ever mentioned slavery or downplayed it in minimalist language. Millett concludes that the 2014 protests on campus, in the wake of Michael Brown's killing, has provided university administrators an opportunity to reexamine SLU's history not only in its involvement with slavery, but also its fraught record on race.

Sean Dempsey's concluding essay is set against the backdrop of world wars, the Great Depression, and the Cold War, reminding readers that Jesuits were intimate witnesses and influential actors in the global twentieth century's often tense history of race relations, racism, and decolonization. "Trial by

Fire: Father George Dunne and Race Relations in Cold War Los Angeles" illustrates each of these points through an examination of the career and political activism of George Dunne, S.J. This Jesuit served as a missionary in 1930s China before returning to the United States to obtain a political science PhD in Sovietology from the University of Chicago. At a point in time when the Cold War and early Civil Rights Movement came to occupy prominent places within the American consciousness, Dunne graduated and began a career combatting segregation and racial injustice in California. Throughout the essay, Dempsey nimbly juxtaposes Dunne's radicalism with institutional and individual Catholic opposition to antisegregationists and Civil Rights advocates by those who embraced a fierce brand of anticommunism. Despite the just nature of Dunne's activism, he was eventually transferred out of Los Angeles by his superiors and, along with likeminded colleagues, left stymied and subject to suspicion.

An epilogue by John McGreevy offers an elegant synopsis of the essays and their relevance in light of the long history of the Society of Jesus and its current multicultural character and antiracist engagement. The durability of the Order and ongoing corporate life of the Jesuits give scholars an opportunity to scrutinize the continuities, transitions, and discontinuities in both the outlook of the Order and the evolution of racial hierarchies. Jesuits have been intricately involved in the world's major historical movements for almost five hundred years, from the Reformation, to colonialism, to global missions, to scientific study, to world wars, to decolonization, and to greater civil rights for more peoples. Going forward into a more just and equitable future requires taking stock of an often less-than-sanguine past. This lively collection of deeply-researched essays reflects a commitment to that project. Jesuits themselves have certainly reflected on that past and, as McGreevy notes, used it and their sustained interaction with peoples around the world to muster a greater commitment to social justice and racial equality.

Notes

1. See Nathaniel Millett, "The Memory of Slavery at Saint Louis University," *American Nineteenth Century History* 16, no. 3 (2015): 329–50.
2. Karin Vélez, *The Miraculous Flying House of Loreto: Spreading Catholicism in the Early Modern World* (Princeton: Princeton University Press, 2019), 3–11.

3. Quoted in Stuart B. Schwartz, *All Can Be Saved: Religious Tolerance and Salvation in the Iberian Atlantic World* (New Haven, CT: Yale University Press, 2009), 161.

4. Margaret Olsen, *Slavery and Salvation in Colonial Cartagena de Indias* (Gainesville: The University Press of Florida, 2004), 17–21; Schwartz, *All Can Be Saved*, 162–64.

5. John M. Monteiro, *Blacks of the Land: Indian Slavery, Settler Society, and the Portuguese Colonial Enterprise in South America*, trans. James Woodard, Barbara Weinstein (Cambridge: Cambridge University Press, 2018), 27.

6. Olsen, *Slavery and Salvation*, 14.

7. Margo Hendricks, "Coloring the Past, Rewriting our Future: RaceB4Race," Folger Shakespeare Library: Advancing Knowledge & the Arts, September 2019, https://www.folger.edu/institute/scholarly-programs/race-periodization/margo-hendricks.

8. Nancy Stepan, *The Idea of Race in Science: Great Britain, 1800–1960* (Hamden, CT: Archon Books, 1982), xii–xiii.

9. Henry Louis Gates, "Writing Race and the Difference it Makes," *Critical Inquiry* 12 (1985), 1–20; Thomas Hahn, "The Difference the Middle Ages Makes: Color and Race before the Modern World," *Journal of Medieval and Early Modern Studies* 3, no. 1 (2001): 6.

10. Colin Kidd, *The Forging of Races: Scripture and Race in the Protestant Atlantic World* (Cambridge: Cambridge University Press, 2006), 54–55 (quote 54).

11. Jean-Frédéric Schaub, *Race is about Politics: Lessons from History* (Princeton: Princeton University Press, 2019), 12.

12. Schaub, *Race is about Politics*, 7.

13. Kathryn Burns, "Unfixing Race," in *Rereading the Black Legend: The Discourses of Religious and Racial Difference in the Renaissance Empires*, ed. Margaret R. Greer, Walter D. Mignolo, and Maureen Quilligan (Chicago: University of Chicago Press, 2007), 201–2.

14. David Nirenberg, "Was there Race before Modernity? The Example of 'Jewish' Blood in Late Medieval Spain," in *The Origins of Racism in the West*, ed. Miriam Eliav-Feldon, Benjamin Isaac, and Joseph Ziegler (Cambridge: Cambridge University Press, 2009), 236.

15. Hendricks, "Coloring the Past"; Dorothy Kim, "Introduction to Literature Compass Special Cluster: Critical Race and the Middle Ages," *Literature Compass* s. 2019; 16:e12549.https://doi.org/10.1111/lic3.12549.

16. Cord J. Whitaker, *Black Metaphors: How Modern Racism Emerged from Medieval Race Thinking* (Philadelphia: University of Pennsylvania Press, 2019), 189–92.

17. Suzanne Conklin Akbari, *Idols in the East: European Representations of Islam and the Orient, 1100–1450* (Ithaca, NY: Cornell University Press, 2009), 4, 114.

18. Whitaker, *Black Metaphors*, 12–21.

19. Craig Kolofsky, "Knowing Skin in Early Modern Europe, c. 1450–1750," *History Compass* 12, no. 10 (2014): 798.

20. Geraldine Heng, *The Invention of Race in the European Middle Ages*

(Cambridge: Cambridge University Press, 2018), 181–82. See also Hahn, "Difference the Middle Ages Makes," 11, 15, 25–26.

21.   Nirenberg, "Race before Modernity," 242, 245.

22.   David M. Whitford, *The Curse of Ham in the Early Modern Era: The Bible and the Justifications for Slavery* (Farnham: Ashgate, 2009), 90, 106, 118–21.

23.   Burns, "Unfixing Race," 191, 197, 199; Ruth Hill, "Toward an Eighteenth Century Transatlantic Critical Race Theory," *Literature Compass* 3, no. 2 (2006), 56–61.

24.   Patricia Seed, *American Pentimento: The Invention of Indians and the Pursuit of Riches* (Minneapolis: University of Minnesota Press, 2001), 132.

25.   Charles King, *The Reinvention of Humanity: A Story of Race, Sex, Gender and the Discovery of Culture* (London: Penguin Books, Bodley Head, 2019); see also Ruth Benedict, *Race, Science, and Politics; including The Races of Mankind* (New York: Viking Press, 1959).

CHAPTER ONE

"The Society of the World"

Antonio Possevino (1533–1611) and the Jesuit Debate over Purity of Blood

EMANUELE COLOMBO

Introduction

During the last thirty years of the sixteenth century, the Society of Jesus experienced a major crisis that led to a series of external and internal debates challenging the identity of the Order. From outside the Society, conflicts with the popes—especially Sixtus V (r. 1585–1590) and Clement VIII (r. 1592–1605)—and with King Philip II of Spain (1527–1598) raised questions about the relationships between Jesuits, the church, and the political powers of the time. At the same time, inside the Order, groups of Italian and Spanish Jesuits called for a reform of the organization and the spirituality of the Society. All of these tensions, which began under the generalates of Francisco de Borja (r. 1565–1572) and Everard Mercurian (r. 1573–1580), came together in an explosive combination during the generalate of Claudio Acquaviva (r. 1581–1615).[1]

One of the issues discussed during this period was the admission to the Society of New Christians, candidates of Muslim and Jewish ancestry.[2] Since its origins, the Society of Jesus has had a policy of not discriminating on the basis of lineage in the admittance of new members. Both *moriscos* (Christians of Muslim origins) and *conversos* (Christians of Jewish ancestry) were welcome in the Society. However, the rule (and the debates connected to it) applied especially to candidates of Jewish origins, since there were not many moriscos who joined the Society.

The nondiscrimination policy was not common among the religious orders in early modern Spain, especially after the statutes of *limpieza de sangre* ("purity of blood"), which required that candidates for ecclesiastical and civil positions had no Moorish or Jewish ancestry, took effect on the Iberian Peninsula.[3] The statutes, issued in 1499, became quite common in Spain and Portugal; in 1547 the archbishop of Toledo, Juan Martínez Silíceo (1486–1557) enforced his own statutes and banned Jewish and Moorish descendants from any position within the Catholic Church. Many confraternities, dioceses, and religious orders enforced these prohibitions; among the exceptions was the Society of Jesus, and as a result, many New Christians, and especially those of Jewish ancestry, joined the Society.[4] Also, friends and admirers of the early Society were from a converso background; among them, Juan de Avila (1500–1569), the apostle of Andalusia, who invited many of his followers—often conversos—to join the Society.[5]

This chapter offers an overview of the Society's nondiscrimination policy, whose origin can be traced back to its cofounder and first superior general, Ignatius of Loyola (1491–1556);[6] it presents the harsh debate on the admission of New Christians that spread within the Society after Ignatius' death, and its evolution in the following decades, when an Iberian problem soon became a global one; and, finally, it highlights the original contribution to the debate of Antonio Possevino, a key figure in the early Society, and the reasons for his strong support of the admission of New Christians to the Society of Jesus.

Ignatius of Loyola and New Christians

Ignatius was born in the region of Guipúzcoa, in the Basque country, an area that was fiercely proud of its Old Christian heritage.[7] Considerable historical evidence confirms his origins. On more than one occasion, during the 1520s, Ignatius defended his "purity of blood," which was questioned by the Inquisition because of his connections with the *alumbrado* movement, in which New Christians were prominent.[8]

In his approach toward Jews and Muslims, Ignatius was consistent with the Catholic view of his time: he aimed at their conversion. This was one of his priorities well before the foundation of the Society of Jesus and became one of his dreams when he became the superior general of the Order.[9] His tone when referring to Muslims and Jews was often harsh, and he supported some of the papal policies that they should be tolerated in view of their possible conversion to Catholicism.[10]

His trust in the transformative power of conversion and baptism brought Ignatius, unlike a large portion of the Iberian environment in which he was educated, to consider the Muslim or Jewish ancestry of converted people not as a "stain" to be condemned or as an impediment to joining the Society; on the contrary, it could be valuable because both moriscos and conversos could help with the conversion of more Muslims and Jews.[11]

His welcoming attitude toward New Christians was displayed especially in the case of those of Jewish ancestry.[12] People of Jewish descent who joined the Society often came from prominent families of the Iberian Peninsula, were well educated, and ended up holding leading roles in the Order.[13]

The growing number of New Christians in the Society raised internal tensions because many Iberian Jesuits advocated excluding candidates based on their lineage. Opponents of the New Christians included one of Ignatius's first companions and a long-time provincial of Portugal, Simão Rodrigues (1510–1579), and one of Ignatius' relatives, Antonio de Araoz (1516–1573). The latter began opposing the admission of New Christians while Ignatius was still alive.[14] Many Jesuits thought that, although New Christians were often known to be constant in their faith, "the Society should hold them at a distance because of their character," for they were "opposed to the purity of true religion." They were considered "enemies of the cross of Christ, restless, scheming men," who sought "the highest offices and wish to be called 'rabbi.'"[15]

Pedro de Ribadeneyra (1527–1611), Loyola's first biographer and a Jesuit of converso origins, reported many episodes in which Ignatius stood against discrimination directed at people of Jewish lineage.[16] In addition to evidence in the rich hagiographic tradition, there are many pieces of historical evidence showing Ignatius's sympathetic approach toward New Christians.

In the long process of the elaboration of the *Constitutions* of the Society of Jesus, there is no evidence that Ignatius considered impurity of blood to be an impediment to joining the Order.[17] It was a bold decision, given the different policy in many other religious orders, and it was often referenced in Jesuit correspondence after Ignatius's death. Diego Laínez (1512–1565), the second superior general of the Society, wrote to the anticonverso Jesuit Antonio de Araoz that "the reason why we cannot exclude [New Christians] is that, if you remember, [you] wrote about this to our Father [Ignatius], and then our Father, after carefully considering the matter and recommending it to our Lord, decided against it, and this is what he put into the *Constitutions*."[18]

Ignatius was well aware of the importance of ancestry in the Iberian ecclesiastical environment and of the tensions caused by the admission of New Christians; for this reason, he often asked his companions to be prudent when dealing with the issue.[19] For instance, he introduced a question about the ancestry of the candidates into the section of the *Constitutions* called the *Examen General*. Reading the passage in context, it is clear that it was not conceived as an impediment, but rather as a way of identifying New Christians, because "if local conditions in Spain or Portugal made it inadvisable for [them] to be received on the spot, [Ignatius] wanted them sent to Italy or some other neutral location for their training and ministry."[20] Later, Ignatius's prudence was interpreted by the anticonverso Jesuits as a reticence to accept New Christians, a view that is, however, not supported by the sources.[21] The absence of impediments to New Christians joining the Society was simply a fact—there were many well-known New Christians in the circle of Ignatius's closest collaborators and protégés, including a convert from Judaism, Giovanni Battista Eliano (1530–1589), the grandson of a famous rabbi.[22]

To Ignatius, New Christians were a resource for the Society and a clear sign of its universality. In 1554, echoing Saint Paul, Ignatius wrote to the provincial of Portugal Diego Mirón that "in the Society *there is no distinction between Jew and Greek* when [its members] are united in the spirit of divine service."[23] Many sources evidence the fact that "to Ignatius, and those successors who inherited his nondiscriminatory spirit, the most important criterion for admitting a candidate was his spiritual and educational suitability, regardless of his lineage."[24]

Jesuits of Jewish Ancestry under Diego Laínez and Francisco de Borja

Upon the death of Ignatius (1556), Diego Laínez (r. 1556–1565) was elected the second superior general of the Order. A remarkable theologian (he participated in the Council of Trent) and an extremely active missionary in France, Laínez tried to avoid the fact of his election, making public his converso origins. Despite the widespread prejudices against New Christians, the members of the congregation disregarded this possible objection and elected him anyway.[25]

Subsequently, another Spaniard, the well-known Old Christian Francisco de Borja, was elected superior general (1565–1572). Instead of demeaning the role of New Christians as might have been expected, he welcomed their presence in the Society. Additionally, Borja gave many Spaniards, and among them several New Christians, important roles within the Society, not only in the Iberian Peninsula, but almost everywhere. It is difficult to quantify the number of Jesuits of converso origins present in the fifteen years of the Laínez and Borja generalates because it is not easy to identify them. Recent research has shown their extraordinary visibility within the Society and their influence as teachers in the most prominent Jesuit institutions.[26]

Among the supporters of their admission, at least two should be mentioned. The first was Juan Alfonso de Polanco (1517–1576), a New Christian himself, the secretary of the Society under Ignatius, Laínez, and Borja, and a man of huge influence within the Society. The second was Jerónimo Nadal (1507–1580), who was close to Ignatius and who spent most of his life traveling on behalf of the Society. It is not known whether Nadal was an Old or New Christian; what is certain is that he was sincerely persuaded that Jewish ancestry should not be an impediment to candidates for the Order.[27] In one instance, while discussing the possible admission of a candidate, he wrote: "We [Jesuits] take pleasure in admitting those of Jewish ancestry."[28]

During the Borja generalate, rumors and complaints about his esteem for New Christians merged with widespread criticism of his spiritual views. His emphasis on prayer and mysticism and his attempts to bring the spiritual practices of the Jesuits closer to those of the traditional religious orders were seen as attempts to "spiritualize" the Society and as being a consequence of his strong connections with New Christians.[29]

At the death of Borja, his logical successor was his vicar general, Juan Alfonso de Polanco. However, as the third General Congregation gathered to elect the new general, the growing tensions within the Society became apparent. An anti-Spanish movement led by Portuguese and Italian delegates aimed at preventing the election of a fourth Spanish general (after Ignatius, Laínez, and Borja); at the same time, a group of Iberian Jesuits lobbied against the election, after the generalate of Laínez, of another New Christian. Polanco, both Spanish and a New Christian, became the target of both movements. An unprecedented series of interventions by Pope Gregory XIII (r. 1502–1585) pressured the delegates—the majority of whom were from Spain—to elect the Walloon Jesuit Everard Mercurian as the fourth superior general.[30] At the end of the congregation, the Portuguese delegates proposed limiting the power of New Christians and even excluding them from the Society; a decision on this proposal was, however, not taken, and it remained in suspension for the next twenty years.[31]

A Divided Society: The *De genere* Decree

The Society's approach toward New Christians radically changed during the Mercurian generalate. Mercurian removed from Rome many converso Jesuits who held important positions, including Ribadeneyra, Polanco, and Nadal, and pressure was applied by Spain and Portugal to stop accepting candidates of Jewish ancestry.[32]

Things became worse after the death of Mercurian and the election of the Italian Jesuit Claudio Acquaviva to the generalate. A growing discontent with both the central and local governments of the Society gave birth to the *memorialista* movement, a group of Spanish and Italian Jesuits who wrote anonymous memorials to civil and ecclesiastic authorities criticizing the general, asking for a renewal of the Society, and even for the independence of the Spanish province. The movement has been often described as being strongly supported by New Christians, and some historians have considered it to have been a converso plot against Mercurian and Acquaviva.[33] More recent and informed research has shown that the movement was complex and nuanced, and that personal considerations, political and religious differences, and internal disagreements unrelated to the New Christian issue also affected its members.[34] The identification of the memorialistas with New Christians, however, was strongly amplified by anticonverso Jesuits in order to demonstrate that New Christian Jesuits had been lobbying against their superior generals.

In the late 1580s, the Italian Jesuit Benedetto Palmio (1523–1598), the long-time assistant to the Italian provinces, wrote a long memorial to Acquaviva. Presenting himself as important to the living memory of the Society of Jesus because of his age and because he had met Ignatius, he offered to Acquaviva his suggestions about how to deal with the divisions within the Society.

According to Palmio, one of the key reasons for these divisions was the growing presence of the New Christians. In his view, neither Ignatius nor Laínez had supported their proliferation among the Jesuits; it was instead Borja who had diverged from the spirit of Ignatius and "opened the doors so wide to this sort of people [New Christians] that almost no other people were being admitted in Spain, and the Old Christians, realizing this situation, were escaping from the Society."[35] Palmio concluded that the presence of New Christians in the Society became so overwhelming that the Order could be defined as a "synagogue of Jews," an expression used by Philip II of Spain.[36]

Acquaviva, influenced by his Jesuit collaborators in the Roman curia, became more and more persuaded that, for the good of the Society, it was necessary to place limits on the admission of New Christians and on the power of those who had already been admitted.[37] In 1590, he sent a secret instruction to the provincials of Spain in which he warned them not to give New Christians leadership roles and suggested that they discreetly make their admission more difficult, but decided "not to prohibit universally the admission of those who somehow have this defect."[38]

Things escalated three years later, during the fifth General Congregation (1593–1594), which was convened under pressure of some Iberian Jesuits who gained the support of Philip II of Spain and Pope Clement VIII and demanded radical changes in the structure of the Society.[39] The congregation approved the *De Genere* decree, which provided for excluding from the Society all candidates with Jewish or Muslim ancestors, no matter how distant in time.[40]

Those . . . who are descended from parents who are recent Christians have routinely been in the habit of inflicting a great deal of hindrance and harm on the Society (as has become clear from our daily experience). For this reason, many have earnestly requested a decree on the authority of this present congregation that no one will hereafter be admitted to this Society who is descended of Hebrew or Saracen stock. And if any one of them will have been admitted by mistake, he should be dismissed from the Society as soon as this impediment has been shown to exist.[41]

The decree, which was stricter than the statement of any other religious order, quoted Ignatius of Loyola, despite clearly opposing his policy regarding the admission of New Christians.[42] How much of it was the price Acquaviva had to pay to the Spanish Jesuits to moderate their discontent, and how much he was persuaded of the real need for the decree, is difficult to say.[43] Only two members of the congregation voted against the decree: José de Acosta (1540–1600), who, ironically, was there as a representative of Philip II of Spain, and Francisco Arias de Párraga (1534–1605).[44]

Despite the huge majority of votes the decree received at the General Congregation and the strong support provided by prominent Jesuits, in the following years it became unpopular because it had certain negative consequences. Many influential converso Jesuits abandoned the Society and the overall number of candidates decreased. Additionally, since it was not always easy to identify the lineage of candidates, rumors and accusations increased the divisions within the Society. After a provincial congregation in 1593, representatives of the Spanish provinces asked Rome to revoke or at least mitigate the decree.[45] As a Spanish Jesuit wrote to Acquaviva in 1594, "The *perturbatores* of the Society of Jesus, with all their memorials, did not do—and could never have done—such a harm to the Society as this decree with all the disunities and division that will arise from it."[46]

The interventions of many influential Jesuits and pressure brought to bear on Pope Clement VIII persuaded the procurators to call a new General Congregation, summoned in 1608.[47] One of its decisions was to mitigate the *De Genere* decree: members of families of Muslim or Jewish ancestry who had been good Christians for four or five generations could be admitted to the Society. Additionally, "to foster union" among the Jesuits, the congregation condemned "uncertain rumors or reports" regarding ancestry and asked members of the Order "not to engage in conversations about these matters."[48]

The mitigation of the decree allowed a relative flexibility in the admission of New Christians during the following decades. However, the difficulties surrounding the issue of New Christians remained latent and reemerged on various occasions.[49] In 1620, for instance, the Jesuit historian Francesco Sacchini (1570–1625) published the second volume of his *History of the Society of Jesus*, which contained information about the Jewish ancestry of Laínez and Polanco.[50] The Jesuit Province of Toledo twice asked that this information be removed from the *History* because it diminished the prestige of the Society. Sacchini's answer was a powerful defense of the admission of New Christians: "I in no way repent what I wrote about Laínez. As a Christian, his Jewish blood was not an ignominy but ennoblement, for he was not a wild shoot, as each of us is, but a fallen branch of the good olive [tree] grafted again sweetly and fitly into the parent stock."[51]

Forms of both discrimination and flexibility in the acceptance of New Christians have continued throughout the history of the Society, including after its suppression (1773) and restoration (1814). The impediment was confirmed, in a mitigated form, during the twenty-seventh General Congregation (1923) but officially eliminated during the twenty-ninth General Congregation (1946), in the wake of the Shoah.[52]

In order to understand the arguments of the proconverso Jesuits, we should go back to the late sixteenth century to analyze the contribution to the debate of the Jesuit Antonio Possevino.

The Contribution of Antonio Possevino

Many prominent Jesuits, during the generalate of Mercurian and Acquaviva, wrote against lineage-based discrimination in the Society. We can mention, among others, Pedro de Ribadeneyra, Diego de Guzmán (c. 1522–1606), Juan de Mariana (1536–1624), and García Girón de Alarcón (1534–1597).[53] One Jesuit, however, contributed to this debate more than anyone else and for more than thirty years: Antonio Possevino, who was particularly influential thanks to his personal connections with Pope Clement VIII.

Possevino is mainly renowned for his diplomatic activity in central and eastern Europe and for his celebrated *Bibliotheca selecta* (1593), a monumental bibliography containing suggested readings on almost any topic; published with a prefatory letter by Pope Clement VIII, the Bibliotheca was instrumental in shaping the Jesuit pedagogical code, the *Ratio studiorum*. Earlier stages of Possevino's life, such as his activity as the secretary of the Society of Jesus (1573–1577) during Mercurian's generalate, should be explored more in depth.[54]

After John Donnelly's pioneering contribution, Thomas Cohen, Robert Maryks, and Marc Rastoin have studied different aspects of Possevino's role in the Jesuit debates over purity of blood.[55] However, a comprehensive analysis of Possevino's long-term contribution to this debate, some questions about his origins—was he a New Christian?—and the study of a number of hitherto neglected primary sources, reveals a more precise and complete image of Possevino's views and actions regarding the admission of New Christians to the Society.

Possevino's first pronouncement on this subject dates back to 1576, when he sent Mercurian a long memorial, probably "the most important effort during the generation after Ignatius's death to call attention to the need to rid the Society of lineage-based discrimination."[56] The memorial was a response to a text written by Benedetto Palmio, who, despite being instrumental in Possevino's vocation, became his adversary on the question of New Christians.[57] Possevino asked Mercurian to write a public letter about the need for unity in order to address the growing divisions among Jesuits. He could boast of a privileged vantage point on the life of the Society at that time: he was the general secretary of the Order, a role that he held for five years (1573–1577), which had allowed him to work closely with the general and in which he was continually exposed to Jesuit correspondence from all over the world.[58] Later, in 1598, five years after the *De Genere* decree, Possevino addressed a memorial to Acquaviva, followed by a series of letters. His tone in these communications was even more dramatic: he identified the policy of discrimination as a betrayal of the "spirit of the Society of Jesus" and the source of dangerous divisions. He tried to persuade Acquaviva to cancel the decree, which, in his view, was issued in a climate of tension as a means of quelling uprisings against the general, and was in blatant contradiction with the *Constitutions* of the Society; he begged the general to "reform what seems irreformable," warning him that it was his duty "to leave the Society of Jesus as God has given it to [him]."[59]

Later, he publicly reiterated this view at the provincial congregations in

Brescia (1599) and Piacenza (1603) and wrote several letters to prominent members of the Society, including to the Jesuit cardinal Robert Bellarmine (1542–1621) and to Francesco Sacchini, to whom Possevino confirmed Laínez's Jewish ancestry.[60]

Perhaps disappointed by Acquaviva's failure to respond, in 1603 Possevino wrote a letter to Pope Clement VIII on the subject of "The Things that Are Considered Necessary Now in the Society of Jesus." Claiming a deep knowledge of the Society, Possevino asked the pope to take action to address several problems. His most important request was that he issue a papal brief against the *De Genere* decree, so that the Society would return to its admission policy as it was before the fifth General Congregation.[61] Some of Possevino's petitions contributed to the 1608 decree that moderated the discrimination;[62] however, not satisfied with this result, Possevino wanted this softening of the impediment to be only a first step, desiring that "over time it would be possible to go back to what our Father Ignatius had ordered in the Constitutions."[63]

Scholars have consistently acknowledged Possevino's battles in favor of the admission of New Christians and have often explained his extraordinary commitment to the issue by the fact that he was "almost certainly a closet-converso."[64] According to some scholars, he was part of a network of converso Jesuits who wanted to protect their roles within the Society.[65] However, evidence of Possevino's Jewish ancestry is very weak, and there are some facts in his life that are hardly compatible with alleged Jewish origins. The most eloquent argument is the stunning silence of everyone involved about Possevino's ancestry: of the superiors of the Society, of his adversaries in the debate on the admittance of New Christians, and of Possevino himself. This silence is very difficult to explain if we consider that, for more than thirty years, his Jewish ancestry might have been used as a weapon by his enemies and as a source of pride by him.[66]

If one believes that Possevino was an Old Christian, his dedication to the cause of New Christians becomes even more interesting. Despite the fact that he had various interlocutors and that he published his writings over a long period of time, he employed some recurring themes in order to demonstrate that blood discrimination was a betrayal of the "spirit of the Society."

First, Possevino supported the acceptance of New Christians by retracing the Society's history. He reminded his readers that the first group of Jesuits was made up of ten people, "some of them Old Christians, and others New, some noble, and others ignoble, because God was not making distinctions."[67] He made the point that the Constitutions were written "with many tears, blood, and prayers," and that "Ignatius did not want to add any impediment, and his desire was respected within the Society until the fifth Congregation."[68] Possevino went on to note that "[Ignatius knew] what a tempest in his own time had been stirred up against the Society [by the debate over the lineage]. He nonetheless believed that the spirit of God did not make distinctions between people, and believed more in Jesus Christ than in worldly caution, and acted on this belief, so that it remained stamped on the souls of the Society, and he shaped the Society in such a way that nothing moved him to alter her, knowing that *what God has joined together, let no one separate*."[69]

Possevino highlighted the extraordinary contributions of New Christians to the early Society, both in Europe and the Indies, and highly praised many of them, including Polanco and Laínez.[70] The latter, in particular, had been elected the second general superior of the Society despite his "stain," namely, his Jewish ancestry, because "the congregation, united by those early fathers who possessed the sincere spirit of the Society, judged that any objection born out of similar respects for the world, was frivolous before God."[71]

Second, Possevino emphasized the importance of conversion and the efficacy of baptism. Baptism was more powerful than lineage and "Jesuits who reject[ed] Paul's affirmation that 'there is no distinction between Jew and Greek'" were questioning—"perhaps inadvertently"—the efficacy of baptism and were "creating a new species of Cathars."[72] A true conversion should cancel out any distinction. Even if a particular ancestry could be seen as a "stain," the sacrament of baptism had the power to eliminate any stain, including real ones, those that came from opposing God.[73] In fact, "No stain coming from the ancestors can eliminate the influence of the gifts provided by God to those He has chosen, in His eternal counsel, for the conversion of the world."[74] Possevino argued that people who did not accept New Christians into the Society were implicitly stating that "baptism is less than baptism."[75] He recalled the fact that Ignatius worked tirelessly to convert the Jews, and in one instance, insisted on "persuad[ing] a [Jewish] neophyte who joined the Society of Jesus not to abandon it."[76]

Possevino answered the common objection that conversos often practiced forms of crypto-Judaism. While it was true that many converted Jews later "went back to their vomit," he thought that this happened because they "falsely converted in order to maintain their property and avoid abandoning their homeland and relatives."[77] In the end, the only issue was whether conversion was sincere: if it was, any distinction based on birth should be discarded.

To those who asked him, "What will you do, Saint Paul, with these Jews?" the Apostle would have certainly answered, "Who can resist God who is calling? I, too, wanted to defy the desire to become a Christian, and Christ himself made of me, a persecutor, a vessel of election and an apostle for the entire world."[78]

A third recurring argument in Possevino's writings was his strong endorsement of the idea that the Society of Jesus "was founded by God following the example of the primitive Church, because it should serve to help the New and the Old world."[79] "Regarding the Christian Church, no one can ignore that Christ gathered it from every nation under the sky and that, Him being the cornerstone, he made two people into one fold; he gathered Jews and Gentiles and made of them not only a sheepfold, but also the shepherds and the doctors of the Church, and stated that, after they became part of His body . . . no tongue should dare to call the Christians 'Jews,' or 'Greeks,' or 'Scythians,' or 'Gentiles,' for all are one in Christ."[80]

In his genealogy, Possevino went back to the origin of the Church, pointing out that the twelve apostles, the seventy-two disciples, and the thirty-three archbishops of Jerusalem were all Jews.[81] The connection between the early church and the Society of Jesus was explicit. "As in the emerging Church, Christ our Lord had made two people into one [*utraque unum*], so much so in the recent times, in which the Church is re-emerging through the Society, He wanted to follow the same method and did not want to close any door to any nation under the sky, nor to prevent the admission of New Christians, Gentiles, converted heretics and illegitimate people and their descendants , . . . or anyone else."[82] These words, written to the Jesuit Sacchini, who was collecting materials for his history of the Society, show Possevino's ratification of a common narrative about the Society's origin. Internal documents, not intended for publication, often described the

Society of Jesus as a "work of God," and conceived of it as a second foundation of the early church. The entire structure of the Society was modeled on the community of the apostles, and its ministries of preaching, explaining the scriptures, teaching Christian doctrine, spreading the Spiritual Exercises, and traveling to mission lands, were apostolic practices recovered from the primitive church.[83] Like the early church, the Society of Jesus had the task of evangelizing the world; at the time these documents were written, after the world had expanded, both the old and new worlds were part of the Jesuit missionary horizon.

This myth of the origins justified the distinctiveness of the Society of Jesus and made it radically different from the other religious orders. The structure of the Society (with its superior general elected for life and the other superiors chosen by him rather than elected) and its name (which seemed to emphasize a unique relationship with Jesus, on the model of the early church) were at the center of lively debates both inside and outside the Society and were threatened during the generalates of Mercurian and Acquaviva by external and internal movements for normalization. It is worthwhile to note that the argument of the perfect analogy between the Society of Jesus and the early Church was usually limited to the internal communication. In fact, in his letter to Clement VIII, Possevino repeated almost all the arguments he had used in his memorials to Mercurian and Acquaviva, with the exception of the narrative of the Society of Jesus as a rebirth of the primitive Church.

Another implicit allusion to Jesuit identity can be found in Possevino's constant reference to Saint Paul. Unlike superiors of other religious orders, who chose not to accept New Christians, Ignatius "remembered the saying of Saint Paul, *we are all one in Christ* and did not want to tie God's hands, allowing God to choose [New Christians] if He wanted, for His greater glory, since God *chose the weak of the world to shame the strong.*"[84] As recent historiography has shown, the Pauline model had a strong influence on the religious experience of Ignatius and on the institutional organization of the early Society of Jesus. The image of Ignatius as an "other Paul" was a key element of the identity of the Society as described by early Jesuits and reinforced the connection of Ignatius and the Society with Paul and the early church.[85] Additionally, during the sixteenth century, the Pauline message had left its mark on a long season of Iberian religious history and the converso tradition had often resorted to the Pauline ecclesiology to justify the inclusion of New Christians in the church. A prominent converso, Juan de Avila, had strongly supported the Society of Jesus against its detractors by highlighting its uniqueness: it was shaped directly on the model of the early church and the apostles.[86]

The connections between the proconverso literature and the myth of the origins of the Society require further exploration. It is striking that many of the Jesuits who elaborated the early historiography of the Society of Jesus were also strong advocates of the acceptance of New Christians; among them were Nadál, Polanco, and Ribadeneyra.[87] The latter, one of the most prominent contributors to the internal historiography of the Society, was also the author of important documents against discriminations based on blood.[88] Banning New Christians meant, in his view, "open[ing] the doors to radical changes to our Institute" and betraying "the spirit and the sentiments of Our Father Ignatius." In a crucial passage, Ribadeneyra reminded his readers that discrimination against New Christians was much more dangerous for the identity of the Order than the structural changes under discussion in his time, such as diluting the power of the superior general and limiting his lifetime term of office.[89]

A fourth and final argument employed by Possevino was that the exclusion of New Christians from the Society would be only the first in a series of discriminatory policies that would change its nature. In 1576, while serving as the secretary of the Society, Possevino wrote to Mercurian: "[This Institute] permits no preference for lineage, or for human concerns (which are vestiges of paganism), or for its own honor, such as not allowing oneself to be touched by others or to greet them, as is the custom of some infidels about whom Father Valignano has recently written to Your Paternity."[90]

As was noted by Thomas Cohen, this passage is crucial because it linked the problem of purity of blood in Europe with similar issues that presented themselves in the Jesuit missions overseas: conflicts over nation and lineage constituted "a pagan survival" that should be "expunged from the Society."[91]

Possevino expanded on this point. If the possible relapse of converted Jews were to be considered a valid argument for preventing their descendants from joining the Society, the same danger was present with every group, among Protestants in Europe and pagans in Africa and Asia. If, because of the possibility of relapse, the Jesuits should refrain from procuring salvation for and admitting New Christians into the Society, they should abandon their goal of converting the Gentiles for the same reason. In these passages, "Possevino foresaw, with a clarity that few men of his generation possessed, that the effort to exclude New Christians would inevitably lead to the exclusion of other groups."[92]

A Global View

Possevino wrote his memorial to Mercurian at a time when he was in epistolary contact with Jesuits from all over the world and had the opportunity to speak with many returning missionaries who stopped in Rome. In these same years, he completed a "plan for world evangelization," one of the early plans for the foundation of what years later would become The Sacred Congregation de Propaganda Fide (1622).[93] During his tenure as secretary of the Society of Jesus, he could "see every day what God was doing with his instruments among Christians, and what other people were doing with the instruments of the world."[94]

Possevino was certainly aware that the debate about accepting New Christians into the Society was not limited to the Iberian Peninsula. Since the early days of the Society, there were often disguised references to the presence of New Christians in the Indies in the letters that arrived in Rome.[95] Especially in Portuguese Asia, Jesuits were pressured to adopt the same anticonverso regulations of other religious orders and often considered accepting and promoting New Christians to be politically unwise.[96]

This discontent with the increasing presence of New Christians grew during the generalate of Mercurian: While in Europe many Jesuits of Jewish ancestry were dismissed from their leadership roles, signs of impatience with New Christians were also clear in the Indies, as witnessed by Jesuit correspondence going in both directions. In 1577, Mercurian wrote to José de Anchieta (1534–1597), the provincial of Brazil, ordering him not to admit New Christians into the Society to avoid the complaints of prominent colonists.[97] In 1578, the provincial of India, Rui Vicente, complained to Mercurian about Portuguese superiors' habit of getting rid of Jesuits of Jewish ancestry in Portugal by sending them to the Indies.[98]

The impediment that applied to New Christians was often used in places outside Europe as a reason to ban Native people from the Society. The debate about Native clergy within the Society, a dispute that divided Jesuits in America, Africa, and Asia, is complex and cannot simply be folded into the debate about New Christians; there are, however, important connections between them.

The timeline of the two debates is very similar. Discussions on the admissions of the descendants of Native people began very early in the history of the Society, but the restrictions started to be enforced systematically under Mercurian.[99] The latter ordered Jesuits in India to impose a ban on admitting Indians and *mestiços* (half-caste) and introduced strong restrictions on *castiços* (the sons of Europeans born in Asia). While exceptions were made in favor of the Japanese, Chinese, Vietnamese, and Koreans based on the perception that they had a high level of civilization, the ban on the admission of Indians was retained up to the time the Society was expelled from the Portuguese empire in 1760.[100] With respect to Brazil, in 1574 Mercurian banned the mestiços from admission into the Society, but his order allowed the admission of castiços after they demonstrated the genuineness of their vocation. Five years later, however, the ban was extended to all castiços.[101]

Also, during this period, the justification for excluding New Christians was applied to converted *indios* and *mestizos* in Spanish America. The case of Peru is especially interesting because it shows the deep connection between the debates about New Christians and those about people with Native ancestry.[102] Since the 1570s, Jesuit rectors and provincials in Peru had applied the limpieza de sangre statutes to their selection of novices. The parallel between New Christians and converted indios was made explicitly: In a letter written from Lima in 1572, the Jesuit Bartolomé Hernández stated that in Peru "the indios are like the *moros*, and they only have the name and practice the exterior ceremonies of Christians; internally, they do not have any idea of the things of our faith."[103]

The idea that the indios were "eternal neophytes" meant that mestizos inherited their defects and could not be considered real Christians; for this reason, after a first period in which they were admitted to the Society, they were banned from joining the Society, and the few of them who had joined in the previous decades were subjected to discrimination.[104] At the same time, suspicion against the descendants of moriscos and conversos who came to Peru from the Iberian peninsula was growing exponentially. At the third (1582) and fourth (1588) Jesuit Provincial Congregations, mestizos were officially banned from the Society and criollos, born in America from European parents, were considered dangerous and discouraged from joining the Order.[105] The fear of a "creolization" of the Society supported a narrative that the creoles were inferior, not because of their lineage, which was entirely European, but because of the allegedly negative effects on them of the place where they were born.[106]

Jesuits had fluctuating views on this topic, as shown by José de Acosta, later one of only two opposers of the *De Genere* decree at the fifth General Congregation. When he was the Jesuit provincial of Peru, from 1576 to 1581, he supported the ban of mestizos from the Society, probably to avoid critiques of the Order. Later, however, he praised the contribution of mestizos to the evangelization of the indios and spoke in favor of their ordination to the secular clergy, a view that was endorsed by the third Council of Lima (1583).[107]

The severity of the bans escalated up to the time of the fifth General Congregation, at which the *De Genere* decree was approved. During the same congregation, a deputation for the Indies voted to place an impediment on mestizos who wished to join the Society of Jesus because, as Acquaviva wrote, "our experience has shown that they are not fit for our ministries."[108] Exceptions were possible for the *cuarterones* (people whose racial origins were three-quarters European and one-quarter Indigenous) and for creoles.

In the following years, Jesuits applied the *De Genere* decree to the viceroyalty of Peru, and the superiors collected information about the lineage of novices for the purpose of identifying New Christians and mestizos among them. The impediment applied to the creoles was softened because the Jesuit superiors saw the need for additional missionaries, but the increased power and autonomy of creoles and their admission into the Society was at the expense of mestizos, conversos, and moriscos. The creoles highlighted their purity of blood, and the limpieza de sangre became an instrument of ethnic and social discrimination.[109]

Conclusion

In the last few years, many scholars have discussed the definition of the term "race" and whether limpieza de sangre could be considered an embodiment of a racial doctrine.[110] The debate within the Society of Jesus shows a variety of factors pertinent to its relationship to New Christians. The possession of Jewish and Muslim blood was considered by some Jesuits to be a stain—to use a term that often recurred in contemporary documents—that had moral consequences. But many other elements were involved in the discrimination against moriscos and conversos, including political, social, cultural, and religious ones.[111]

The De Genere decree of 1593, despite its subsequent softening, had long-lasting effects on the Society, supporting various forms of discrimination and exclusion; it provided the Jesuits an excuse to ban from their order entire groups of people on the basis of their ancestry, exclusions born from the idea that they were not fit for the Society's ministries.

Many Jesuits vocally opposed this view. As many scholars have shown, in the first seventy years of the Society, a network of Jesuits of Jewish ancestry lobbied for the elimination of any form of discrimination, and in doing so, defended their own lineage. It is also interesting to note the role of some Old Christian Jesuits who supported the presence of conversos in the Society, from Ignatius to Possevino.

Like Ignatius, Possevino was strongly attracted to the opportunity to convert Jews and Muslims.[112] Also like Ignatius, he thought that if their conversion was authentic, they and their descendants should be allowed to join the Society. For him, the acceptance of New Christians within the Society was theologically sound and, even more, was based on a clear understanding of the Society's identity. To him, discrimination based on lineage was a betrayal of the Society's history and of all the significant accomplishments of many Jesuits of Jewish ancestry; it was a denial of the power of baptism and conversion; and, above all, it represented disloyalty to what made the Society distinctive, a distinctiveness that was modeled on Paul and the early church.

Possevino considered the acceptance of New Christians to be one of the most radical elements of Jesuit distinctiveness: it was a habit of the early church, supported by Paul, and fostered by the Society of Jesus—but not supported by the majority of other contemporary religious orders. He had in mind the importance of the name of the Society of Jesus, a name that during the first decades of its history had been at the center of many scandals because of its radicalness; it was his view that by banning the New Christians, "the Society . . . while professing to be holy and to model itself after Jesus its leader, could ultimately be complicit in harming Jesus, and be a Society of the world [Societas mundi] rather than of Jesus."[113]

Notes

1.   On the crisis under Acquaviva, see Alessandro Guerra, *Un generale tra le milizie del papa. La vita di Claudio Acquaviva scritta da Francesco Sacchini della Compagnia di Gesù* (Milan: Franco Angeli, 2001); Michela Catto, *La Compagnia divisa. Il dissenso nell'ordine gesuitico tra '500 e '600* (Brescia: Morcelliana, 2009); Esther Jiménez Pablo, *La forja de una identidad. La Compañía de Jesús (1540–1640)* (Madrid: Polifemo, 2014), 87–314; Guido Mongini, "The Persecutions of the Jesuits: Religious Identity and Political Myth," in *The Acquaviva Project: Claudio Acquaviva's Generalate (1581–1615) and the Emergence of Modern Catholicism*, ed. Pierre-Antoine Fabre and Flavio Rurale (Boston, MA: Institute of Jesuit Sources, 2017), 43–57; Guido Mongini, "La crisi della Compagnia di Gesù all'epoca di Acquaviva: Pedro Ribadeneira e la definizione dell'identità gesuitica," in *Padre Claudio Acquaviva S. J. preposito generale della Compagnia di Gesù e il suo tempo*, ed. Martín Maria Morales and Roberto Ricci (L'Aquila: Colacchi, 2018), 183–229.

2.   See Thomas M. Cohen, "Nation, Lineage, and Jesuit Unity in Antonio Possevino's Memorial to Everard Mercurian (1576)," in *A Companhia de Jesus na Península Iberica nos secs. XVI e XVII*, 2 vols (Porto: Universidade do Porto, 2004), 1, 543–61; Thomas Cohen, "Racial and Ethnic Minorities in the Society of Jesus," in *The Cambridge Companion to the Jesuits*, ed. Thomas Worcester (Cambridge: Cambridge University Press, 2009), 199–214; Thomas Cohen, "Jesuits and New Christians. The Contested Legacy of St. Ignatius," *Studies in the Spirituality of Jesuits* 42, no. 3 (2010): 1–46; Robert A. Maryks, *The Jesuit Order as a Synagogue of Jews. Jesuits of Jewish Ancestry and Purity of Blood Laws in the Early Society of Jesus* (Leiden: Brill, 2009); Robert A. Maryks, "The Jesuit Order as a 'Synagogue of Jews': Discrimination against Jesuits of Jewish Ancestry in the Early Society of Jesus," *AHSI* 78 (2009): 339–416; Marc Rastoin, *Du même sang que Notre Seigneur: juifs et jésuites aux débuts de la Compagnie de Jésus* (Paris: Bayard, 2011); José Martínez Millán, "El problema judeoconverso en la Compañía de Jesús," *Chronica nova* 42 (2016): 19–50.

3.   The literature on this topic is huge. See the classic works by Marcel Bataillon,

Erasmo y España: estudios sobre la historia espiritual del siglo XVI (Mexico City: Fondo de Cultura Económica Mexico, 1966) and Albert Sicroff, *Los estatutos de limpieza de sangre: controversias entre los siglos XV y XVII* (Madrid: Taurus, 1985).

4. James Reites states that "[b]y the time Ignatius was writing the *Constitutions of the Society* (chiefly from 1547 to 1556), all of the major and most influential religious orders of Spain enforced clauses in their rules for admission excluding those of Jewish origin." "St. Ignatius of Loyola and the Jews," *Studies in the Spirituality of Jesuits* 13, no.4 (1981): 20.

5. On the Iberian converso environment at the origin of the Society of Jesus and the role of Juan de Avila, see Marcel Bataillon, *Les Jésuites dans l'Espagne du XVIe siècle*, ed. Pierre-Anoine Fabre (Paris: Les Belles Lettres, 2009); Stefania Pastore, *Il Vangelo e la spada. L'Inquisizione di Castiglia e i suoi critici (1460–1598)* (Rome: Edizioni di Storia e Letteratura, 2003); Stefania Pastore, "Tra conversos, gesuiti e inquisizione: Diego de Guzmán e i processi di Ubeda (1549–1552)," in *Le Inquisizioni moderne: percorsi di ricerca*, ed. Giovanna Parolin (Trieste: EUT, 2002), 216–51; Rady Roldán-Filgueroa, "Ignatius of Loyola and Juan de Ávila on the Ascetic Life of the Laity," in *A Companion to Ignatius of Loyola: Life, Writings, Spirituality, Influence*, ed. Robert A. Maryks (Leiden: Brill, 2014), 159–78; María Amparo López Arandia, "¿Caminos encontrados?: Juan de Ávila y la Compañía de Jesús," in *El maestro Juan de Ávila (1500?–1569): Un exponente del humanismo reformista*, ed. María Dolores Rincón González and Raúl Manchón Gómez (Madrid: Fundación Universitaria Española-Universidad Pontificia de Salamanca, 2014), 567–91.

6. See James W. Reites, *St. Ignatius and the People of the Book: An Historical-Theological Study of St. Ignatius of Loyola's Spiritual Motivation in His Dealings with the Jews and Muslims* (Rome: Pontificia Universitas Gregoriana, 1977); Reites, "St. Ignatius of Loyola and the Jews"; Francisco de Borja Medina, "Ignacio de Loyola y la 'limpieza de sangre,'" in *Ignacio de Loyola y su tiempo. Congreso Internacional de Historia (9–13 Septiembre 1991)*, ed. Juan Plazaola (Bilbao: Universidad de Deusto, 1992), 579–615; Robert A. Maryks, "Ignatius of Loyola and the Converso Question," in *A Companion to Ignatius of Loyola: Life, Writings, Spirituality, Influence*, ed. Robert A. Maryks (Leiden: Brill, 2014), 84–102.

7. See José Luis Orella Unzué, "La Provincia de Guipúzcoa y el tema de los judíos en tempos del joven Iñigo de Loiola (1492–1528)," in *Ignacio de Loyola y su tiempo: Congreso internacional de historia* (Bilbao: Mensajero, 1992), 847–68.

8. Cfr. Stefania Pastore, "Unwise Paths: Ignatius Loyola and the Years of Alcalá de Henares," in *A Companion to Ignatius of Loyola* (Leiden: Brill, 2014), 25–44; Sabina Pavone, "A Saint Under Trial: Ignatius of Loyola Between Alcalá and Rome," in *A Companion to Ignatius of Loyola* (Leiden: Brill, 2014), 45–65; Stefania Pastore, "Jesuits, Conversos, and Alumbrados in the Iberian World," in *The Oxford Companion to the Jesuits*, ed. Ines G. Županov (Oxford: Oxford University Press, 2019), 128–49.

9. See, for instance, Ignatius's involvement in the foundation of the House of Catechumens of Rome in 1543. The house, which was in principle for "infidels" (that

is, any kind of nonbeliever), actually hosted primarily male Jews. See Domenico Roc-
ciolo, "Documenti su catecumeni e neofiti a Roma nel Seicento e Settecento," *Ricerche
per la storia religiosa di Roma* 10 (1998), 391–452; Lance Gabriel Lazar, *Working in the
Vineyard of the Lord: Jesuit Confraternities in Early Modern Italy* (Toronto: University of
Toronto Press, 2005), 106.

10.   Reites, "St. Ignatius of Loyola and the Jews," 16. On Ignatius and Islam, see
Emanuele Colombo, "Defeating the Infidels, Helping their Souls: Ignatius Loyola and
Islam," in *A Companion to Ignatius of Loyola* (Leiden: Brill, 2014), 179–97.

11.   On many occasions, for instance, Ignatius encouraged the acceptance of moriscos emphasizing that "some of them will be able to learn that language [Arabic] and
could help us in our mission in the Maghreb" (Ignatius to Pedro Navarro, June 18, 1555,
in *Epp. Ign.* 9: 209–10).

12.   There were not many candidates with Muslim origins who joined the Society
of Jesus; for some case studies on Jesuit moriscos, see Francisco de Borja Medina, "La
Compañía de Jesús y la minoría morisca. 1545–1614," *AHSI* 57 (1988): 3–135; Youssef El
Alaoui, *Jésuites, morisques et indiens: Étude comparative des méthodes d'évangélisation
de la Compagnie de Jésus d'après les traités de José de Acosta (1588) et d'Ignacio de Las
Casas (1605–1607)* (Paris: Honoré Champion, 2006).

13.   Israel-Salvator Révah, "Les origines juives de quelques jésuites hispano-portugais
du XVIe siècle," in *Études ibériques et latino-américains: IV congrès des hispanistes fran-
çais* (Paris: Presses Universitaires de France, 1968), 87–96.

14.   On the confrontations between Araoz and Jerónimo Nadal, see Maryks, "Ignatius of Loyola and the Converso Question," 101.

15.   Manuel Rodrigues, "De baptizatis ex progenie Judaeorum" (1593), ARSI, *Inst.*
186e, 337v, quoted in Francisco Borja de Medina, "Ignacio de Loyola y la 'limpieza de
sangre,'" 586 (trans. by Cohen, "Jesuits and New Christians," 3).

16.   See, for instance, *Mon. Rib* 2:375 and *Font. Narr.* 2:476.

17.   See Pierre-Antoine Fabre, "La conversion infinie des conversos. Des 'nouveaux-
chrétiens' dans la Compagnie de Jésus au 16e siècle," *Annales HSS* 4 (1999): 875–93.

18.   Laínez to Araoz, quoted in Reites, "St. Ignatius and the Jews," 23.

19.   See. *Epp. Ign.* 1:336. Reites, "St. Ignatius and the Jews," 22–23; Maryks, *The Jesuit
Order*, 63–66.

20.   John W. O'Malley, *The First Jesuits* (Cambridge, MA: Harvard University Press,
1993), 188.

21.   See, for instance, Benedetto Palmio's memorial (here, footnote 35), Acquaviva's
secret instruction (here, footnote 38) and de *De genere* decree (here, footnote 40).

22.   For a list of converso Jesuits, see Rastoin, *Du même sang*, 275–300. On Eliano,
José C. Sola, "El P. Juan Baptista Eliano, un documento autobiográfico inédito," *AHSI* 4
(1935): 191–221 (a French translation in Rastoin, *Du même sang*, 261–74). Robert Cline
observes that Eliano's missionary work and autobiography were affected by the rise
of an anticonverso culture in the Society of Jesus during the generalate of Mercurian.
See Robert John Cline, *A Jewish Jesuit in the Eastern Mediterranean. Early Modern*

Conversion, Mission, and the Construction of Identity (Cambridge: Cambridge University Press, 2020), 95–99, 198–219.

23. *Mon. Ign.* 12:569 (Ignatius wrote through his secretary, Alfonso de Polanco). There is a reference to Rom. 10:10 and Gal. 3:28.

24. Maryks, "Ignatius of Loyola and the converso question," 93.

25. As witnessed by Possevino's memorial to Acquaviva (1598), ARSI, *Inst.* 184/II, ff. 349–52, here 350v (two copies in ARSI, *Cong.* 26, ff. 28–30 and 288–92). Comments on this memorial in John P. Donnelly, "Antonio Possevino and the Jesuits of Jewish Ancestry," *AHSI* 109 (1986): 3–29 and Maryks, *The Jesuit Order*, 162–81. See also Possevino's letter to Sacchini, ARSI, *Vita* 162, 59r–60v, published in Maryks, "'A true Israelite in Whom there is Nothing False,'" 439–44.

26. Rastoin, *Du même sang*, 119–22.

27. On his persuasion that the *Constitutions* did not include any discrimination, see *Mon. Nad.* 1:233.

28. *Mon. Nad.* 2:21, quoted in Maryks, *The Jesuit Order*, 86–87. Maryks supposes that Nadal was a New Christian, but there is no certainty about that.

29. Later, Benedetto Palmio observed that "'the excessive credit and favor' given by Francisco de Borja to converso Jesuits was due to the monastic influences by which he had been affected before becoming a Jesuit. That impact would have inclined Borja to a spirituality that—according to Palmio—was alien to the spirit that God had communicated to Ignatius and resulted from Devil's deceit." Maryks, *The Jesuit Order*, 112. On Borja, see Mario Scaduto, *L'opera di Francesco Borgia, 1565–1572* (Rome: Edizioni La Civiltà cattolica, 1992); Catto, *La Compagnia divisa*, passim. See also Enrique García Hernán and María del Pilar Ryan, eds., *Francisco de Borja y su tiempo: Política, religión y cultura en la Edad Moderna* (Rome: Institutum Historicum Societatis Iesu, 2011).

30. John W. Padberg, "The Third General Congregation. April 12–June 16, 1573," in *The Mercurian Project. Forming Jesuit Culture*, ed. Thomas M. McCoog (Rome: Institutum Historicum Societatis Iesu), 49–75.

31. Padberg, "The Third General Congregation," 56.

32. Maryks, quoting Palmio, describes "Everard Mercurian's 'house cleansing'" *The Jesuit Order*, 123–25.

33. See, for instance, Antonio Astrain, *Historia de la Compañía de Jesús en la asistencia de España*, 7 vols. (Madrid: Administración de Razón y Fe, 1902–1925).

34. José Martínez Millán, "La crisis del 'partido castellano' y la transformación de la monarquía Hispana," *Cuadernos de Historia Moderna* 2003: 15–27; Francisco Borja de Medina, "Los precursores de Vieira,"; Catto, *La Compagnia divisa*.

35. Benedetto Palmio's memorial, ARSI, *Institut.* 106, ff. 92^r–132^v, here 95^{rv}, quoted in Maryks, *The Jesuit Order as a Synagogue*, 133. The memorial is published in Maryks, *The Jesuit Order as a Synagogue*, 219–56.

36. Benedetto Palmio's memorial, 95^v. For a reference to this expression, see Catto, *La compagnia divisa*, 50. The insistence of Palmio on the problem of the New

Christians is striking: five out of seven reasons for the divisions within the Society are attributed to them. He even makes clear that he does not have anything against Spanish Jesuits who are Old Christians, and his target is very clear. Palmio interpreted the question regarding ancestry that Ignatius added in the *Examen general* of the Constitutions as the attempt to identify New Christians and limit their number.

37.   On the role of three assistants of Acquaviva, Paul Hoffaeus (c. 1530–1608), Manuel Rodrigues (1534–1596), and Lorenzo Maggio (1531–1605), in creating an anti-converso culture, see Maryks, *The Jesuit Order*, 143–46.

38.   Claudio Acquaviva, Rome, April 18, 1590 (ARSI, *Instit. 184/II*, ff. 347 and 366–67), quoted in Maryks, *The Jesuit Order*, 146–48. In 1584 the provincial Congregation of Portugal had decided to stop admitting New Christians to the Society. See Josef Wicki, "Die 'cristão-novos' in der Indischen Provinz der Gesellschaft Jesu von Ignatius bis Acquaviva," *AHSI* 92 (1977): 342–61, here 354.

39.   The fifth General Congregation was the first one held during the lifetime of a general. The main concerns were the excessive powers in the hands of the General and complaints against Acquaviva's government. A group of Spanish Jesuits requested a commissary for the Spanish provinces. Acquaviva was confirmed in his government. See John W. Padberg, Martin D. O'Keefe, and John L. McCarthy, eds., *For Matters of Greater Moment. The First Thirty Jesuit General Congregations: A Brief History and a Translation of the Decrees* (St. Louis, MO: Institute of Jesuit Sources, 1994), 10–13; Astrain, *Historia de la Compañía de Jesús*.

40.   Padberg, O'Keefe, and McCarthy, *For Matters of Greater Moment*, 204–5.

41.   Padberg, O'Keefe, and McCarthy, *For Matters of Greater Moment*, 204.

42.   "It is more suited to the greater glory of God and the more perfect pursuit of the ends it [the Society of Jesus] proposes to itself that it possess[es] workers who are very acceptable to other nations throughout the world and who might be more freely and reliably employed in the Church of God by those people whose good or ill will towards us (as Father Ignatius, of happy memory, says) has much influence to open or to keep closed our access to the divine service and the help of souls." Padberg, O'Keefe, and McCarthy, *For Matters of Greater Moment*, 204.

43.   In a letter sent to Possevino (November 7, 1598), Acquaviva "admitted quite frankly that a major consideration in passing the decree . . . was pressure from Spain: important people had warned him that 'we will never have peace with the King, with his principal ministers, and with the Inquisition nor would the Society ever have the status it deserves unless the decree was passed'" Donnelly, "Possevino and Jesuits of Jewish Ancestry," 11.

44.   This information is confirmed by Possevino, ARSI, *Congr. 20b, 309r*. On Acosta, see Claudio M. Burgaleta, *José de Acosta, S. J. (1540–1600). His Life and Thought* (Chicago: Loyola University Press, 1999). Many prominent Jesuits, on the contrary, supported the decree, among them, the Jesuit theologian Francisco Suárez (1548–1617), who argued that the Congregation had the power to amend the Jesuit *Constitutions* by adding the impediment of origin. See Joseph A. Munitiz, "Francisco Suárez and the

Exclusion of Men of Jewish or Moorish Descent from the Society of Jesus," *AHSI* 73 (2004): 327–40.

45.   See Borja de Medina, "Precursores," especially on Andalusia.

46.   Luis de Santander to Acquaviva, November 4, 1594, ARSI, *Hisp.* 137, 299–300, quoted in Borja de Medina, "Precursores," 498.

47.   Padberg, O'Keefe, and McCarthy, *For Matters of Greater Moment*, 217–46. The sixth General Congregation was the first and the only one, in the history of the Society of Jesus, called as a result of a procurators' congregation.

48.   Padberg, O'Keefe, and McCarthy, *For Matters of Greater Moment*, 232.

49.   For a series of case studies, see the thematic issue of the *Journal of Jesuits Studies* on "Jesuit and Conversos," ed. Claude B. Stuczynski, forthcoming.

50.   Francesco Sacchini, *Historiae Societatis Iesu. Pars Secunda sive Lainus* (Antwerp: Ex officina filiorum Martini Nutij, 1620). For Antonio Possevino's contribution in demonstrating Laínez' Jewish ancestry, see here footnote 61.

51.   See *Mon Laínez* 8:833–55, translated and published in James Brodrick, *The Progress of the Jesuits (1556–1579)* (Chicago: Loyola University Press, 1986), 314–21. See also Maryks, *The Jesuit Order*, 94–96 and Maryks, "'A True Israelite in Whom There is Nothing False.' The Controversy Over the Jewish Ancestry of Diego Laínez," in *Diego Laínez (1512–1565) and his Generalate: Jesuit with Jewish Roots, Close Confidant of Ignatius of Loyola, Preeminent Theologian of the Council of Trent*, ed. Paul Oberholzer (Rome: Institutum Historicum Societatis Iesu, 2015), 419–44.

52.   Padberg, O'Keefe, and McCarthy, *For Matters of Greater Moment*, 534, 625.

53.   For an analysis of some of these writings, see Maryks, *The Jesuit Order*, 159–214; for Ribadeneyra, see also Claire Bouvier, "Les controverses à propos des Nouveaux-Chrétiens dans la Compagnie de Jésus: la défense des conversos du père Pedro de Ribadeneyra (1526–1611)," *Atlante* 2 (2015): 117–60 and here, footnote 89.

54.   The only biography of Antonio Possevino dates back to the eighteenth century: Jean Dorigny, *La vie du Père Antoine Possevin de la Compagnie de Jésus* (Paris: Ganeau, 1712). For an updated bibliography, see Emanuele Colombo, "Possevino, Antonio," *Dizionario biografico degli Italiani*, vol. 85 (Rome: Istituto dell'Enciclopedia, 2016), 153–58.

55.   See Donnelly, "Antonio Possevino and the Jesuits of Jewish Ancestry." For the other works, see note 2.

56.   Cohen, "Jesuits and New Christians," 9. Possevino's memorial to Mercurian (1576), ARSI, *Congr.* 20b, ff. 206–12.

57.   On Possevino's vocation to the Society of Jesus, see Giuseppe Castellani, "La vocazione alla Compagnia di Gesù del P. Antonio Possevino da una relazione inedita del medesimo," *AHSI* 14 (1945–1946): 102–24; Adriano Prosperi, *La vocazione: Storie di gesuiti tra Cinquecento e Seicento* (Turin: Einaudi, 2016).

58.   John Patrick Donnelly S.J., "Antonio Possevino: From Secretary to Papal Legate in Sweden," in *The Mercurian Project: Forming Jesuit Culture, 1573–1580*, ed. Thomas M. McCoog S.J. (St. Louis, MO: Institute of Jesuit Sources, 2004), 323–50.

59.   Possevino's letter to Acquaviva (1598), ARSI, *Opp. NN.* 333, 85, my translation. Possevino was aware that the superior general did not have the power to reform a decree approved by the Congregation.

60.   Possevino's letter to Bellarmine (September 28, 1599), ARSI, *Congr.* 26, 49–50; See also Possevino's letter to Sacchini, in which Possevino criticized Ribadeneyra, who in his biography of Laínez had omitted the reference to Laínez's Jewish ancestry.

61.   Possevino's letter to Clement VIII (Venice, October 11, 1603), ARSI, *Congr.* 26, 115r–112r, partially published in Donnelly, "Antonio Possevino and the Jesuits of Jewish Ancestry," 24–28.

62.   See Donnelly, "Antonio Possevino and the Jesuits of Jewish Ancestry," 20–21.

63.   Possevino's letter to Antonio Barisone (Ferrara, after March 1608), ARSI, *Opp. NN.* 333, 305r–306r, published in Donnelly, "Possevino and the Jesuits of Jewish Ancestry," 28–30.

64.   See Maryks, *The Jesuit Order*, 123, 160; Cohen, "Jesuits and New Christians," 8; Rastoin, *Du même sang*, 143. For a different view, see Luigi Balsamo, *Antonio Possevino S. I. bibliografo della Controriforma e diffusione della sua opera in area anglicana* (Florence: Olschki, 2006), 19.

65.   See Maryks, *The Jesuit Order*; Rastoin, *Du même sang*.

66.   For a more detailed analysis, see Emanuele Colombo, "The Watershed of Conversion: Antonio Possevino, New Christians and Jews," in *The Tragic Couple. Encounters Between Jews and Jesuits*, ed. James Bernauer and Robert A. Maryks (Leiden: Brill, 2013), 25–42.

67.   Possevino's memorial to Acquaviva (1598), 350v–51r.

68.   Possevino's letter to Sacchini, 60r.

69.   Possevino's memorial to Mercurian (1576), quoted in Cohen, "Jesuits and New Christians," 14. There is a reference to Matt. 19:6.

70.   Possevino's memorial to Acquaviva (1598), 350v–51r.

71.   Possevino's memorial to Acquaviva (1598), 351r (quoted in Maryks, "A True Israelite," 428). See also Possevino's letter to Sacchini, 59r.

72.   Possevino's memorial to Mercurian (1576), quoted in Cohen, "Jesuits and New Christians," 13. There is a reference to Rom. 10:10 and Gal. 3:28.

73.   See Possevino's letter to Sacchini, 60r.

74.   Possevino's letter to Sacchini, 59v.

75.   Possevino's letter to Clement VIII, f. 121r.

76.   Possevino's letter to Antonio Barisone, f. 305v. The neophyte quoted in the letter is almost certainly Giovanni Battista Eliano (see here, footnote 22).

77.   Possevino's memorial to Acquaviva (1598), 350rv, (quoted in Maryks, *The Jesuit Order*, 177).

78.   Possevino's memorial to Acquaviva (1598), 349v–350r. References to 2 Cor. 3:15 and Acts 9:15.

79.   Possevino's memorial to Acquaviva (1598), 350v.

80.   Possevino's memorial to Acquaviva (1598), 349rv. Reference to Col. 3:11.

81.   Possevino to Sacchini, 60r; see also Possevino's memorial to Acquaviva (1598), 349v.

82.   Possevino to Sacchini, 59v. Reference to Eph. 2:14 (*utraque unum*).

83.   For an in-depth analysis of this narrative, see Guido Mongini, *Maschere dell'identità: alle origini della Compagnia di Gesù* (Rome: Storia e Letteratura, 2016), 373–429; Mongini, "The Persecutions of the Jesuits."

84.   Possevino's letter to Clement VIII, f. 120v. References to Eph. 4:4 and 1 Cor. 1:27.

85.   On Ignatius as an "alter Paul," see Rogelio García Mateo, *Ignacio de Loyola. Su espiritualidad y su mundo cultural* (Bilbao: Mensajero, 2000), 65–88 and especially Mongini, *Maschere dell'identità*, 313–71. The narrative of Ignatius as "other Paul" was developed in the early stage of the life of the Society, but it did not disappear and was used, for instance, during the process of beatification of Ignatius Loyola, that ended in 1609 (Mongini, *Maschere dell'identità*, 364–65.

86.   See Mongini *Maschere dell'identità*, 341–47, with a rich bibliography.

87.   On their role in shaping the identity of the Society, see Mongini, *Maschere dell'identità*, passim.

88.   Pedro de Ribadeneyra, "De prognatis genere hebreorum Societatis aditu non excludendis," ARSI, *Instit.* 184/I, 292r–295v, published in *Mon. Rib.* 2:374–84, my translation. A French translation in Rastoin, *Du même sang*, 169–88. See also another important contribution by Pedro de Ribadeneyra, "Letter to the Member of the sixth General Congregation (1608)," *Mon Rib* 2:247–54.

89.   Ribadeneyra, "De prognatis genere hebreorum," 383–84. According to Ribadeneyra, Juan de Avila predicted that the Society of Jesus would be lost in two circumstances: if it accepted too many members and if it made distinctions according to lineage and blood (*Ibid.*, 381).

90.   Possevino's memorial to Mercurian (1576), f. 207r., quoted in Cohen, "Jesuits and New Christians," 12–13.

91.   See Cohen, "Jesuits and New Christians," 13.

92.   Cohen, "Jesuits and New Christians," 27.

93.   John Patrick Donnelly, "Antonio Possevino's Plan for World Evangelization," *Catholic Historical Review* 74 (1988): 179–98; Emanuele Colombo, "Il libro del mondo. Un documento di Antonio Possevino," in *Milano, l'Ambrosiana e la conoscenza dei nuovi mondi (secoli XVII–XVIII)*, ed. Michela Catto and Gianvittorio Signorotto (Milan: Bulzoni, 2015), 335–62.

94.   Antonio Possevino, "Ragionamento di Antonio Possevino alla signoria di Venetia in collegio di detta repubblica sopra il fatto e il modo della lega, il di 12 di agosto 1582," in Paul Pierling, *Bathory et Possevino: documents inédits sur les rapports du Saint-Siège avec les Slaves* (Paris: Leroux, 1887), 181.

95.   See Wiki, "Die 'Christão-Novos.'"

96.   See Ines G. Županov, *Missionary Tropics. The Catholic Frontier in India (16th–17th Centuries)* (Ann Arbor: University of Michigan Press, 2005), 199, 313.

97.   Dauril Alden, *The Making of an Enterprise: The Society of Jesus in Portugal, Its*

Empire, and Beyond, 1540–1750 (Stanford: Stanford University Press, 1996), 257–58. On Brazil, see also José Gonçalves Salvador, *Cristãos-novos, jesuítas e Inquisição: Aspectos de sua actuação nas Capitanias do Sul, 1530–1680* (São Paulo: Livraria Pioneira, 1969), 136–46.

98.   Wiki, "Die 'Christão Novos,'" 359.

99.   For the early debates, see for instance the exchanges between Ignatius and Francis Xavier, in John Correia-Alfonso, "Ignatius and Indian Jesuit Vocations," in *Jesuits in India: In Historical Perspective*, ed. Teotónio R. de Souza and Charles J. Borges (Macau: Instituto Cultural de Macau-Xavier Center of Historical Research, 1992), 73–82.

100.   See Mercurian to Ruy Vicente, provincial of Goa, 1579, in Carlos Mercês de Melo, *The Recruitment and Formation of the Native Clergy in India, 16th–19th Century: An Historico-Canonical Study* (Lisbon: Agência Geral do Ultramar, 1955), 166.

101.   Metcalf, "Jesuit in Brazil: Defining the Vision," 787–814.

102.   See Alexandre Coello de la Rosa, "El estatuto de Limpieza de Sangre de la Compañía de Jesús (1593) y su influencia en el Perú Colonial," *AHSI*, 80 (2011): 45–76; Coello de la Rosa, "De mestizos y criollos en la Compañía de Jesús (Perú, siglos XVI–XVII), *Revista de Indias*, 68 (2008): 37–66; Larissa Brewer-García, "Bodies, Texts, and Translators: Indigenous Breast Milk and the Jesuit Exclusion of Mestizos in Late Sixteenth-Century Peru," *Colonial Latin American Review* 21, no. 3 (2012): 365–90. "In the Jesuit case, in particular, the question of ordaining Native and mestizo priests in the Americas and other satellite missions arose alongside (and sometimes in dialogue with) questions of ordaining conversos and moriscos in the Peninsula" (ibid., 368).

103.   Bartolomé Hernández to Juan de Ovando, president of the Council of the Indies, Lima, April 19, 1572, quoted in Emilio Lissón Chaves, *La Iglesia de España en e Perú. Colección de documentos para la historia de la iglesia en el Perú, que se encuentran en varios archivos*, II, (Sevilla: Edit. Católica Española, 1944), 600. See also Bernard Lavallé, "La admisión de los americanos en la Compañía de Jesús. El caso de la provincia peruana en el siglo XVI," *Historica* 11 (1985): 137–53.

104.   See the case of the Jesuit mestizo Blas Valera (1545–1597): Francisco de Borja Medina, "Blas Valera y la dialéctica 'exclusión-integración del otro,'" *AHSI* 68 (1999): 229–67; Lavallé, "La admisión de los americanos," 143–47; Sabine Hyland, *The Jesuit and the Incas: The extraordinary life of Padre Blas Valera, S. J.* (Ann Arbor: University of Michigan Press, 2003); Sabine Hyland, *Gods of the Andes: An Early Jesuit Account of Inca Religion and Andean Christianity* (University Park: Pennsylvania State University Press, 2011); Aliocha Maldavsky, *Vocaciones inciertas: misión y misioneros en la provincia jesuita del Perú en los siglos XVI y XVII* (Madrid: Consejo Superior de Investigaciones Científicas, 2012).

105.   See *MP* 3:205–6 for the third provincial congregation and *MP* 3:333 for the fourth one. In both cases, the congregation banned the mestizos and discouraged the acceptance of criollos. See also Acquaviva's letter to the Peruvian province, January 1584, *MP* 3:341–50, here 343.

106.   Francesca Cantù, "'Come ese nuevo mundo está tan lexos destas partes.' Strategie e politiche di governo della Compagnia di Gesù nella provincia peruviana (1581–1607)," in *I gesuiti ai tempi di Claudio Acquaviva. Strategie politiche, religiose e culturali tra Cinque e Seicento* (Brescia: Morcelliana, 2007), 119–55.

107.   See Brewer-García, "Bodies, Texts, and Translators." For Acosta's support of anti-mestizo views, see José de Acosta, *De procuranda indorum salute* [1577], trans. L. Pereña (Madrid: Consejo Superior de Investigaciones Científicas), 2:69. For his statement in favor of admitting mestizos to the secular clergy, see José de Acosta, *Declaración judicial*, Lima, August 5, 1583, in *MP*, 3:271–74. See Borja de Medina, "Blas Valera y la dialéctica," 240–41.

108.   Acquaviva to the visitor of Peru, October 1596, in *MP*, 6:224–25, quoted in Borja de Medina, "Blas Valera y la dialéctica," 266. Later, exceptions were made for Japanese and Chinese, but not for Native people of America.

109.   Coello de la Rosa, "De mestizos y criollos."

110.   For a recent reassessment, see David Nirenberg, "Was There Race Before Modernity? The Example of 'Jewish' Blood in Late Medieval Spain," in *The Origin of Racism in the West*, ed. Miriam Eliav-Feldon, Benjamin Isaac, and Joseph Ziegler (Cambridge: Cambridge University Press, 2009), 232–64.

111.   For an overview of the development of the discrimination of conversos in Portugal, in connection with local politics, see Claude B. Stuczynski, "Negotiated Relationships: Jesuits and Portuguese 'Conversos:' A Reassessment," in *"The Tragic Couple": Encounters between Jews and Jesuits*, ed. James Bernauer and Robert Maryks (Leiden: Brill, 2014), 43–61.

112.   There are fascinating parallels in Ignatius' and Possevino's views on Jews and Muslims. On Ignatius, see Reites, "St. Ignatius of Loyola and the Jews"; Reites, *St. Ignatius and the People of the Book*; Francisco de Borja Medina, "Ignacio de Loyola y los judíos," *Anuario del Instituto Ignacio de Loyola* 4 (1997): 37–63; Colombo, "Defeating the Infidels." On Possevino, see Colombo, "The Watershed of Conversion"; Colombo, "Entre guerre juste et accommodation. Antonio Possevino et l'islam," *Dix-septième siècle* 268, no. 3 (2015): 393–408.

113.   Possevino's memorial to Mercurian (1576), 209rv, quoted in Cohen, "Jesuits and New Christians," 19–20.

CHAPTER TWO

Eternal Blackness

*Body and Soul in Jesuit
Martín de Roa's Afterlife*

ERIN KATHLEEN ROWE

DURING THE GLOBAL EXPANSION of Iberian powers, missionaries and colonial administrators grappled with one crucial question: Could non-Europeans become Christians? The question appears simple on its surface, but it contained within it a complex variety of early modern attitudes about social inclusion, understanding, reason, climate, and race. As Spanish Jesuits fanned the globe, taking prominent positions in colonial cities, they carried with them a series of assumptions about conversion that flowed along networks that connected disparate sites. One central node for these networks was the city of Seville, a hub of the Spanish empire as well as the peninsular province of Andalusia. While the missionary experiences of Jesuits in Andalusia remained distinct from their confreres in Cartagena de Indias, Manila, or Japan, they shared a set of theological, sacramental, and logistical concerns about race and conversion.

Spanish missionaries encountered a multiplicity of non-European people as they took to the oceans, and each encounter was shaped by the political and religious contexts of that particular meeting. Jesuits could be colonizers or suppliants, major power brokers or dependent hangers-on. In the colonial context, of course, Spaniards created hierarchical structures of power that oppressed Indigenous people and promoted the trafficking of millions of West and Central Africans. While the numbers of Indigenous people brought to Seville remained small, the traffic of enslaved Black Africans accelerated rapidly from the late fifteenth to the mid-seventeenth century. Seville maintained the largest population of enslaved and free Black Africans in the kingdom of Castile, although enslaved people could be found in relatively high numbers throughout Andalusia.

In the 1620s, Jesuits in Seville took center stage working within enslaved communities, evangelizing newly arrived Black Africans while participating in Atlantic debates over color difference, race, and slavery. One highly respected Jesuit scholar who was also a lifelong resident of Andalusia, Martín de Roa, produced sacred histories and lives of local saints that were marginal to such concerns. Yet, as a Jesuit living in Seville, he lived in and among such conversations, and they appeared in unexpected places in his scholarship. The most vivid example of this appeared in a text about the ensouled body after the Final Judgment, which included a section about Black bodies in heaven. In a brief but astonishing passage, Roa put forward an erudite theology of racial difference, salvation, and the spiritual body. His striking analysis originated out of the ongoing debates about the spiritual capacity of Black Africans that swirled around his Jesuit brothers. While expounding on the appearances of resurrected bodies in heaven, Roa launched a sharp critique of contemporary notions about the vileness of the Black body, instead insisting on the divine celebration of the diversity of nature in the eternal kingdom.

The Jesuits and Slavery in Andalusia

The institution of slavery had a long history throughout the Mediterranean, persisting from antiquity throughout the Middle Ages, passing along thriving networks of trade between Mediterranean societies across religious and geographic boundaries. Slave markets in medieval Iberia largely consisted of captives taken during the long series of wars between the Christian and Islamic polities.[1] While the fifteenth century saw an influx of enslaved people from the Canary Islands, the slave trade took a dramatic turn in the latter half of the fifteenth century as Portuguese merchants began to traffic large numbers of enslaved people from West and Central Africa, many of whom were sold into Spain. Domínguez Ortiz calculates that there were 14,670 slaves in the archbishopric of Seville by 1565.[2] But its enslaved population remained diverse through the period. For example, Francisco Farfán, a resident of Seville in the middle of the sixteenth century, owned four enslaved people: a *morisca*; a "Berber" (that is, North African Muslim); a *mulata*; and an "Indian." Berber, Moorish, and *morisco* slaves were sometimes described as white [*esclavo blanco*], though descriptions of individual enslaved people often made more fine-tuned descriptions of skin color.[3] In spite of such diversity, however, the preponderance of enslaved people in sixteenth- and seventeenth-century Iberia transitioned from esclavos blancos to those of Black African origin or descent, referred to as Black slaves [*esclavos negros*].

Black Africans, then, joined a society familiar with both slavery and the problem of large-scale conversions. The Spanish monarchy initiated several waves of forced baptisms, including a series of mass conversions of Jews beginning in the late fourteenth century, the 1492 expulsion of all Jews who refused to convert, and the 1502 requirement of all Muslims to convert after the fall of the last Nasrid kingdom of Granada. These large populations of the newly baptized and their descendants—so-called New Christians—posed a series of theological and logistical issues for Castilian clergy, which sought to persuade and coerce these groups into "proper" Christian behavior, with mixed success.[4] Following similar patterns, Spanish missionaries participated in the wholesale (forced) conversion of hundreds of thousands of Indigenous people in the Americas. In all these cases, clerical ideas about evangelization unfolded in diverse ways, with tactics swaying between two main poles: persuasion and coercion.

In Seville, attempts at persuasion involved public gatherings of enslaved people and other marginalized groups such as criminals and moriscos, where they would be ministered to by Jesuit priests. The Jesuits appeared in Seville in 1554, and quickly took up missionary activities of the city. Alonso de Avila (d. 1556) and Francisco Arias de Párraga (d. 1605), for example, preached to prisoners, the poor, moriscos, and enslaved people.[5] Martín de Roa's *Historia de la Provincia de Andalucía de la Compañía de Jesús* [*History of the Jesuit Province of Andalusia*] included brief hagiographic entries that celebrated the Society's domestic missionary labor. For example, Roa praised Father Ambrosio de Castillo, who helped found the first Jesuit house in Cádiz: "And it was not small, the fruit that Father Ambrosio produced in all types of people, mostly children and slaves, with his teaching of Christian doctrine."[6] Roa's account of Father Jorge Álvarez's life and ministry in Seville discussed his great charity for the poor. In one anecdote, Álvarez encountered an (unnamed) enslaved Black woman who was deathly ill of a "disgusting and foul smelling" diarrhea; the priest entered her home and ministered to her with gentleness and kindness, administering the sacraments.[7] Álvarez's ability to withstand a particularly repellent disease was a common marker of sanctity in early modern hagiography, casting Jesuit dedication to spiritual healing as a form of holiness.

Martín de Roa was himself a lifelong resident of Andalusia. Little is known about his early years before his profession to the Society of Jesus in 1578, when he was about eighteen years old. Once a Jesuit, he moved around Andalusia, getting a degree in theology at the University of Osuna and working in Écija and Jerez de la Frontera before becoming a rector at the Colegio de San Hermenegildo in Seville in 1614. In 1628, Roa left Seville, eventually dying in Montilla in 1637. Like many scholars of early modern Spain, Roa was primarily preoccupied with sacred history; he wrote ecclesiastical histories of Écija, Cordoba, and Málaga as well as the histories of the three patron saints of Jerez de Frontera, eventually producing around twenty-one works.[8] In 1647, Jesuit author Juan de Santibáñez described Roa as "one of the most illustrious men of the century."[9]

The Jesuit houses in Seville where Roa resided between 1614 and 1628 hummed with intellectual and theological activity. Out of the six Jesuit colleges established in the city in the second half of the sixteenth century, San Hermenegildo separated from the Casa Profesa and was formally dedicated in 1579. At this college, Jesuits oversaw the education of local boys in the liberal arts, while the Casa Profesa was their main residence. Under the leadership of theologian Juan de Pineda, San Hermenegildo was transformed into a "center of literary production."[10] The period from 1600 to 1630 witnessed an explosion of Jesuit scholarship radiating out from the college.[11] The deep engagement of Jesuit scholars at San Hermenegildo and the Casa Profesa on three major issues—evangelization of the marginalized, discoveries of ancient relics, and the Immaculate Conception—made them ideal partners for the Archbishop of Seville, Pedro de Castro Quiñones, who arrived in 1610 from Granada. Ardent supporter of ecclesiastical liberty, defender of the authenticity of sacred artifacts in Granada, critic of efforts to make Teresa of Avila co-patron saint of Spain, and vocal devotee of the Immaculate Conception, Castro participated in the most important political-ecclesiastical debates of his day, as well as being connected with the most famous intellectuals in Seville's vibrant humanist culture.[12]

Castro also turned his attention to the evangelization of enslaved people in Seville, choosing to partner with the Jesuits when looking into the baptismal state of enslaved Black Africans. By 1614, Castro was requiring owners to interrogate their slaves about baptism, but he handed the real questioning over to the Jesuits, whose efforts revealed that many enslaved people evinced little to no understanding of the sacrament they had performed on them or what it meant, in direct violation of canon law.[13] Castro's main Jesuit ally, Diego Ruiz de Montoya (d. 1632), was a professor of theology whose extensive experience in domestic missionary work made him an ideal choice to draft new instructions on how to properly baptize enslaved people.[14] Ruiz asked Black Christians what they thought baptism meant, how it had been performed, and whether or not they had wanted to be baptized (as opposed to coercion at the hands of enslavers and missionaries). Shocked at his findings, the Jesuit father declared that in cases where the catechumen had received the sacrament without proper understanding, the sacrament was to be re-administered following proper catechesis.[15]

While consent (requiring understanding) had always been the legitimating factor of the sacraments, ecclesiastical authorities had consistently resisted their re-administration, worried that reapplication would dilute belief in sacramental grace. As a result, theologians typically viewed coerced baptisms of Jews and Indigenous people as exhibiting some degree of consent, no matter how minimal. Forced baptisms, therefore, had commonly been upheld by theologians and canon law from the Middle Ages on, in spite of some equivocation on the problem of forcing consent.[16] Castro's and Ruiz's refusal to accept the legitimacy of such sacraments, then, set them dramatically apart from their predecessors and contemporaries.[17]

Ruiz's instructions on baptism appeared within Alonso de Sandoval's *Naturaleza, policia sagrada y profana*, which was printed in Seville in 1627, in the same year as a standalone reprint of the instructions.[18] Although Sandoval's work was printed in Seville, it was written in Cartagena de Indias during the Jesuit's work in the port city ministering to newly arrived slaves. Sandoval, like Ruiz, was privy to the spiritual state of enslaved people and the problems surrounding correct baptism. The Jesuit decrees reached far into Latin America to cities such as Lima, Mexico City, and Puebla de los Ángeles, where local provincials discussed the problem of baptism and what came to be called the "Jesuit method" throughout the first half of the seventeenth century.[19] The Jesuit node in Seville, therefore, circulated texts and ideas throughout the Spanish Atlantic, and the Atlantic world refracted back into Seville and Andalusia more broadly. Questions about slavery and the entrance of Black Catholics into the fold of the Church reverberated even in peninsular spaces that might seem on the surface to be far removed.

Color Difference and the Body

The twin problems of catechesis and forced baptism were entangled with larger debates over the spiritual and moral capabilities of different groups of people. The oppressive hierarchies that were entrenched throughout medieval and early modern Europe began to coalesce in ever-harsher ways along with the consolidation of state power and global colonial expansion. The military conquests in the Americas and acceleration of the slave trade from West Africa at the end of the fifteenth century led Europeans to systematize ethnic differences in ways both cultural and embodied. The idea that difference was embodied had evolved throughout the Middle Ages; anti-Semitism drew from ideas about lineage and inheritability of virtue and vice.[20] But the "discovery" of the Indigenous peoples of America and the increasing numbers of Black Africans in the Spanish Atlantic led to intense theological debates about the origin and meaning of color difference, and its relationship to cultural difference, potential for conversion, and legal enslavement.

Humanist scholar Juan Ginés de Sepúlveda (in)famously argued in favor of Indigenous enslavement, proclaiming: "God has given great and exceedingly clear instructions respecting the destruction of these barbarians . . . and that it is lawful not only to subject these barbarians, polluted with heinous acts of lasciviousness and the impious worship of false gods, to our dominion in order to bring them to spiritual health."[21] While some of Sepúlveda's positions were contested deeply within Spain, almost all theologians agreed that colonial rule would remedy the "barbaric" customs of Indigenous people, particularly their idolatry. Indigenous systems of belief corroded their spiritual health, leading to unnatural and sinful behavior. The metaphor of the spiritual body here allowed Sepúlveda to connect lack of reason (barbarism) with culture (idolatry) and sinful acts (lasciviousness).

Jesuit missionaries found themselves in a complicated position, as they had to defend universal application of baptism while drawing on a number of circulating beliefs about spiritual potential and race. The most well-known Jesuits who worked with enslaved Africans in the Americas—Alonso de Sandoval, Pedro Claver, and Antonio Vieira—attempted to convince white enslavers to baptize the enslaved and to treat them "well." The treatise in which Sandoval included Ruiz's and Castro's instructions for baptism was written in part to attack common beliefs that Africans were too barbaric to understand the Christian faith. Sandoval insisted that the inability to speak Spanish did not render Africans without intelligence or understanding: "From this two things can be inferred: First, that Black people are not animals, as some say, that for this reason they believe they [black people] are incapable of becoming Christian, nor that they are to be called children, or babies, because they are adult men, and as such ought to be baptized."[22] Sandoval paired animals and infants here as representing physicality without reason; resisting such common characterizations of Black men, he argued that because African men were indeed *men* (adult humans) they were endowed with reason and understanding. As a result, they could and should be baptized and folded into Christian society.[23] Yet it is crucial to note that Sandoval never suggested that Black Africans be manumitted or treated as equals to white Spaniards (other than in their equal promise of redemption).

It was, therefore, the duty of Christian rulers to force their subjects into proper, Christian behavior, and concepts about inheritability of vice made the subjection of Indigenous people and Africans justifiable over many generations. The idea of being stained with an inheritable punishment was enshrined in Christian thought through the doctrine of Original Sin, according to which every human—except the Virgin Mary—was born with the stain of the first sin committed by Adam and Eve. Such beliefs deepened against heretics and Jews in the Middle Ages and became systemized in Castilian law in the fifteenth and sixteenth centuries in a series of laws banning New Christians from holding certain offices, particularly in the Church. Alexandre Coello de la Rosa asserts that these so-called blood purity laws could have less to do with race than theological strictures about the inheritability of a propensity to sinfulness or virtue that connected being newly baptized with the potential for heresy.[24] Scholars such as María Elena Martínez have argued that these blood purity (*limpieza de sangre*) laws were transported to the New World, where they became the foundation of racist hierarchies.[25] While the Jesuits initially resisted the establishment of blood purity statutes in their order, they eventually put them in place following 1593, which meant not only that moriscos and *conversos* were officially denied entry into the Society, but so were Indigenous people and Africans, which created racialized hierarchies within the Church.

Barbaric and beastly, ugly and deformed, stained and divinely ordained slaves—such attitudes about West and Central Africans permeated early modern Iberian culture on both sides of the Atlantic. By the early seventeenth century, some thinkers began to describe the enslavement of Africans as divine punishment, a hereditary legacy from the Curse of Ham. Dissemination of this specific exegesis of the Genesis story about Noah and his sons added a critical new element to ideas about inheritability, as it entwined divinely-mandated, perpetual punishment (enslavement) with bodily blackness (that is, dark skin pigmentation).[26] While debates about natural slavery could focus most intently on assessments of reason and culture, ideas about racial difference were always embodied. In the early seventeenth century, Prudencio de Sandoval—a historian, monk, and bishop—framed his vitriol against conversos with a rhetorical question: "Who could deny that the descendants of Jews remain, and persist in the evil tendencies stemming from their ancient ingratitude and poor understanding, just as Black people are inseparable from the accident of their blackness?"[27] This brief moment in Sandoval's biography of Charles V illuminates much about early modern attitudes about race, virtue, and inheritability—Jews and their descendants retained their vile rejection of Christ, which would be passed from generation to generation in a similar way to Original Sin itself. To make his point, Sandoval reached out to a version of "Can an Ethiopian be washed white?" (a popular early modern Spanish aphorism) by comparing the inability of conversos to free themselves of their genetic stain with the inability of Black Africans to no longer be black. While it is possible to read blackness here operating in parallel to the entrenched sin of Jews, his use of the qualifying adjective "accident" in describing the black skin of Africans suggests that Sandoval viewed "evil tendencies" of Jews/conversos inherent in the same way as naturally occurring physical traits. The pairing of negative inheritable qualities with physical traits clearly demonstrates the ways in which Iberian thinkers understood race.

The connection between bodies and virtue had ancient roots. Ancient Greek physicians, particularly Galen, developed theories about bodily composition in which all humans were composed of four humors (blood, yellow bile, phlegm, and black bile), each with their own qualities (hot, cold, dry, and moist, respectively). While individuals contained all humors and the ideal was to achieve balance, they also had dominant humors and qualities that affected both physical and emotional/intellectual development. For example, femaleness derived from damp and cold humors, while males were dry and hot, which endowed men with energy, strength, and advanced intellectual capabilities.[28] While shaping basic gender and personality, however, humors could fluctuate based on age, health, and climate. The role of climate in the development of dark skin was repeated throughout the early modern period as one main explanation for physical difference. Roxann Wheeler argues that when considering early modern ideas about race, we need to contextualize them within the humoral system. The qualities of humors constituted complexion, and the term "complexion" during this period did not refer to flesh tones; rather, as Valentin Groebner describes it: "As a person's behavior, appearance, aptitude, and moral stature were perceived to be intricately connected to his or her physical, humoral, 'natural' condition, the term complexion was thus employed for a relatively wide range of meanings."[29] Because complexion fluctuated, many early modern thinkers increasingly attempted to "fix" or stabilize the body. For example, Spaniards who traveled to the Americas worried a great deal about what would happen to white, European bodies in the colonies.[30] The desire to stabilize European bodies led in turn to the fixing of brown and black bodies as unchangeably inferior.

While humoralism had ancient Greek roots, the embodied nature of humanity was foundational to Christian theology and eschatology. Christian ideas about the body were ambivalent—it could be viewed as the dialectic of the soul, the gateway to sin, a path to spiritual transcendence, and the final promise for all those saved during the Last Judgment when all bodies would be resurrected intact. All of these teachings about the body existed simultaneously, each playing its own part in belief and practice. Scholars have sometimes focused predominantly on the Church's attitude about sinfulness residing in bodily pleasure—most clearly seen in the evolution of the seven deadly sins, in which all major sins were located in the body and embodied emotion. Yet because the redemption of all people had been achieved through Christ's body and God Himself created the first bodies, flesh was part of God's gift to humanity. Christ's own humanity, suffering, and bodily resurrection meant that the saints could imitate Christ's sacrifice through martyrdom, either literal martyrdom at the hands of the enemies of Christianity or metaphorical martyrdom through extreme self-imposed asceticism. The body, in short, could act as a site of salvation, while the bodies of saints transformed into loci of the miraculous. Further, the incorruption of the bodies of many saints presaged the eventual bodily resurrection of all people.[31] While believers were reminded that earthly death awaited everyone as a warning that the things of the secular world were transitory, the eternal "true life" that existed after death also, importantly, included one's body.

The relationship between flesh and spirit led to a series of questions about the literal state of both, especially after death. When one died, for example, and before the Last Judgment, what form did the person's spirit take in the afterlife and to what extent did it mirror bodily functions such as sight and smell? Such questions were far more than the curiosity of the laity but serious theological questions that philosophers had grappled with since the days of Saint Augustine, and that subsequently had been taken up by major theologians following Tertullian, Jerome, and Augustine. Although they agreed that before the Final Judgment all souls remained incorporeal, they pondered how, then, souls could be tormented in hell and purgatory. If people did not have bodies, could they feel? Were the fires of hell dreams or material? As Michael Barbezat shows, medieval theologians argued that "imaginary" hell fire could still burn, and that it was possible to have sensation outside of one's body.[32]

But it was bodily resurrection and its aftermath that concerned medieval and early modern theologians most intensely. Caroline Bynum describes the theological stakes succinctly: "Theologians agreed that body is crucial. What is and must be redeemed is a psychosomatic unity, a person, full individual both in its physicality and its consciousness. Although what survived death immediately was separated soul, soul was not person. Without its body, it was incomplete."[33] But once the person was reintegrated with his or her body following the Final Judgment, what would that look like, especially for those in heaven? How old would one be? What height and weight? Would bodily imperfections ("defects" in their language) be healed? Would people still inhabit gendered bodies? The permutations of such questions were almost endless, especially those concerning bodies that were dispersed or destroyed in some fashion at the moment of death. Augustine of Hippo even raised the issue of what happens to the bodies of those who had been consumed by cannibals (and presumably digested and integrated into another person's body). Augustine detailed his thoughts on all these questions in *City of God*, arguing that all people will most likely be resurrected around the age of thirty regardless of what age they died, because this was Christ's age at death. Furthermore, we resurrect with our gender, insisting (contrary to some theologians of late antiquity) that being female is not, in fact, a defect, but rather "natural," and originating from God. He continued by arguing for resurrected bodies as returning to wholeness following any kind of deformity, mutilation, or dispersal.[34]

This long theological tradition continued into the early modern period. While most commonly known as a historian, Martín de Roa detailed the same questions and concerns for an early modern audience lay people as well as clergy in one of his most popular works. His *Estado de los bienaventurados en el cielo. De los niños en el limbo. De los condenados en el infero, y de todo este Uniuerso despues de la resurrection y juizio uniuersal* (State of the blessed in heaven. Of children in limbo. Of the condemned in hell, and the whole universe after the resurrection and last judgment) first appeared in Seville in 1624, followed by a series of printings in 1626, 1627, and 1628, as well as in Gerona (1627), Barcelona (1631), Madrid (1653), and Alcalá de Henares (1663). It quickly traversed Europe, appearing in translated editions in Portuguese (Lisbon) in 1630, in Italian in 1626 and 1643 (Orvieto and Venice, respectively), and French (Lyon) in 1643. This work followed the major questions set forth by his medieval and early modern antecedents, systemically explored every facet of people's experiences after death in heaven, purgatory, and hell following the Last Judgment. Roa organized the work around specific questions that he perceived as the most important—or those that were most heavily debated—including how bodies looked when resurrected, at what age individuals are resurrected, what Limbo was like for babies, what heaven and earth looked like after the Judgment, etc. Much time was also spent detailing how the senses operated in heaven—could people see and smell, did they talk and sing, did their bodies smell good, etc. While such questions emerged out of long-standing theological debates, they also spoke to deep seated anxieties from early modern laypeople seeking to understand what the afterlife portended. Roa was clear about his desire to write to a broad audience in his dedication to his (lay) noble patron, Rodrigo Ponce de León, Duke of Arcos: "I also serve the honest curiosity that stems out of just devotion from those who, with generous ardor, aspire to the eternal good."[35]

Roa followed Augustine's template by opening his study with the basic question of whether people were resurrected in their own bodies, declaring in nearly identical terms as the Bishop of Hippo that "they will preserve the difference between male and female, in the same bodies that they each had on earth; because this distinction between women and men is not a defect, but the perfection of nature."[36] The idea that the body resurrected needed to be the same as the person's body before death attests to the premodern belief that specific physical qualities—including humors—constituted personhood. The dead were not only to have a body, but *their* body, without which they could never achieve wholeness. Roa even noted that the bodies would have "their same humors," and in the subsequent chapter, their same hair color and facial hair. Yet in both chapters 1 and 2, Roa engaged with a serious philosophical problem: if the body needed to be the same, it also needed to be different—different because it would be perfected. Just as one's soul in heaven would be without sin or failure, so the body would be "robust, without scars, or another fault in the body."[37] The erasure of fault, then, extended to the body in the same way that it manifested in the soul, and theologians carefully separated out faults from nature. While clearly some considered the female sex a defect, Roa pushed back. Gender, humors, and hair color resided in the realm of the "natural"—they were variations, not flaws.

Breaking away from his antecedents, Roa next tackled a question deeply pressing to his seventeenth-century readers that did not concern the medieval: "Whether everyone will be resurrected in one color, or in white or black as they had been." While the chapter addressed several types of difference, his question about skin color came first, and the chapter began immediately with the sentence: "Color is an accident that results from the mildness of the first qualities. These the Philosophers called the cold, heat, dryness, and humidity that mix together in diverse proportions. . . . In regions where there is more heat, men become blacker in color, just as they are whiter where it is colder."[38] Roa then added that in mild climates, a person could be black or white depending on which qualities dominated over the others, leading to greater variety, which was why some nations had both black and white residents. This assertion was fully in line with the humoral-climate theory of the day.

Yet clearly some of Roa's contemporaries claimed that all people would be resurrected "in the same color" rather than different ones. The question of skin color in heaven originated in a common belief in Christian thought: monogenesis. If all humans were descended from Adam, what was the "original" skin color of humankind? Unsurprisingly, all Europeans espousing monogenesis agreed that Adam and Eve had been white. Roa cited those who argued for original whiteness and their position that people in heaven would all be white "since because it is filled with more light, it is first among all." Whiteness, then, was closer to divinity than blackness.

Roa agreed that the first men must have been white because of the perfect mildness and balance of the original world, but he elaborated that after the expulsion from Eden, people spread out across the globe and physical diversity evolved. The new variety of conditions gave rise to a diversity of humors, which "degenerated" original whiteness to varied colors, including blonde, red, brown, olive-skinned, and yellowish, "which are now the signs of different nations."[39] This is a fascinating insertion to the common discussions of skin color and climate because his list of colors referred to general appearance, especially hair color, and less obviously to skin tone. Missing from this particular list were the adjectives "black" (negro) and "white," (blanco) which featured prominently in the preceding sentences. The inclusion of *rubio* and *gualdado* (blond and yellowish) suggest that the degeneration of traits following postlapsarian climate change included those often associated with racial whiteness, such as yellow hair, and in turn begs the question whether or not any postlapsarian people retained the perfect "whiteness" of Adam and Eve. Roa concluded this section by explaining that over a long period of time, these "defects" (e.g., the movement away from prelapsarian whiteness) transformed into natural qualities and were therefore no longer flaws.[40]

After establishing the history of difference in human appearance, Roa announced that as natural qualities, such differences transformed from degenerative to natural, no matter where a person lived. He managed, therefore, to resolve a conundrum that affected Iberian thought in the seventeenth and eighteenth centuries that led to significant questioning of humoralism—that is, if climate theory were correct, why did Black people retain darker skin in cold climates even generations later? While some might respond by rejecting or questioning humoralism, Roa returned to the idea that over time difference became "natural"—an accident, like hair color, that would no longer change with climate. Of course, black skin—and possibly other complexions—were considered defects along with physical markers such as scars or missing limbs. But the former, unlike the latter, could, through time, become part of the diversity of nature. Roa concluded that Black Africans would be resurrected with their blackness, because this reflected humanity; it was truthful (verisimil), and therefore divinely ordained.

Roa then responded to his earlier statement that some argued that whiteness was superior to blackness because it was closer to divine light. Turning this on its head, he declared that in heaven black skin would be equally admirable and beautiful to white skin because both the skin (tez) and features (faicones) of Black Christians would be infused with "such light and grace. It will be a black not dull or dingy, but alive, luminous, like a jet stone shot through with blood, penetrating everywhere with more light than a sun, which will provide such a gift of brightness that it will endow incredible charm and grace."[41] The repeated use of words related to light (resplandeciente, luz, sol, claridad) were crucial to his overarching argument that Black Christians were as endowed with heavenly light as white ones, that being light-filled had nothing to do with skin tone or whiteness, but with divine grace. Other adjectives in this passage focused on life or being alive (*vivo*, *sangre*). Bringing together light and life connected the divine (light) to the flesh (blood), the soul and the body, with the blood acting as a light-giving source. The body completes the wholeness promised to all believers after the Final Judgment.

After this extraordinary passage, Roa returned to the idea of humors to provide further evidence. None, Roa declared, "will deny blackness this beauty," because the beauty did not originate in color ("*no consiste tanto en el color*") but rather in its pleasantness (*suavidad*) "that makes blackness and whiteness equal and gives great pleasure to the eyes." The variation in appearance acted in heaven as another facet of nature just as humoral difference did. For example, Roa pointed out, there would also be variation in the humoral balance of those in heaven. Even though the sanguine humor was the "most perfect," everyone would retain their individual dominant humor. The same, he concluded, would happen with color.[42] This section highlights Roa's awareness of entrenched negative views of blackness in contemporary society. Because the emphasis here is on appearance, rather than behavior, we can see how the discussion of skin tone acted as a stand-in for complexion more broadly. Yet he also accepted the idea that in life, blackness was less desirable—less "perfect"—than whiteness.

The subsequent paragraph is the last one in which Roa discussed skin color before moving on to hair color and more general forms of appearance or bodily states (age, health). Here he stated that those who were born white but for "external causes" degenerated (*degeneraron*) to a browner color (*tostado, oscuro*) that was aesthetically displeasing, as was common for those who work in the fields—clearly here he was referring to tanning—they would be returned to their original skin tone (i.e., become paler) with the resurrection. In this case, then, skin tone is a "defect" rather than a natural variation because it was not how the individual had been born. Here we see a fascinating colorism emerging among whites, where paler skin tone is marked as more pleasing and more perfect, and browning by the sun is equated with an injury, that is, bodily harm.[43] While the passage described tanning as a form of degeneration, its purpose is to highlight for the reader that some changes in skin tone constituted a defect requiring repair in the afterlife, while difference in skin color (and other forms of appearance such as hair color) did not. How we are born, versus what we become, was key to the relationship between soul and body in the resurrection, and to understanding what constituted wholeness and perfection in God's eyes and, of course, in society's.

While I have frequently translated various terms used by Roa as "skin color" or "skin tone," Roa himself only used the term "*tez*" (literally, the color of the face) once in his text. This term along with more general words like color, black, or white stress appearance generally, rather than skin specifically. Because references to blackness and whiteness clearly referred to the early modern beliefs about the essential embodied nature of race, I translated his terms to reflect this understanding. Yet the fact that Roa did not do this himself provides an important reminder that skin itself was not a concept that most early seventeenth-century thinkers considered, as their ideas derived from theology or humoralism, rather than anatomy. Complexion is not skin, as Wheeler and Groebner make pains to point out; it refers to a multifaceted series of signification and possibilities that cannot be reduced to fleshtone or medical notions of what comprises the skin. Skin as a subject of study by anatomists and physicians did intensify in the seventeenth century, which added a new series of theories and conceptions about body and identity, or body and being.[44] The theory of complexion was, of course, itself embodied, but it operated in ontologically distinct ways from the anatomy of skin.

If the diversity and accidents of the body are natural and divine, then the whole variety of humanity could be included in the divine embrace, rather than some having lesser souls or being denied access to God. The Jesuits, like all early modern Iberian clergy, straddled multiple discursive and administrative registers—they sought to evangelize Black Africans while at the same time engaging in the slave trade. They argued for the spiritual capabilities of people of color while expressing complacency regarding earthly oppressive hierarchies, including brutality to Black and brown bodies. Yet a careful look at Roa's conceptualization of the perfect merging of body and soul in the afterlife emphasized that after death, the blessed in heaven could retain their natural diversity, perfected through divine grace; this diversity itself was divinely mandated. Such a view had the potential to elevate the social status of enslaved and free Black Iberians, and to construct positive discourses of blackness. For Roa, blackness, radiated by divine light, transformed into eternal beauty.

Notes

1.   Charles Verlinden, *L'esclavage dans l'Europe médiévale* (Bruges: De Tempel, 1955); Debra Blumenthal, *Enemies and Familiars: Slavery and Master in Fifteenth-Century Valencia* (Ithaca, NY: Cornell University Press, 2011), 9–16; and Olivia Remie Constable, "Muslim Spain and Mediterranean Slavery: The Medieval Slave Trade as an Aspect of Muslim-Christian Relations," in *Christendom and its Discontents: Exclusion, Persecution, and Rebellion, 1000–1500,* ed. Scott Waugh and Peter D. Diehl (Cambridge: Cambridge University Press, 1996), 264–85.

2.   Alessandro Stella, *Histoires d'esclaves dans la péninsule ibérique* (Paris: Ed. de l'Ecole des Hautes Etudes en Sciences Sociales, 2000); and Antonio Domínguez Ortiz, *La esclavitud en Castilla en la edad moderna y otros estudios de marginados* (Granada: Editorial Comares, 2003), 9. See also R. M. Pérez García and M. F. Fernández Cháves, "La cuantificación de la población esclava en la Andalucía moderna. Una revisión metodológica," *Varia historia, belo horizonte* 31 (2015): 711–40.

3.   Manuel F. Fernández Chaves and Rafael M. Pérez García, *En los márgenes de la ciudad de Dios. Moriscos en Sevilla* (Valencia: Publicacions de la Universitat de València, 2009), 38.

4.   The literature on these two conversion efforts is vast. I cannot do justice to its complexity here, but for a few examples, see James S. Amelang, *Parallel Histories: Muslims and Jews in Inquisitorial Spain* (Baton Rouge: Louisiana State University Press, 2013); Mercedes García Arenal and Gerard Wiegers, eds., *Polemical Encounters: Christians, Jews and Muslims in Iberia and Beyond* (University Park: Penn State University Press, 2018); and Mark D. Meyerson and Edward D. English, eds., *Christians, Muslims, and Jews in Medieval and Early Modern Spain: Interaction and Cultural Change* (Notre Dame, IN: University of Notre Dame Press, 1999).

5.   Charles E. O'Neill and Joaquín María Domínguez, eds., *Diccionario histórico de la Compañía de Jesús: Biográfico-Temático,* vol. 3 (Rome: IHSJ, 2001), 1:304.

6.   Martín de Roa, *Historia de la Provincia de Andalucía de la Compañía de Jesús (1553–1602),* ed. and intro. Antonio Martín Paradas (Écija: Asociación de Amigos de Écija, 2005), 181.

7.   Roa, *Historia,* 269.

8.   Agustín Quirós, "Varones ilustres de la Provincia de Andalucía de la Compañía de Jesús que han florecido desde el año de 1552 hasta el de 1650," Biblioteca Nacional de España, MSS/23111, 19r. Many of Roa's principal works can be found in modern edition; for a full list, see Alexander S. Wilkinson, ed., *Iberian Books/ Libros ibéricos,* Vol. III (Leiden: Brill, 2010), 2083–85.

9.   Antonio Martín Paradas, ed. and intro., *Historia de la Provincia de Andalucía de la Compañía de Jesús (1553–1602)* (Écija: Asociación de Amigos de Écija, 2005), 28–31.

10.   José Antonio Ollero Pina, "La biblioteca del Colegio de San Hermenegildo y la Universidad de Sevilla," in *Fondos y Procedencias: Bibliotecas en la Biblioteca de la Universidad de Sevilla* (Seville: Universidad de Sevilla, 2013), 81.

11.   Pineda was given an entry in Francisco de Pacheco's famous *Libro de descripción de verdaderos Retratos de Ilustres and Memorables varones*, produced in 1599, 11r-12v. In addition to Pineda and Roa, this group included Luis de Alcazar, Diego Ruiz de Montoya, Diego de Granado, Alonso Rodríguez, and Antonio de Quintanadueñas.

12.   For a comprehensive overview of Seville's intellectual culture in the late sixteenth and early seventeenth centuries, see Guy Lazure, "To Dare Fame: Constructing a Cultural Elite in Sixteenth-Century Seville" (PhD thesis, Johns Hopkins University, 2003); and Luis Méndez Rodríguez, *Velázquez y la cultura sevillana* (Seville: University of Seville, 2005). For more on Castro and his controversies, see A. Katie Harris, *From Muslim to Christian Granada: Inventing a Christian Past in Early Modern Spain* (Baltimore, MD: Johns Hopkins University Press, 2007); Mercedes García-Arenal and Fernando Rodríguez Mediano, *The Orient in Spain: Converted Muslims, the Forged Lead Books of Granada, and the Rise of Orientalism*, trans. Consuelo López-Morillas (Leiden: Brill, 2013); and Erin Kathleen Rowe, *Saint and Nation: Santiago, Teresa of Avila, and Plural Identities in Early Modern Spain* (University Park: Penn State University Press, 2011).

13.   Aurelia Martín Casares and Christine Delaigue, "The Evangelization of Freed and Slave Black Africans in Renaissance Spain: Baptism, Marriage, and Ethnic Brotherhoods," *History of Religions* 52, no. 3 (February 2013): 214–35; and James Sweet, *Recreating Africa: Culture, Kinship, and Religion in the African-Portuguese World, 1441–1770* (Chapel Hill: University of North Carolina Press, 2003), 198–9.

14.   Ruiz de Montoya was celebrated by the Jesuits for his work in baptism and catechesis of black slaves: *ARSI*, Baet. 19/I, Litt. Ann.1632, 119; and *Carta del Padre Iuan Muñoz de Galvez rector del colegio de San Hermenegildo de la Compañia de Iesus de Sevilla para los superiors, y religiosos desta provincial de la Andalucia sobre la muerte, y virtudes del Padre Diego Ruiz de Montoya (1632)*, Biblioteca Nacional de España, VE/1375/9. "Muy sabida, y celebrada es la diligenicia, que puso, en que los Negros, y Negras, que vienen de Guinea, y Angola, se baptizassen."

15.   Diego Ruiz de Montoya, *Para remediar, y assegurar, quanto con la divina gracia fuere possible, que ninguno de los Negros, que vienen de Guinea, Angola, y otras partes de aquella costa de Africa, carezca del sagrado Baptismo* (Seville: Alonso Rodriguez Gamarra, 1614), ARSI, FG 720/III/4(b), 2r-v.

16.   On the larger history of medieval legal and theological debates surrounding forced baptism, see Marcia L. Colish, *Faith, Force and Fiction in Medieval Baptism Debates* (Washington, DC: Catholic University Press, 2014), 227–310.

17.   *Para remediar, y assegurar*, 4v.

18.   Alonso de Sandoval, *Naturaleza, policia sagrada i profana, costumbres i ritos, disciplina i catechismo evangelico de todos los etiopes* (Seville: Francisco de Lira, 1627). For more on Sandoval's career and beliefs, see Margaret M. Olsen, *Slavery and*

Salvation in Colonial Cartagena de Indias (Gainesville: University Press of Florida, 2004); and Ronald J. Morgan, "Postscript to his Brothers: Reading Alonso de Sandoval's *De Instauranda Aethiopum Salute* (1627) as a Jesuit Spiritual Text," in *Atlantic Studies: Global Currents* 5, no. 1 (2008): 75–98.

19. Of course, this effort tells us nothing about the ways in which black slaves understood the sacrament they received even with "proper catechesis."

20. David Nirenberg, "Was There Race before Modernity? The Example of 'Jewish' Blood in Late Medieval Spain," in *The Origins of Racism in the West*, ed. Miriam Eliav-Feldon, Benjamin Isaac, and Joseph Ziegler (Cambridge: Cambridge University Press, 2009), 232–64; Geraldine Heng, *The Invention of Race in the European Middle Ages* (Cambridge: Cambridge University Press, 2018).

21. Bartolomé de las Casas, *An Account, Much Abbreviated, of the Destruction of the Indies, with Related Texts*, intro. Franklin W. Knight and trans. Andrew Hurley (Indianapolis, IN: Hackett, 2003), 105.

22. Sandoval, *Naturaleza*, 241v.

23. Black Africans could even be saints (a point made by Sandoval himself), and their cults spread throughout the seventeenth century Iberian Atlantic: Erin Kathleen Rowe, *Black Saints in Early Modern Global Catholicism* (Cambridge: Cambridge University Press, 2019).

24. Alexandre Coello de la Rosa, "El estatuo de Limpieza de Sangre de la Compañía de Jesús (1593) y su influencia en el Perú," *Archivum Historicum Societatis Iesu* 80, no. 159 (January–June 2011): 45–93. José de Acosta and Francisco Arias de Párraga were among the Spanish Jesuits opposed to the Society's acceptance of *limpieza* statutes.

25. María Elena Martínez, *Genealogical Fictions: Limpieza de sangre, Religion, and Gender in Colonial Mexico* (Stanford, CA: Stanford University Press, 2008).

26. Didier Lahon, "Black African Slaves and Freedmen in Portugal," in *Black Africans in Renaissance Europe*, ed. T. F. Earle and K. J. P. Lowe (Cambridge: Cambridge University Press, 2005), 261–79; Benjamin Braude, "The Sons of Noah and the Construction of Ethnic and Geographical Identities in the Medieval and Early Modern Period," *The William and Mary Quarterly* 54, no. 1 (January 1997): 103–42; David Whitford, *The Curse of Ham in the Early Modern Era: The Bible and the Justifications for Slavery* (Burlington, VT: Ashgate, 2009). Braude and Whitford both trace the emergence of the Curse of Ham justification for enslavement, which did not become firmly entrenched until the mid- to late seventeenth century.

27. "Mas quien podra negar, que en los descendientes de Judios permanece, y dura la mala inclinacion de su Antigua ingratitude y mal conocimiento, como en los negros el accidente inseparable de su negrura?" Prudencio de Sandoval, *Historia de la vida y hechos del emperador Carlos V*, Part II (Antwerp: Heronymo Verdussen, 1681), 470 (año 1547).

28. On gender and humors, see Joan Cadden, *Meanings of Sex Difference in the Middle Ages: Medicine, Science, and Culture* (New York: Cambridge University Press, 1993).

29.   Valentin Groebner, "*Complexio*/Complexion: Categorizing Individual Natures, 1250–1600," in *The Moral Authority of Nature*, ed. Lorraine Daston and Fernando Vidal (Chicago: University of Chicago Press, 2003), 364; Roxann Wheeler, *The Complexion of Race: Categories of Difference in Eighteenth-Century British Culture* (Philadelphia: University of Pennsylvania Press, 2000). Fewer studies have traced the term's use in early modern Spanish thought, but Covarrubias defined it: "Comúnmente se toma por el temperamento de humores que cada uno tiene, de donde resulta ser de buena y fuerte complexión o delicada, frágil y enfermiza." Sebastián de Covarrubias Orozco, *Tesoro de la lengua castellana o Española*, 2nd ed. (Madrid: Editorial Castilia, 1995), 340.

30.   For colonial anxieties about the potential of the Americas to transform (or degenerate) creole bodies, see Rebecca Earle, *The Body of the Conquistador: Food, Race, and the Colonial Experience in Spanish America, 1492–1700* (Cambridge: Cambridge University Press, 2012); and Jorge Cañizares-Esguerra, "New World, New Stars: Patriotic Astrology and the Invention of Amerindian and Creole Bodies in Colonial Spanish America, 1600–1650," *American Historical Review* 104, no.1 (February 1999): 33–68.

31.   On the body and its role in salvation in medieval thought, see Matthew Kemp, "Most Evident to Us, Most Distant from God: The Body as Locus of Salvation in Bonaventure's *Breviloquium*," *Essays in Medieval Studies*, 34 (2018): 53–64. On the bodies of saints, see Carlos M. N. Eire, *From Madrid to Purgatory: The Art of Dying in Sixteenth-Century Spain* (Cambridge: Cambridge University Press, 1995), ch. 3.

32.   Michael D. Barbezat, "In a Corporeal Flame: The Materiality of Hellfire before the Resurrection in Six Latin Authors," *Viator* 44, no. 3 (2013): 1–20.

33.   Caroline Walker Bynum, "The Resurrection of the Body in the Middle Ages: Some Modern Implications," *Proceedings of the American Philosophical Society* 142, no. 4 (Dec. 1998): 594; Caroline Walker Bynum, *The Resurrection of the Body in Western Christianity, 200–1336* (New York: Columbia University Press, 1995).

34.   Augustine of Hippo, *De civitate Dei*, rev. ed, ed. P. G. Walsh, Loeb Classical Library (Cambridge, MA: Harvard University Press, 2014), book 22, ch. 12, 17, 19, and 22. For discussions about such issues among important medieval theologians, see: Thomas Aquinas, *Summa contra Gentiles, Book 4: Salvation*, intro. and trans. Charles J. O'Neil (Notre Dame, IN: University of Notre Dame Press, 1956), ch. 79, 80, and 82; and Peter Lombard, *The Sentences: Book 4. On the Doctrine of Signs*, trans. Giulio Silano (Toronto: Pontifical Studies: University of Toronto Press, 2010), 43–44.

35.   "Sirvo igualmente a la onesta curiosidad, que a la justa devocion de aquellos, que aspirando con generoso ardor a la possession de los bienes eternos" (4r). Martín de Roa, *Estado de los bienaventurados en el cielo. De los niños en el limbo. De los condenados en el infero: y de todo este Uniuerso despues de la resurrection y juizio uniuersal* (Seville: Francisco de Lyra, 1624). This work expanded his earlier treatise *Estado de las almas de purgatorio*, which was printed several times in Seville from 1619 to 1628.

36.   Roa, *Estado de los bienaventurados*, 7r–v.

37.   Roa, *Estado de los bienaventurados*, 5v–6v.

38.   Roa, *Estado de los bienaventurados*, 8v–9r.

39.   Roa, *Estado de los bienaventurados*, 9r–v: "De aqui los rubios, los bermejos, morenos, trigueños, gualdados, etc. que son ya como sello de diferentes naciones" (9v).

40.   Roa, *Estado de los bienaventurados*, 10r.

41.   Roa, *Estado de los bienaventurados*,10r–v: "Porque la tez, i faiciones del senblante seran tan ermosas, de tanto lustre, i gracia, que haran en aquella ciudad soberana una no menos admirable, que agradable varied. Serà el negro no deslavado, ni desluzido, sino vivo, resplandeciente, qual fuera el de un azabache quajado con sangre, penetrado todo de luz mas que de un sol, qual tendran por el don de claridad, que les dara incredible donaire, i gracia."

42.   Roa, *Estado de los bienaventurados*, 10v–11r.

43.   Roa, *Estado de los bienaventurados*, 11r.

44.   For an excellent overview that includes some discussion of anatomy, see Craig Koslofsky, "Knowing Skin in Early Modern Europe, c. 1450–1750," *History Compass* 12, no. 10 (October 2014): 794–806, https://onlinelibrary.wiley.com/doi/full/10.1111/hic3.12195. The University of London, King's College is engaged in a multi-year research project (2016–2021) entitled "Renaissance Skin," which brings together an interdisciplinary perspective on early modern notions of human and animal skin.

CHAPTER THREE

Jesuits and Unfree Labor in Early Modern East Asia

LIAM MATTHEW BROCKEY

MONARCHS, MANDARINS, AND MUSKETEERS filled the streets of Macau in early July 1642. News reaching that farthest Portuguese outpost in Asia two months earlier gave ample cause for celebration. A new king had been acclaimed in Lisbon, bringing an end to sixty years of Castilian dominion, and public displays of joy were in order. Befitting a colony, Macau's shows were distinctly imperial, and they had a distinct Asian flavor. According to one report, there were the customary artillery salvos, fireworks, and bullfights as well as pageants where noblemen and clergy exalted King João IV. Actors representing other regional powers likewise exhibited their enthusiasm for the new monarch. In one such display on July 7, Chinese officials in mandarin pomp marched before Japanese bearing lanterns and parasols and wearing kimonos. These were, in turn, followed by Persians in turbans and Dutch in broad-brimmed hats, with a substantial Portuguese contingent bringing up the train.

In these pageants of freedom, the unfree also joined the show at several reprises. The most magnificent episode resulted from the petitions of one parish's slaves and servants to mount their own procession. On July 11, they sallied forth across the city dressed in crimson and bearing the "arms, drums, muskets, and harquebuses of their masters." They assembled in the form of a well-drilled civic militia before Macau's city hall. Completing this procession across the breadth of the colonial city came an East African man, "representing one of the Kings of the Coast of Melinde, or Mombasa." Wrapped in silk embroidered with red roses, and wearing a crown of rooster feathers, this king was accompanied by two servants of his own bearing his royal bow and arrows. To shouts and shots from his mustered troops, this king acclaimed his royal brother in Lisbon before the city fathers, loudly applauded by the onlookers, "so that truly it can be written that in this city there was no status of people who did not show especial joy." Once this ceremony ended, however, the militia was again disarmed, and the king left his robes behind to return to the Jesuit Colégio de Madre de Deus, where he was a slave.[1]

The Jesuits' colleges in the early modern period were reflections of the societies in which they were found. Where activity was supported by broad networks of free and unfree servants the priests and brothers of the Society of Jesus enjoyed pride of place in these communities. That the Jesuits in Macau should have owned slaves is unremarkable since any major institution in a colonial context would have possessed at least a few. Religious communities were no different in this regard from other civic institutions, whether noble or mercantile. Moreover, in Macau, a colonial port with longstanding contacts across Maritime Asia, the population of slaves was drawn from a vast geography stretching far to the West. Given the large scale of the Jesuit presence in Macau and the nature of the Society's links to the city's merchant and noble communities, it is surprising that few contemporary documents attest to the presence of slaves there. Indeed, the Society's archives from the Province of Japan and Vice-Province of China (as the administrative units comprising East and Southeast Asia were called) contain few explicit mentions of slaves. External sources, such as the one cited above, likewise give only fleeting references, such as the one to the East African king as *hum cafre dos Religiosos da Companhia*. What accounts for this lacuna? Perhaps the routine presence of slaves in considerable numbers throughout the Portuguese empire; perhaps the unquestioned assumption that owning slaves or indentured servants was permissible, even for members of religious communities.

The preceding observations suggest that there are serious problems for historians investigating Jesuit use of unfree labor in East Asia. In addition to a lack of sources making direct mention of the numbers of slaves or the conditions of their servitude in the Society's colleges and residences, there is a problem of terminology.[2] By far the most prevalent term used to indicate servitude in sources produced in Iberian East Asia and areas beyond colonial control is the paternalistic euphemism *moço/mozo*, boy.[3] But this term is ambiguous: In the case of the account of the 1642 celebrations, for example, it was the moços who petitioned their *senhores* for the ability to form their celebratory militia, but these could be either slaves, indentured servants, or even hired servants. Other terms are also seen in contemporary documents: *escravo/a* or *esclavo/a* (slave), *cativo/a* (captive), *criado* (servant), or *bicho/a* (servant or slave). Designations linked to perceived skin color are also found, such as *negro/a* (black), but this term did not necessarily indicate enslavement in contemporary documents unless linked to a possessive: *seus negros* or *os negros do colégio*. At times, geographic origins are indicated in names with the implication of servitude. The term *cafre* mentioned above derives from *kaffir*, Arabic for unbeliever (and a racial slur in today's parlance), and in early modern sources typically denoted a person from East Africa. But unfree individuals mentioned in Jesuit sources on Asia came from a variety of geographical and ethnic origins and were often referred to by shorthand: *Malabar, Bengala, Jao, China, Japão*, etc.

In addition to the principal challenge of identifying unfree individuals in Jesuit sources, there is also the difficulty of determining the precise nature of their servitude. It has long been accepted among scholars (as is evident from the other contributions to this volume) that there were multiple forms of bondage practiced across the early modern globe. Masked by the reductive terminology used in Portuguese- or Spanish-language sources were variants of bondage derived from the different cultures of servitude in East Asia, Southeast Asia, South Asia, and East Africa.[4] Even within the cities and territories of the Iberian empires, a range of forms of bondage often coexisted. Working in colonial spaces and far beyond the limits of Portuguese dominion, the Jesuits relied on unfree assistants who entered servitude according to the local economic and legal arrangements. These conditions frequently varied in terms of the span of servitude, the kind of work, the requirements for manumission, and the nature of the relation between masters and servants. Not all of the Jesuits' menial laborers in East Asia were slaves, as some were indentured servants and other hired servants; the distinctions depended on the context of their acquisition and labor. Such variations, however, are difficult to detect in the succinct references and pejorative or euphemistic terms used in early modern documentation where moços, criados, and escravos abound.

A further factor complicating the analysis of Jesuit documents that follows concerns the use of racial categories. As pointed out in the introduction to this volume, premodern categories do not mesh well with modern ones. While there may have been implicit notions of status based on skin color within the Iberian colonial sphere in Maritime Asia—documentary references to negros or cafres who belonged to individuals or communities typically signal enslaved status—across the quarter of the globe between Mozambique and Honshu, race was not a shorthand for status. So, the Jesuits' use of descriptors of ethnic origin do not generally reveal degrees of unfreedom. Moreover, as will be shown below, the Jesuits' reliance on indentured or enslaved labor in East Asia gradually shifted from East African and South Asian men to East Asian men. As the missionaries—whose numbers included Japanese and, later, Chinese Jesuits—increasingly worked farther away from the zones of European colonial control, the unfree labor that they acquired and controlled more closely resembled the populations to whom they ministered. The distinction of unfree individuals working for the Jesuits amid communities of East Asian Christians by the seventeenth century therefore became one of legal and economic status, not skin color.

Despite all these difficulties, this chapter endeavors to survey the evolution of Jesuit reliance on unfree labor in East Asia from Francis Xavier's time through the end of the seventeenth century. Following the development of the Society's missions in the region, our focus will begin in Japan and shift toward the China coast and finally inside the Ming, and later Qing, Empire. This study is nevertheless not a comprehensive examination; a discussion of Jesuit attitudes toward slavery practiced in Asia, whether by Asians or Europeans, falls outside its scope.[5] The principal sources of information for this analysis are Jesuit documents, although these are not always as revelatory as desirable. The variety of print and manuscript sources used here will hopefully serve as a starting point for others in finding further descriptions of the Jesuits' use of unfree labor in the archives.

As is the case with many of the characteristics of the Society's presence in

Asia, the initial pattern of Jesuit relations with individuals in bondage was established by Francis Xavier. After he arrived in South Asia in 1542, he quickly set to creating institutions for the Society's pastoral ministries in the colonial capital Goa and farther afield. In order to aid with these enterprises, Xavier accepted donations from members of the local elite and royal patrons, as his brethren did in Europe.[6] Already in 1546, rules for the newly founded Colégio de São Paulo in Goa mentioned the expectation of receiving slaves from benefactors, along with alms and devotional or liturgical objects. These same rules, however, stipulated that the numbers of slaves at the college not be excessive, setting a limit of "six male slaves for the garden and for burying the poor, and sweeping and chopping wood, and for the kitchen either two or three."[7]

Outside of Jesuit communities, Xavier's personal example also established a pattern for acceptable behavior for his brethren in Asia. During his travels around the Fishery Coast in the mid-1540s, he was accompanied by translators and a cook. While these individuals are not referred to as slaves, his letters clearly mention purchasing individuals to perform these functions. For instance, in 1544 he instructed Francisco Mansilhas to use a donation received from a benefactor to *comprar hum topaz*, that is, to purchase an interpreter.[8] Likewise, the way in which Xavier that same year requested of Mansilhas that another man, called António Paravá, be sent to him to serve as a cook, suggests that the Apostle of the Orient was often accompanied by unfree laborers—whether slaves or indentured servants.[9] The subordinate place of these individuals in Xavier's train is indicated by their names: António Paravá (Paravar), much like other figures who appear in Xavier's letters such as Manuel China (Chinese), Joanne Japão (Japanese), Amador Malabar (Malabari) and Francisco Bengala (Bengali), are referred to by the combination of their baptismal names and crudely-conceived ethnic labels.

When Francis Xavier sailed farther east in the late 1540s, he took these attitudes toward servants with him to East Asia. Indeed, during his first voyage in 1549, he brought with him individuals from South Asia including Amador Malabar.[10] Xavier also traveled in the company of the former servants of Yajirō, who was known as Paulo da Santa Fé after his conversion to Christianity. Some of them served as interpreters in Japan and others were donated to the Colégio de São Paulo in Goa.[11] It is nevertheless unclear precisely what the status of these individuals was since contemporary sources do not call them escravos, and even later ones referring to Xavier's 1549–1551 stay in Japan use the term moço.[12] It appears that Amador Malabar was the moço in this case, while Joanne Japão was an interpreter who returned to his homeland impoverished but no longer in bondage.[13] In any case, the sources do not raise doubts about the legitimacy of the Jesuits' acquisition of, or reliance upon, unfree labor.[14] The missionaries were men of experience in colonial contexts for whom such arrangements were commonplace and unremarkable.

Where Francis Xavier had permitted the purchase and retention of individuals in bondage for domestic service, his brethren would do likewise. This was seen in the incipient Japan mission in the 1550s, when the early Jesuits kept a handful of moços at their residences at Yamaguchi as well as at Funai in the Bungo domain. Cosme de Torres, one of Xavier's first companions in Japan, mentioned in a 1554 letter the presence of a Bengali cook named Francisco and a gardener, perhaps Japanese, named João, at Yamaguchi; while another pair, Amador Malabar and a man named Bertholomeu, resided with Baltasar Gago at Funai.[15] Lest there be confusion about the status of these individuals, Gago wrote to his fellow Jesuits in 1555 that Torres tended to two thousand Christians with *dous japões que pregão, e dous escravos*: "two Japanese who preach, and two slaves."[16]

The pattern for the acquisition of individuals in bondage in these early years of the Japan mission was, unsurprisingly, similar to that employed elsewhere within the Portuguese Empire. Three examples will suffice to demonstrate how such individuals passed into Jesuit control. Here again, the missionaries' benefactors were the principal conduits early on. Baltasar Gago described how Duarte da Gama, the captain of a carrack that plied the route between India and Japan, had always seen to the missionaries' needs: "With his silver and clothes and slaves and wax and everything else that we lacked, he provided us with everything in Yamaguchi and Bungo."[17] Another set came into the missionaries' possession when Fernão Mendes Pinto, a successful merchant (and later fabulist), joined the Society for a brief span in 1554. According to one Jesuit confrere, Mendes Pinto freed his slaves before making his vows, "telling each one of them that from then on they should only have God as master." Of these, some he simply freed while others he entrusted to the care of the Goa Jesuits to catechize and educate. "Among these slaves, there were three who saw his determination," reads this source, "and threw themselves at his feet, crying that they wanted to go die with him in Japan."[18] This trio sailed east with Mendes Pinto, although it is not clear what happened to them after they reached their destination.

The third case is that of Luís, a moço originally from Java. Like Mendes Pinto's slaves, this man served the Jesuits after his master joined the Society: When Luís de Almeida left his career as a merchant, he offered his belongings to the missionaries, including a substantial sum of money and at least one of his moços. It is not clear if Luís the Javanese was manumitted at that point in 1556—the sources continue to refer to him as *o moço jao* through 1562— since he accompanied Almeida for several years afterward. Almeida had been trained as a physician and devoted his first years in Japan to curing the sick at the Jesuits' modest hospital in Funai before turning his attention to proselytization and diplomacy. Moço Luís was an invaluable auxiliary as a healer during that time; Xavier's onetime companion Juan Fernández averred that he had performed cures "that clearly were not because of the surgeon's wisdom nor due to the virtue of the medicine" but seemed to be divine interventions.[19] Yet despite this testimony of Luís's skill, the sight of which "left the Japanese greatly amazed," and his successful interventions with elite Japanese patients, he did not receive the credit that Almeida did.[20]

It was at Luís de Almeida's hospital that the Jesuits began to rely on Japanese moços alongside those they brought from elsewhere in Portuguese Asia. His letters speak of *moços, assi japões como da India*, "boys, Japanese as well as from India," here understood to include South and Southeast Asia.[21] Both types were referred to by the same term, but the precise status of the Japanese servants is unclear. As the Jesuit enterprise completed its first decade, the numbers of non-Japanese moços declined and in their place, Indigenous moços were acquired to provide menial labor. In 1559, for instance, a report from the Funai residence recorded the presence of nine priests and brothers, as well as *moços servidores de casa, japões* (Japanese household servants) and "some who serve in the hospital" (presumably the Javanese Luís and other non-Japanese). The total number of servants at this one major residence was seventeen, nearly double the number of Jesuits.[22] The local superior, Baltasar Gago, noted that these moços were entrusted with protecting the mission station "with rifles and arms" during a period of upheaval in which Funai was occupied by an invading army.[23] When peace returned, their occupations included serving as "buyer, dispenser, cook, and gardener," in addition to their daily obligation to "commend themselves to Our Lord like the brothers do." Brother Juan Fernández noted that some of these moços required "spur and rein" in order for them to behave, something that demanded sending three of them to India in 1562.[24]

One clear indication of the diminishing presence of non-Japanese unfree labor used in the Jesuit mission to Japan was the stir caused by the presence of an African slave in the retinue of a visiting superior in the early 1580s. As will be discussed below, African or South Asian slaves were commonly owned by Jesuit communities in the Iberian colonies of Maritime Asia, and Jesuit superiors often had attendants as was befitting of their status. So, it was unsurprising that Alessandro Valignano, the plenipotentiary representative of the superior general of the Society of Jesus, would have traveled with slaves during his inspection of the Japan mission. By the time of Visitor Valignano's tour, the Jesuits had residences spread across Japan and had become recognized by competing authorities as minor players on the political stage. Both Japanese and Jesuit sources mention the slave who accompanied Valignano to his meeting with the hegemon Oda Nobunaga in the spring of 1581. Luís Fróis's eyewitness account mentions the boisterous crowds that swarmed at the Miyako residence to see the cafre, and Nobunaga's subsequent request to see him as well. The warlord "celebrated in a strange way the sight of him, making him strip from the waist up and being incapable of believing that such a thing was natural and not artificial," and summoned his kin who "greatly enjoyed seeing him."[25] A contemporary Japanese chronicle confirms these impressions, noting the arrival of a "blackamoor from the Kirishitan Country" whose "formidable strength surpassed that of ten men."[26] As part of the gift exchange that took place during their subsequent meeting, Valignano offered the slave to Nobunaga.[27]

It was during the same official inspection in the early 1580s that the Jesuit hierarchy decided to regularize the presence of Japanese servants within the mission. As their enterprise expanded, they claimed, they needed a support staff that would permit them to accommodate themselves to Japanese customs. In contrast to the Society's European provinces, Japan lacked a sufficient number of Jesuit brothers or novices who typically handled menial tasks. The missionaries thus turned to different types of Indigenous men, the most prevalent of which were *dōjuku* and *komono*.[28] Dōjuku, which translates literally as "cohabitant," were individuals who served Buddhist religious communities as lay associates, some of whom might enter the ranks of the clergy. It is important to note that dōjuku were not indentured servants, and certainly not enslaved; nevertheless, they occupied a subordinate position to priests and brothers within the mission. According to one contemporary Jesuit description, "In Japan, certain men are called *dogicos* who, whether young or old, shave their heads in order to renounce the world, professing to serve in the church, some studying to enter into religious life and be clergy, some to perform various household ministries which in Japan can only be done in the church by shaved men of this type, such as the duties of sacristan, of doorman, of *chanoyuxa*,[29] of giving and receiving messages, of helping with masses, funerals, baptisms, and other church solemnities, and of accompanying the priests."[30] Indeed, with the exception of the tasks specific to Japan, many of these tasks would be performed by brothers in the Society's European colleges and residences. In Valignano's estimation, dōjuku were "very beneficial and necessary for our men, and it was a blessing from our Lord to find in Japan the use of such a type of people, because without them we neither would nor could do anything in Japan."[31]

By contrast, menial tasks at the Jesuits' residences were handled by *moços* or *gente de serviço*, men sometimes called *comono* in Jesuit sources. Whether the reductive Portuguese moço or the generic Japanese komono, such terms masked a variety of regional forms of bondage. There is no doubt that the Jesuits had purchased slaves (*moços cativos*) who had been sold into captivity in the context of Japan's political upheaval but it is difficult to quantify how many were acquired in this manner.[32] To be sure, Jesuit voices in Asia and Europe repeatedly condemned the illicit traffic in Japanese, Korean, and Chinese slaves conducted by Portuguese and other traders in Eastern Maritime Asia.[33] Concerned that the link in Japanese eyes between the European Jesuits and Portuguese slavers would tarnish the image of Christianity, the Jesuits avoided acquiring many moços in this manner. More frequently, it appears, they purchased servants for a specific term of indenture.[34] Valignano averred that there was an abundance of such people in Japan—"many more than in our land"—and that their presence was obligatory in Jesuit residences. To this end, he stipulated that each missionary should be accompanied on their travels by at least a pair of moços, as well as a dōjuku.[35] But what did these moços do? One glimpse comes in the translation of the Japanese term komono, which the Jesuits defined as a "moço who serves to remove sandals & other lowly tasks."[36] Other contemporary definitions give more details: Moços accompanied the missionaries on their circuits through villages "to take their shoes when they enter in churches and in houses, and to care for the horse, and to make food, wash clothing, and attend to various other services."[37]

While documents attesting to the numbers of gente de serviço are few, some of them give a sense of how many moços the Jesuits owned in Japan. Late sixteenth-century tallies of Jesuits and their dependents testify to substantial numbers. A distinction is made in the sources between moços and dōjuku, who also occupied a subordinate position in the Order, inferior to both priests and brothers. One accounting from 1592 attested that the Japan mission had six principal houses and eighteen other residences, in addition to 207 churches, all of which were staffed by more than 660 individuals. Setting aside the 154 priests and brothers, as well as the 180 dōjuku, this enumeration estimated that there were about 330 moços de serviço.[38] Just over a decade later, in 1603, the total number of people associated with the mission exceeded 800. Of that total, 122 were Jesuit priests and brothers, 254 were dōjuku, and over 420 were moços de serviço.[39] In 1609, when the mission was at its height, the Society's College of Nagasaki—its largest establishment in Japan by far—housed twenty-seven priests and brothers, sixty students, and 120 moços de serviço.[40] And in 1613, on the eve of the expulsion of the Jesuits from Japan, orders from Rome mentioned the unseemliness of the provincial officer having "ten or twelve moços who do nothing but spend their time serving, in addition to three dōjuku who are always at the door of his cubicle."[41]

As this last quote suggests, the ballooning numbers of servants over the final years of the sixteenth century and the early years of the seventeenth century caused concern among the Jesuits both within Japan and without. Like the disputes over the missionaries' use of silk, their reliance on indentured help seemed to fly in the face of their vows of poverty and, more broadly, their detachment from worldly honors.[42] A provincial consultation called by Visitor Valignano in 1590 mooted a few moral questions related to the presence of moços in Jesuit employ, a subject considered in parallel to that of the role of dōjuku. Perhaps surprisingly, the Jesuits' primary consideration concerned the appointment of specific moços to individual priests, making them "like proprietors or individual masters" instead of being shared by the community as a whole. Those who argued for communal ownership were opposed by those who saw bad eggs among the moços, including some who "would not know how to cook, or who would be a thief or would be a ruffian," citing instances where chalices and altar cloths were stolen.[43] In his resolution, Valignano reiterated the need for gente de serviço, insisting that only those who had seen the "customs, qualities, and way of living in Japan" would understand why so many were necessary. Nevertheless, he asserted their numbers and apportioning could easily exceed "the just and rational mean," and so moderation was essential if the Jesuits were to avoid the appearance of pomp while still projecting *autoridad y reputación*.[44] In order to maintain in the Society's houses, "the necessary cleanliness and to be able to deal with guests, and to shelter those who come to our houses according to the mode and custom of Japan," Valignano asserted, moços (and dōjuku) were crucial. To those who imagined Jesuit colleges staffed only by Jesuits, he noted that in "all of the houses in India, those who live among Christians do not dispense with this type of service, and in the same houses and colleges that are among the Portuguese there are great numbers of moços, such as there are in Évora and in Coimbra and in other colleges in Europe as well."[45]

Valignano's comparison of the Japan mission's use of moços with the presence of servants and slaves elsewhere in the colonial world, as well as in Europe itself, offers the occasion for a shift in focus toward Macau and China. As suggested in the introduction to this chapter, the Portuguese colonial outpost on the Chinese coast bore many similarities to other such settlements: Malacca, Cochin, Diu, Bassein, and Goa. In all of these, a substantial Indigenous population lived beside a small Portuguese and Luso-Asian community. Slaves who had been trafficked around Maritime Asia could be found in large numbers in these settlements, serving secular and religious masters. According to one late sixteenth-century report, Jesuits in Macau taught doctrine on Sundays and feast days to "close to a thousand slaves."[46] Another account from a century later outlined the tasks of the *Pai dos Cristãos* (Father of the Christians), a post held by a Jesuit, whose task it was to minister to the destitute and slaves, "with whom the houses are filled," and to intercede with masters to mitigate the rigor of their punishments.[47]

As we have seen, the Jesuits at the Cólegio de Madre de Deus owned slaves of African origin, as well as other slaves or indentured servants they referred to as moços. Reports of such individuals are scarce in the archival record. No tallies appear in the annual or triennial personnel reports sent from East Asia to Rome, and only infrequently are they mentioned in narrative accounts of Jesuit activities in Macau. At times, however, they do appear in reports of festivals and upheaval. For instance, during a revolt led by the parish clergy in 1624, the Jesuits' slaves who had been doing construction on the college adjacent to the city's principal fortress barred that garrison's soldiers from entering it for three months. In one commentator's estimation, the fortress was "not more poorly guarded by their negros than it would be by the king's soldiers."[48] And in a report of a fire that broke out in the college on 28 December 1667, Visitor Luís da Gama recorded how diligently the moços and cafres threw pails of water upon the flames. This same Jesuit superior also mentioned the presence of "our cafre Agostinho," one of the few slaves to be referred to by name in early modern sources.[49]

Given the commonplace presence of indentured servants and slaves in Jesuit colleges and residences in Japan and Macau, it is not surprising that the missionaries who entered the Ming Empire after 1582 also acquired unfree laborers. But given the difficulty of entering China (foreigners were typically limited to attendance at the biannual Canton trade fairs and not permitted to proceed farther inland unless as part of an official tribute embassy), the Jesuits could not bring moços with them from Macau. Inside the Ming Empire and far from the coastal colony, the missionaries adopted the domestic modes of Chinese society, acquiring moços in a manner similar to that of their brethren in Japan. While there are few studies of the scale of human trafficking and servitude in premodern China, Jesuit sources are unambiguous about the widespread availability and ease of acquisition of indentured labor.[50] Perhaps the best description comes from António de Gouvea, who wrote a lengthy ethnographic preface to his 1644 mission history entitled *Ásia Extrema*. At the start of a chapter dedicated to "Customs, Superstitions, Abuses, and Auguries," he asserted that bondage existed on a massive scale in China but that it differed from forms practiced elsewhere:

> Many who, owing to poverty, can neither purchase a wife, as is custom-
> ary, nor live without one, sell themselves to the rich, who from among
> those in their service and households give them one; and thus not only
> husband and wife, but also children and descendants become captives of
> that household and family. Of this sort there are millions. Others, upon
> reaching the point at which they cannot provide for their children, sell
> them for three or four *cruzados*, and sometimes for much less. There
> are always buyers who traffic and trade this way, carrying the captives to
> various provinces within China where they get more for them. As such,
> the Empire is filled with captive servants, not from war, nor from other
> Kingdoms, but sold by their parents or older siblings, which the laws of
> China permit in cases of necessity and prohibit with punishment those
> who steal children and sell them. This servitude is a little easier than that
> of the Europeans, both because they are considered ordinary people, and
> because at any time they wish they can be freed, paying only the price for
> which they were sold; and finally because to each is given a wife for them
> to marry and enough to sustain them for their whole lives.[51]

Given the standard Jesuit practice of accomodating themselves to other cultures for domestic arrangements, the missionaries bought servants in China under both the Ming and Qing regimes. References to moços in the sources produced by the China missionaries are abundant for the seventeenth century, a fact that reflects the expansion of the mission during that period and the Jesuits' continual need for menial laborers.

As the China mission expanded beyond the foundations laid by Matteo Ricci in the late sixteenth century, and as the Jesuits were recognized at the imperial court, they acquired indentured domestic help. As soon as 1612, two years after Ricci's death, mission superior Niccolò Longobardo requested permission to purchase more moços for the priests in Beijing.[52] In contrast to the Japan mission, where the Jesuits could count on dōjuku to assist them with ritual, catechetical, and hospitality-related tasks, there were no such auxiliaries in China. For some of these tasks the Jesuits recruited Chinese or Luso-Chinese men as Jesuit brothers, but these were never many. At some residences in the mid-seventeenth century, the Jesuits accepted Chinese students to be trained as brothers, but neither these men nor the brothers were intended for menial service of the type moços would provide.

Since it was accepted that the missionaries would require domestic service, the first rules drawn up in Asia in 1621 to govern the newly-created Vice-Province of China contained a specific section "on matters relating to moços." While lists of rules do not provide the same testimony as narratives, they do give some indication of the tenor of relations between them and their Jesuit masters. For instance, it is clear that not all moços were baptized: "Our men should seek to catechize well the moços who serve us, preaching to them a little from time to time, teaching doctrine and other devotional matters to the ones who are Christians, so that in this way they will serve with more love and fidelity. They should also seek to teach good doctrine to those who are heathens either through words or through works and good examples, neither doing nor saying anything to shock them that they will later recount outside." Another of the rules in this short list nevertheless recalls that the moços were not always treated kindly: "The priests will not punish the moços themselves, nor speak to them harshly, since it is against decorum and religious gravitas, but when they are guilty have the brothers or students punish them, not with anger or exasperated words, but with some lashes on top of their pants."[53]

Another set of rules governing the China mission's moços was compiled when André Palmeiro conducted his inspection tour as a visitor in 1629. This Jesuit superior evidently drew on the experience of the Japan mission (as reflected in the compendia of rules mentioned above) along with the counsel of veteran missionaries when he tried to balance the need for domestic service with the obligation to respect the Order's vows of poverty. Palmeiro granted the vice-provincial officer permission to determine the total number of moços to be retained, as well as the amount of food they were to receive daily. He also reiterated the 1621 prohibition of priests' meting out punishments, as well as a demand for modesty in the form of an order that moços not go about "undressed from the waist up" but rather with a long hemp shirt. Drawing on the experience of the Japan mission, Palmeiro also stipulated that they work for communities, not individuals.[54]

Palmeiro's rules give some indication of the various types of individuals who served the Jesuits in China. It appears that their moços ranged in age from young boys to men, and in degrees of indenture. One group were adult men, who served according to a contract with what appears to be financial benefits. Adopting a rule used in Japan, Palmeiro stipulated that each residence possess "a special book be kept wherein is recorded the year and day when each begins to serve, and the salary he is given, and how he accounts for it over the course of the year." Another group consisted of young boys, whom the Jesuits seem to have preferred: "It is most convenient for us to abide by the custom of this whole Kingdom and to purchase children for our service, since experience shows us that these are the only ones who can be tolerated in the house to maintain cleanliness and show fidelity." Palmeiro also insisted that these younger moços be "raised with much care and love, not permitting them to sleep in the rooms of the older ones, nor to deal with them often." The final group were moços cativos, the enslaved. As with the other two groups, these men had a term of service, but one which counted not on dismissal but rather on sale (or potentially manumission). Palmeiro ordered that such men "should be dressed decently so that they go about clean and content," noting that some, after being freed, may want, "out of love of God, to serve without salary."[55]

One of the most striking aspects of Palmeiro's rules for moços is the ambiguity that he showed toward their religious practice. On the one hand, he insisted that none be allowed to work on Sundays and feast days and urged that child moços be taught "doctrine and the things of God according to their capacity." Moreover, he insisted that Christian moços be preached to occasionally, and that they be "exhorted to confess, something that should happen at least during Lent." On the other hand, he showed ambivalence about taking domestic service as an opportunity for making Christians. "With those who are heathens," Palmeiro ordered, "even though it is good to seek that they come to like our Holy Law, there should be no great rush to have them be baptized, principally those who reveal that they will not be tolerated for long in the house."[56] Given Jesuit superiors' repeated complaints about the perennial lack of conversions in China, for the missionaries not to have sought to evangelize their own households is paradoxical. But given how much attention they paid to constructing an image of priestly authority and lay piety, their desire to safeguard the reputation of Christianity from undesirable associations with disgruntled former servants makes sense.[57]

The patterns established by Visitor Palmeiro appear to have persisted largely intact until the late seventeenth century, at least according to the sources considered for this analysis. It does not seem that the numbers of moços expanded as they had done in Japan, although this was most likely due to the continual penury of the mission. One report from the 1650s tells of Étienne Faber, a missionary in remote Sha'anxi Province, showing remarkable humility in his attitude toward his one and only moço: "He only had one *moço de serviço* or, better put, he only had one companion, because between the *Padre* and the moço there was only a nominal difference; in serving, in ordering, in dressing, in eating at home and outside of it they were equal companions and brothers. From this holy disguise it arose that often, when they were invited by heathens, the Padre and the moço would sit at the same table without anyone's being offended or finding such prideful boldness on the part of the moço strange. . . . In the household service, the moço only took care of what the Padre could not. Everything else he did by himself."[58] Perhaps more common was the arrangement documented in the Latin account book of François de Rougemont from the mid-1670s. There, this Flemish missionary recorded clothing and food purchases as well as small monetary gifts to his three *famuli*, the moços who served him at the Changshu residence in the Jiangnan region.[59]

A few documents from the end of the seventeenth century further attest to the continued presence of moços in the Jesuits' Chinese residences and gives details about the nature of their service to the missionaries. The first of these describes an intervention made by Vice-Provincial Jean Valat, who in early 1689 sought to restrain his subordinates at Beijing from abusing the college's servants. Valat left written orders "given in virtue of Holy Obedience, and *sub precepto gravi, et gravi pecato*," that is, to be observed in evocation of the Jesuits' vows and under pain of sin, which barred anyone from punishing moços except the *padre ministro*, the priest in charge of the domestic economy. Moreover, all punishments were to "always be less than what is deserved," and that moços were to be fed at the table "in such a quantity that suffices for them to leave satisfied."[60] It is perhaps unsurprising that these rules sparked a vociferous complaint from the college's rector, Tomás Pereira, who saw his authority challenged. Pereira appealed the orders to the Visitor in Macau, calling this imposition too much to bear, not only for its inversion of the college's hierarchy, but also for its watering down of what he deemed were necessary and immediate punishments. "Consider, Your Reverence Father Visitor, if I can take any more?" Pereira riposted. "I am not so confident in myself. I'll commit a mortal sin if, as Rector, I do not obey Father Minister! Or if, without his permission, I give a spanking to a bicho who serves me, or stop him from having an antipasto!"[61]

Pereira's complaints in other letters further inform us about the Jesuits' acquisition of moços at the imperial capital in the early Qing period. In his constant battles with the French missionaries and their allies, he reported to his superiors about how they misused the missions' funds and misgoverned its personnel. In 1689, not long after Joachim Bouvet arrived in Beijing, Vice Rector Antoine Thomas "bought him a moço de lingua Tartara," that is, a Native Manchu speaker. This was the second such servant purchased by Thomas and was to teach this politically useful language to the newly arrived priests. According to Pereira, he had cost fifty silver taels. The reason for this second purchase was to replace the first moço Tartaro who had been contracted "for twelve years for a few taels," but in the meantime was to be married and so, "according to Chinese custom," must be released from service. These mix-ups, the college rector bemoaned, were what happened when "power was handed over to the inexperienced."[62] Pereira's barbs against his fellow Jesuits notwithstanding, these passages show the ease with which the Jesuits acquired indentured labor in China during the Kangxi era, and how they sought to expand not only their domestic service but also their language training by purchasing moços.

Despite the ambiguity of the terms used in contemporary documents, it is clear that the Jesuits in East Asia relied on unfree labor in the early modern period. In some instances, such as in the colony of Macau, they owned slaves whose conditions of servitude were similar to others elsewhere in the Portuguese Empire. Outside of colonial settings, whether in Japan or China, however, they also depended on indentured servants, but these were employed in local fashion. In both of these lands, unfree labor could be readily purchased for contractually stipulated periods of indenture. Buying moços was therefore a common occurrence in Jesuit mission stations, and dealing with indentured servants was a part of everyday life for most, if not all, missionaries in the early modern period. While this labor was primarily domestic, it carried with it the threat of physical violence that characterized social relations in the early modern period. Evidence of abuse can be seen in Jesuit sources, even if it is equally easy to detect paternalistic expressions of empathy for moços in the same documents. In sum, indenture and enslavement existed across early modern East Asia, and, just as they are so famous for having done with the political, artistic, and linguistic cultures of the lands where they worked, here, too, the Jesuits zealously practiced accommodation.

Notes

1. João Marques Moreira, *Relação da Magestosa, Misteriosa, e Notavel Acclama-çam, que se fez a Magestade d'El Rey Dom IOAM O IV. nosso Senhor na Cidade de nome de Deos do grande Imperio da China* (Lisbon: Na Officina de Domingos Lopes Roza, 1644), 20–24; translation in C. R. Boxer, *Seventeenth Century Macau in Contemporary Documents and Illustrations* (Singapore: Heinemann Asia, 1984), 145–74.

2. Most scholars who have confronted this topic with regard to early modern East Asia have recognized the problem of terminology. Recent discussions are found in Tara Alberts, *Conflict & Conversion: Catholicism in Southeast Asia, 1500–1700* (Oxford: Oxford University Press, 2013), 180–87; Rômulo da Silva Ehalt, "Jesuits and the Problem of Slavery in Early Modern Japan" (PhD diss., Tokyo University of Foreign Studies, 2017), 108–20 and 291–314; and Lúcio de Sousa, *The Portuguese Slave Trade in Early Modern Japan: Merchants, Jesuits and Japanese, Chinese, and Korean Slaves* (Leiden: Brill, 2019), 5–8.

3. The lingua franca of the Jesuits in East Asia was Portuguese, so terms here are primarily rendered in that language. Spanish was also used, though, in a smaller portion of Jesuit documents, and some equivalents are given here.

4. Useful overviews of broad patterns are in Anthony Reid, "Slavery and Bondage in Southeast Asian History" in *Charting the Shape of Early Modern Southeast Asia* (Chiang Mai: Silkworm, 1999), 181–216; Pamela Kyle Crossley, "Slavery in Early Modern China" in *Cambridge World History of Slavery*, ed. David Eltis and Stanley Engerman, 4 vols. (Cambridge: Cambridge University Press, 2011), 3:186–213; and Thomas Nelson, "Slavery in Medieval Japan," *Monumenta Serica* 59, no. 4 (Winter 2004): 463–92.

5. Jesuit attitudes toward slaving in Japan has recently attracted scholarly attention while China and Southeast Asia await similar treatment. See Ehalt, "Problem of Slavery" and Sousa, *Portuguese Slave Trade*.

6. For example, Simão Rodrigues accepted a royal donation of "ten blacks to work

on the construction of the college" at Lisbon. See Rodrigues to Martim de Santa Cruz, [Lisbon, 1547?] in *Epistolae PP. Paschasii Broëti, Claudii Jaji, Joannis Codurii et Simonis Rodericii Societatis Jesu* (Madrid: Lopez del Horno, 1903), 571.

7.   Niccolò Lancilotto, "Constitutions of the College of St Paul in Goa," in *Documenta Indica*, ed. Josef Wicki (Rome: IHSI, 1948–1988), 1:123.

8.   Francis Xavier to Francisco Mansilhas, Punnaikayal, 23 February 1544, in *Epistolae S. Francisci Xaverii aliaque eius scripta, nova edition*, ed. Georg Schurhammer and Josef Wicki (Rome: IHSI, 1944), 1:189–90.

9.   Francis Xavier to Francisco Mansilhas, Punnaikayal, 29 August 1544, ibid, 1:221.

10.   Francis Xavier to Micer Paul, António Gomes, Baltasar Gago, Malacca, 20–22 June 1549, ibid., 2:131.

11.   Tomé Lobo to King João III, Goa, 13 October 1548, in *Documentos del Japon, 1547–1557*, ed. Juan Ruiz de Medina (Rome: IHSI, 1990), 37. It is not clear, however, if Xavier considered these men slaves according to common Iberian terminology. His writings are ambiguous on the subject. See Ehalt, "Jesuits and the Problem of Slavery," 113–15.

12.   See, for example, Francisco Cabral to Francisco de Borja, Nagasaki, 5 September 1571, Archivum Romanum Societatis Iesu [=ARSI], *Japonica-Sinica* Collection [=*Jap-Sin*] 7-I: 21r.

13.   Francis Xavier to Gaspar Barzeus in Goa, Singapore Straits, 22 July 1552, in Schurhammer and Wicki, eds., *Epistolae*, 2:479.

14.   Early Jesuits in South Asia did call attention to the moral perils of Portuguese slaveowning, pointing out that slave girls were often acquired as concubines. See Ehalt, "Problem of Slavery," 106–8.

15.   Cosme de Torres to Jesuit Brethren in Bungo, Yamaguchi, Nov/Dec 1554, in Ruiz de Medina, *Documentos*, 463; and Duarte da Silva to Jesuit Brethren in India, Bungo (Funai), 10 Sept. 1555, ibid., 517.

16.   Baltasar Gago to Jesuit Brethren in India and Portugal, Hirado, 23 Sept. 1555, ibid., 555. This point is of particular importance since the most recent editor of these letters, Juan Ruiz de Medina, S.J., describes these individuals as *los empleados de la iglesia de Yamaguchi y los colaboradores de los misioneros*, "the employees of the church of Yamaguchi and the collaborators of the missionaries." While this definition may be valid for the "two Japanese who preach," it was certainly not the case of the two slaves.

17.   Baltasar Gago to King João III, Hirado, 20 Sept. 1555, ibid., 543.

18.   Aires Brandão to Jesuit Brethren in Coimbra, Goa, 23 December 1554, ibid., 494.

19.   Juan Fernández to António de Quadros, Funai, 8 October 1561, in *Documentos del Japon, 1558–1562*, ed. Juan Ruiz de Medina (Rome: IHSI, 1995), 415.

20.   Ibid.; Luís de Almeida to Jesuit Brethren in Europe, Yokoseura, 25 October 1562, ibid., 567.

21.   Luís de Almeida to Melchior Nunes Barreto, Funai, [20] November 1559, ibid., 226.

22. Baltasar Gago to Jesuit Brethren in India, Funai, 1 November 1559, ibid., 177.

23. Ibid., 192.

24. Juan Fernández to António de Quadros, Funai, 8 October 1561, ibid., 441.

25. Luís Fróis to [Jesuit superior], Miyako, 14 April 1581, in *Segunda Parte das Cartas de Iapão que escreverão os padres, & irmãos da companhia de Iesus* (Évora: Manoel de Lyra, 1598), 3v.

26. Ōta Gyūichi, *The Chronicle of Lord Nobunaga*, ed. and trans. J. S. A. Elisonas and J. P. Lamers (Leiden: Brill, 2011), 385–86.

27. Luís Fróis to Claudio Aquaviva, Kuchinotsu, 5 November 1582, in *Segunda Parte das Cartas de Iapão*, 65v.

28. This brief enumeration leaves aside peasants who belonged to villages granted to the Jesuits by elite benefactors. See Rômulo Ehalt, "From Tenants to Landlords: Jesuits and Land Ownership in Japan, 1552–1614" in *Trade and Finance in Global Missions (16th–18th Centuries)*, ed. Ines Županov and Hélène Vu Thanh (Leiden: Brill, 2021), 97–123.

29. *Chanoyu* is the Japanese tea ceremony.

30. "Role of Jesuit Houses and Personnel in Japan, November 1592," in *Monumenta Historica Japoniae I: Textus Catalogorum Japoniae*, ed. Josef Franz Schütte, S.J. (Rome: IHSI, 1975), 295–96.

31. Alessandro Valignano, *Sumario de las Cosas de Japon (1583); Adiciones del Sumario de Japon (1592)*, ed. José Luis Alvarez-Taladriz (Tokyo: Sophia University, 1954), 1:191.

32. Alvarez-Taladriz cites a consultation that specifically mentions *mozos que se compraren*, the legitimacy of whose enslavement had to be verified. If the conditions of captivity were deemed unjust, these individuals would serve for a number of years rather than being permanently enslaved. See, ibid., 2:488, n. 54.

33. In addition to the treatment by Ehalt and Sousa, a briefer yet dated overview is found in Alvarez-Taladriz, *Sumario*, 2:498–511.

34. A consultation from 1590 refers to contracting (*contratar*) *mozos de servicio*, suggesting a term of indenture. See ibid., 2:657.

35. Ibid., 1:9, 73, and 151.

36. Jesuits of the Japan Mission, *Vocabulario*, s.v. *comono* in *Supplemento*, 341r.

37. Alvarez-Taladriz, *Sumario*, 2:638.

38. "Role of Jesuit Houses and Personnel in Japan, November 1592," in *Monumenta*, ed. Schütte, 296.

39. "Catalogue for the Vice-Province of Japan, October 1603," ibid., 450–51.

40. "Role of Jesuit Houses, People, Rents, and Expenses, 12 November 1609," ibid., 517.

41. Various authors, Compendium of Orders from Jesuit superiors for the Japan mission, [1587–1620], Rome, Archivum Romanum Societatis Iesu, *Japonica-Sinica* Collection Codex [=ARSI *Jap-Sin*] 3:42v-43r.

42. On silk, see Liam Matthew Brockey, "Authority, Poverty, Vanity: Jesuit

Missionaries and the Use of Silk in Early Modern East Asia," *Anais de história de Além-Mar*, XVII (2016): 179–222.

43.   Various authors, "Segunda Consulta General, Hecha por El Padre Alejandro Valignano, Visitador de la Compañia de Jesus en Japon, en Agosto del Año de 1590," in Alvarez-Taladriz, *Sumario*, 2:638, 640

44.   Valignano and later visitors would further compile rules for dealing with moços. See, for example, "Obediencias do *Padre* Alexandre Valignano, Vizitador da Provincia de Japão e China, Revistas e concertadas pello *Padre* Francisco Pasio Visitador da mesma Provincia para Instrucção dos Reytores," Lisbon, Biblioteca da Ajuda, *Jesuítas na Ásia* Collection Codex [=BAJA] 49-IV-56: 148v-150r.

45.   Alessandro Valignano, "Resoluciones del Padre Visitador sobre dicha Consulta (1590)," in Alvarez-Taladriz, *Sumario*, 2:654–55.

46.   "Memoria do Principio do Collegio de Macao," BAJA 49-IV-55: 82r.

47.   "Annual Letter for the College of Macau and the Canton Residences, 1692," BAJA 49-V-22: 100r/v.

48.   "Manifesto sobre o sucedido em Macau entre 10 de Outubro de 1624 e 1625," in *Fontes para a História de Macau no Séc. XVII*, ed. Elsa Penalva and Miguel Rodrigues Lourenço (Lisbon: CCCM, 2009), 288.

49.   João F. Marques Pereira, ed., "Uma Resurreição Histórica (Páginas inéditas d'um visitador dos Jesuítas, 1665–1671)," *Ta-Ssi-Yang-Kuo: Arquivos e Anais do Extremo-Oriente Português*, 2:12 (1901), 747–63, at 747; and 1:3 (1899): 181–88 at 184.

50.   Recent studies have focused primarily on concubines and female domestics, leaving aside the type of boys and men the Jesuits purchased. Moreover, these studies concentrate on the nineteenth and twentieth centuries, largely ignoring the earlier period. See, for example, Hsieh-Bao Hua, *Concubinage and Servitude in Late Imperial China* (Lanham, MD: Lexington Books, 2014); Johanna Ransmeier, *Sold People: Traffickers and Family Life in North China* (Cambridge, MA: Harvard University Press, 2017); Angela Schottenhammer, "Slaves and Forms of Slavery in Late Imperial China (Seventeenth to Early Twentieth Centuries)," in *The Structure of Slavery in Indian Ocean Africa and Asia*, ed. Gwyn Campbell (Portland, OR: Frank Cass, 2004), 143–54.

51.   António de Gouvea, *Ásia Extrema*, ed. Horácio Araújo (Lisbon: Fundação Oriente, 1995–2005), 1:281. Gouvea's comment about these servants being *povo sem distinção* (ordinary people) underscores the fact that they did not look different from other commoners, unlike African or Indian slaves in European colonies.

52.   Niccolò Longobardo, "Informação da Missão da China," ARSI Jap-Sin 113:273v.

53.   Gabriel de Matos, "Ordens dos Vizitadores e Superiores Universaes da Missão da China com algumas respostas do nosso Reverendo Padre Geral. 1621," BAJA 49-V-7: 227r/v.

54.   André Palmeiro, "Ordens que o Padre Andre Palmeiro Vizitador de Japão e China deixou a Viceprovincia da China vizitandoa no anno de 1629 aos 15 de Agosto," Macau, 15 January 1631, ARSI *Jap-Sin* 100: 35v-36r.

55.   Ibid., 35v-36v.

56.   Ibid., 36v.

57.   A fuller discussion of Palmeiro's vision for the Chinese church and its pastors is found in Liam Matthew Brockey, *The Visitor: André Palmeiro and the Jesuits in Asia* (Cambridge, MA: Harvard University Press, 2014), 278–325.

58.   Gabriel de Magalhães, "Rellação da vida e morte do Padre Estevão Fabro da Sancta e Saudoza memoria Vice Provincial da China," Beijing, 20 March 1658, BAJA 49-V-14: 189v.

59.   Noël Golvers, *François de Rougemont, S.J., Missionary in Ch'ang-shu (Chiang-Nan): A Study of the Account Book (1674–1675) and the Elogium* (Leuven: Leuven University Press, 1999), 319–20.

60.   Jean Valat, "Treslado da Carta e Ordenações do Pe. João Valat depois da Visita de Pekim," Beijing, 14 March 1689, ARSI Jap-Sin 164: 49r-50r.

61.   Tomás Pereira to Filippo Saverio Philippucci, Beijing, 24 April 1689, in Tomás Pereira, *Obras*, coord. Luís Filipe Barreto (Lisbon: CCCM and FCT, 2011), 1:281–82.

62.   Tomás Pereira to Francesco Saverio Filippucci, Peking, 20 October 1689, ibid., 299–300.

CHAPTER FOUR

Jesuits and "Race" in Early Modern Chile

*Valdivia's Letters to
the King, 1604–1618*[1]

ANDREW REDDEN

"RACE," AS WE KNOW, is a problematic concept; common contemporary categories of race (in particular, those considered biological or genetic or based on phenotype) become even more problematic when used as frameworks with which to study socioreligious structures, phenomena, and groups in the early modern period given the marked differences in meaning over time. We certainly run the risk of distorting historical realities if we seek to impose contemporary preoccupations, however important and justifiable, on earlier societies; yet, at the same time, current societal injustices perpetuated by discrimination and structural violence embedded in what society now perceives to be racial difference often have their roots in colonial hierarchies. As Peter Wade argues in his work *Race and Ethnicity in Latin America*, while it is one thing to be aware of the problem of "presentism" or "the judging of previous historical eras by the standards of our own," to swing the pendulum too far the other way runs the risk of producing histories that are "rather divorced from [their] social context."[2] Wade's point, which acts as the theoretical starting point for this chapter, is that "ideas about human difference, while they may have involved a concept of race that was diverse, contested and even not very central, were certainly powerfully structured by ideas of European superiority."[3]

The purpose of the following chapter is to test the above statement with respect to the Society of Jesus in colonial Hispanic America and, more specifically, on the war-torn frontier of Chile. To this end, this study analyses a series of letters written from Chile to the Spanish monarch Philip III (b. 1578, r. 1598–1621) or his representatives by the Jesuit priest (and also diplomat, crown agent, and peace broker) Luis de Valdivia (1561–1642) from 1604 to 1618.[4] If the findings do not wholeheartedly endorse Wade's statement to its furthest extent, they nonetheless add nuance to our understanding of "ideas about human difference" amongst Jesuits in Hispanic America and highlight potential areas for further study. This chapter shall first introduce the sociopolitical context on the Chilean frontier before moving to discuss the methodology used to analyze the letters. Once the letters have been analyzed, the chapter will turn to the ideas of one of the most important Jesuit thinkers of the time, Valdivia's close contemporary, José de Acosta (1540–1600), for an explanation and contextualization of the findings.

Context: Luis de Valdivia, Chile, and the Defensive War

Luis de Valdivia was part of the first contingent of Jesuits to establish a mission in Chile in 1593 and, as a group, they cultivated close links with an important patron of the Society, Martín García Óñez de Loyola, the nephew of Ignatius Loyola, who was appointed governor of Chile in 1592. In 1598, however, Óñez de Loyola was killed at the start of a major uprising of Indigenous Mapuche, which brought about the collapse of Spanish dominion in Araucanía, the stretch of territory south of the river Biobío, and the destruction of six of the principal Spanish towns of the colony—Valdivia, Villa Rica, La Imperial, Osorno, Angol, and Santa Cruz de Coya.[5] The shock of this uprising and the speed with which Spanish authority collapsed provoked a bitter reaction from the secular and ecclesiastical dignitaries of the colonial capital, Santiago, who petitioned the king to allow the enslavement of the Indigenous Mapuche who had, as they saw it, rebelled against his authority. This intensive lobbying from those in favor of a continuation and escalation of the war was successful because, on May 26, 1608, notwithstanding papal prohibition, Philip III published a decree that permitted the enslavement of Indigenous males over the age of ten-and-a-half and Indigenous females over the age of nine-and-a-half by those who captured them in the course of the frontier war.[6]

Valdivia, then rector of the College of San Miguel (founded in 1595), also signed this petition to allow the enslavement of the Indigenous Mapuche, who had rebelled against the king.[7] Nevertheless, in 1602 he was recalled to Lima, and there his Jesuit brothers persuaded him that the cause of the Mapuche insurgents was, in fact, just and he revised his opinion completely.[8] While there, during the years 1604–1605, Valdivia and his fellow Jesuits developed a proposal for a new colonial policy of defensive war, which was to withdraw troops to a line of forts along the river Biobío and to only engage in defensive military activity to defend the settlements of the Spanish and those Mapuche who had chosen to ally themselves with them. In the meantime, they could agree to terms with those who had rebelled and negotiate exchanges of captives.

To keep the peace, Spanish incursions for the purpose of capturing slaves from enemy Indigenous Mapuche populations would be forbidden. The plan won the approval of the outgoing viceroy of Peru, the Marquis of Salinas, Luis de Velasco (in office 1595/6–1604) and his successor the Count of Monterrey, Gaspar de Zúñiga Acevedo y Fonseca (in office 1603/4–1606) and, with the viceroy's approval, Valdivia traveled back to Chile to implement it.[9] Such was the ferocity of resistance from both secular and ecclesiastical residents of Chile, however, that he returned to Lima in 1606, and then journeyed to Spain to seek the approval of Philip III and his Council of the Indies. The plan was even more controversial for Spanish settlers in Chile because it also sought to address one of the key causal factors of the uprising by calling for an end to obligatory forced labor for the Indigenous Mapuche (tantamount to slavery in all but name). Such a policy change threatened the very basis on which the colonial economy functioned and, as such, was unacceptable to those whose wealth depended on this exploitation of the Indigenous Mapuche.

Valdivia's campaign to implement this policy of defensive warfare (thereby ending the enslavement of the Indigenous Mapuche and removing their reasons to remain at war with the Spanish) had the backing of his superior, the provincial Diego de Torres Bollo. This approval was crucial to Valdivia obtaining the support of the superior general Claudio Acquaviva (b. 1543, d.

1615; in office 1581–1615) bearing in mind that engaging in political controversies and representing secular authorities contravened the *Constitutions* of the Society of Jesus. These stated: "So that the Society may be able to devote itself more entirely to the spiritual pursuits pertaining to its profession, it should abstain as far as possible from all secular employments . . . through not accepting such burdens and not employing itself in them because of any requests."[10]

Acquaviva blocked Valdivia's appointment as bishop of Concepción (which again contravened the *Constitutions*), but acquiesced when, in 1610, Valdivia was appointed crown representative with the authority to implement the policy of defensive war. This authority also extended to put into effect the peace treaty with the insurgent Indigenous Mapuche, and Valdivia was simultaneously made ecclesiastical administrator (vicar general) of the diocese of Concepción until such time as a bishop could be named. Acquaviva even facilitated this appointment by naming Valdivia "the independent superior of the missions already established and those yet to be established south of the Biobío."[11]

Valdivia returned to Chile in 1611 and began to put into action the defensive war strategy. Despite having the support and authority of King Philip III; his council; the viceroy of Peru, Juan de Mendoza y Luna; the Marquis of Montesclaros (b. 1571, d. 1628; in office 1607–1615); and, initially at least, the newly appointed governor Alonso de Ribera (b. 1560, d. 1617; in office 1612–1617), reaction by Spanish colonists (both lay and ecclesiastical) was, as might be expected, extremely hostile due to the economic dependence of the colony on the forced labor of the Indigenous Mapuche, which the Jesuit strategy threatened.[12] Such were the terms of the defensive war that they were to be deprived of the only real source of wealth in the colony— Indigenous labor.

In 1612, negotiations went awry, and renewed fighting led to the killing of three Jesuits (two priests and one brother), numerous warriors and Indigenous Mapuche leaders who had accepted the terms offered by Valdivia, and the enslavement of their wives and children by forces that were hostile to the Spanish.[13] The defensive war strategy started to unravel and then hung on by a thread as the governor decided to back those opposed to it. Nevertheless, if Valdivia's accounts are to be believed, notwithstanding the tragic setback, the policy was successful in that it brought an uneasy peace to the frontier that had not been experienced since the beginning of the uprising in 1598. There were still powerful interest groups (on both sides of the border), however, which continued to oppose this negotiated peace and time was not on Valdivia's side.

The support given to Valdivia in his peace-brokering efforts by his superiors Torres Bollo and Acquaviva was not continued by their successors. Torres Bollo's successor, Pedro de Oñate (d. 1646; in office 1615–1624), vigorously opposed Valdivia's continued political involvement and resented his unusual independence of action. Meanwhile, Acquaviva's successor, Muzio Vitelleschi (b. 1563, d. 1645; in office 1615–1645), who was elected superior general after Acquaviva's death in 1615, was keen to reinforce the Society's conformity with the *Constitutions*. In 1621, attentive to the criticisms of Oñate in Paraguay, Vitelleschi withdrew the authority Valdivia had been given to act independently as an agent of the crown. Valdivia, who had returned to Spain the previous year, was dealt a further blow from which he never really recovered, when Vitelleschi ordered him to remain in Spain.[14] This coincided with the death of Philip III and the coronation of his son Philip IV in 1621 who, receiving new counsel, decided in 1625 to reverse his father's policy of supporting the strategy of defensive war. With the royal decree of April 13, 1625, ordering a return to an offensive strategy, Valdivia, sadly, saw his life's work to bring peace to the Chilean frontier and prevent the enslavement of the Indigenous Mapuche, dismantled around him.

Sources and Methodology

What follows is an examination of thirteen letters or reports written by Luis de Valdivia over the course of fourteen years.[15] The first to be analyzed was written in 1604 to the outgoing viceroy of Perú, the Marquis of Salinas, Luis de Velasco and the incoming viceroy, the Count of Monterrey, Gaspar de Zúñiga Acevedo y Fonseca. Another document, published in 1611, is a printed apologia for the policy of defensive warfare championed by Luis de Valdivia and the Jesuits in the provinces of Peru and Paraguay (which included Chile) and which, as mentioned above, was being severely criticized by numerous colonial interests in Chile.[16] It was a lengthy point-by-point explanation of the Jesuit position and refutation of those who supported the return to a more aggressive campaign against the Indigenous Mapuche, who were fiercely resisting Spanish conquest. The remaining eleven letters, meanwhile, were reports penned by Valdivia to the king, delivering updates on the situation on the frontier and defending himself and the policy he was implementing from his many detractors.

The selection of letters gives particular insight into Jesuit typologies with respect to wider, secular society. Rather than being intended to be circulated internally (such as the edifying and formulaic annual letters sent back to Rome by the superior of each province, which were then copied and circulated amongst Jesuit colleges to encourage novices and clergy), these letters were political polemics and descriptive reports (also formulaic, but in a different way than the annual letters) written to a nonecclesiastical readership to explain a sociopolitical situation from a particular perspective. For the most part, the intended audience (the king and his council) was consistent across the body of letters, as even the two documents not directly written to the king (the 1604 letter to the viceroys and the printed polemical pamphlet of 1611) were meant to inform the ongoing debate at court. One might expect clear hierarchical stereotypes to emerge in such letters, given that the Spanish court and the Council of the Indies, who advised the monarch on matters relating to the Americas, were at the pinnacle of the colonial structures of the Spanish empire. Nevertheless, just these thirteen letters include a staggering number of human categories: 203 in total, mentioned 1,401 times. Such a broad typological spectrum cannot help but shed light on the complexity of categorization by Valdivia, a Jesuit with considerable authority in Chile and who was largely representative of a much broader political position.

The methodology uses a dual premise as its starting point. The first is that seeking to superimpose modern, primarily phenotypical racial hierarchies, on the reality of seventeenth-century Jesuits would be at best ahistorical and, at worst, a distortion of what was lived and understood at the time. The second part of the premise is a counterpoint to the first, which is that the Jesuits, in seeking to describe contemporary events with a particular salvific agenda, did nevertheless classify groups of people according to particular criteria. This dual premise allows us to ask to what extent (if at all) seventeenth-century Spanish Jesuit thought and practice reflected exploitative colonial and discriminatory hierarchies. In order to address this question, the analysis in this chapter uses a combination of quantitative and qualitative methodologies. The quantitative element involved counting the total number of categories that Valdivia used to describe human groups and dividing them into related subgroups in order to permit statistical comparisons. The qualitative analysis involves a qualitative consideration of the context of specific categories the letters use to draw out Valdivia's meaning and intentionality followed by contextualizing Valdivia's letters in a consideration of the universalism of the Catholic Church and the categorization of the highly influential writings of Valdivia's near-contemporary, José de Acosta.

As with all methodologies and short studies, this approach can only give us a partial picture and a number of important caveats should be borne in mind. The scope of this study is necessarily small, and the chapter is essentially a microhistory—a close analysis of just thirteen letters written primarily to the king by one individual in a particular historical and sociopolitical context. The survey sample of thirteen documents is relatively small even though a temporal spread of fourteen years is covered, which does allow us to gauge slight changes over time. Questions might legitimately be raised as to how much can be extrapolated and how representative these documents are with respect to understanding early modern, Jesuit, typological categorizations more generally. A key issue, for example, is that the particular context of these letters means that enslaved Africans and their descendants are almost completely absent from the documents; they refer almost exclusively to Indigenous Americans and Europeans.

No specialist software was used in the quantitative data collection and processing. I tried to be as consistent as possible in the selection process of what was a typological category and what was merely description—nouns were considered categories, while nouns followed immediately by adjectives (descriptors) were subcategories. Descriptions (that were not nouns immediately followed by adjectives) were not considered categories per-se. Spelling variations of the same word (such as "*indio*" vs. "*yndio*") were considered orthographical rather than typological differences and were therefore considered as the same categories. Nevertheless, variations that phrased similar types differently, such as "*nuevos amigos nuestros*" ("new friends of ours"), "*yndios amigos*" ("Indian friends"), and "*yndios amigos de paz*" ("peaceful Indian friends") have all been considered as different categories. Categories that say the same thing but distinguish gender, such as "*yndias de paz*" ("peaceful Indian women") as opposed to "*yndios de paz*" ("peaceful Indians" or "peaceful Indian men") similarly, have been considered as different categories.

The Quantitative Analysis

The thirteen documents studied here, written by Valdivia over a period of fourteen years, used a remarkable 203 categories to describe human typologies with a total frequency of 1,401.[17] Of these categories, 125 referred to Indigenous people (62%), while sixty-four referred specifically to Spaniards (31%). Only eight categories referred to neither Indigenous people nor Spaniards (4%), while a further six (3%) were nonspecific and either referred to humankind in general or both Spaniards and Indigenous Mapuche (fig. 1).

Indigenous categories were mentioned 871 times (62%); Spanish categories, 485 times (35%); non-Indigenous and non-Spanish 17 times (1%); and nonspecific categories were used 28 times (2%). The frequency of use of Indigenous and Spanish categories matches the number of typological categories almost exactly (fig. 1). This is perhaps not surprising given the context of the letters, which sought to inform the king and others of the situation on and beyond the frontier in order to shore up a policy that essentially tried to protect the Indigenous Mapuche from Spanish aggression and remove the causal factors for corresponding Mapuche aggression toward Spanish settlers. The protagonism of Indigenous people in these letters (whether as victims, perpetrators, or allies) is highlighted by the number and frequency of use of Indigenous typological categories.

As mentioned above, people of African descent were almost entirely absent from these letters, only being mentioned twice in two categories. The category "mulatto," referring to mixed Spanish and African parentage, was mentioned once in the letter of 1604 alongside "*mestizo*," which referred to mixed Spanish and Indigenous parentage. In an attempt to persuade the outgoing and incoming viceroys of the unjust nature of the Indigenous forced-labor tribute, Valdivia proposed as a solution that Indigenous laborers

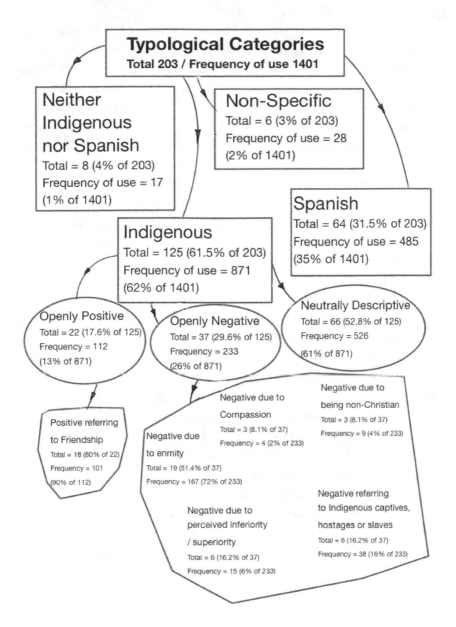

Figure 1. Typological Categories: Indigenous, Spanish, Neither, Non-Specific.
Courtesy of Andrew Redden.

be remunerated, just as "mestizos and mulattos were hired."[18] He continued, reasonably, "He who treats them [his Indigenous workers] better will receive better service."[19] He used the category "black" only once, in a letter to Philip III in 1614.[20] Valdivia was trying to persuade the king of the absolute necessity of continuing with the defensive war policy so that the peace could be kept in order to reduce the military forces on the frontier. In this way they would relieve the pressure on the Indigenous Mapuche groups who were allied to the Spanish and sustained them: "And if this does not happen . . . the peaceful Indians that are in Concepción and those of Arauco and Catiray with the work that will fall on them to provision the troops and the forts, will either rise up and become restless again, and when those of Concepción do not rebel, they will die out and this kingdom will be finished, because it does not have [the resources] to bring blacks from outside."[21]

Even though his proposed solution was to keep the peace rather than import enslaved Africans, the argument he uses is an uncritical repetition of the Lascasian conundrum outlined below—that relief could only be granted to Indigenous laborers if it were replaced with that of enslaved peoples from elsewhere. By the time Valdivia was writing, however—a century after Bartolomé de las Casas considered this same possibility—there was no ambiguity about who would be the ones to be enslaved. Valdivia did not think to question the legitimacy of the institution of slavery as a whole or whether enslaved peoples might be other than African. Unfortunately, the only reason Valdivia did not consider this a viable alternative to Indigenous labor in Chile was because he thought that Spaniards there could not afford to purchase sufficient numbers to sustain the colony, rather than that it was morally abhorrent. Had the financial resources been there, the implication is that he would have accepted, even encouraged, the importation of enslaved Africans as a preferred option to the forced labor of Indigenous Mapuche. A hierarchy of exploitation is clearly evident here. Nevertheless, it is worth noting as a caveat the fact that Valdivia only mentioned this possibility once in a survey of thirteen documents over a fourteen-year period. That it was one typological category out of 203 and mentioned only once out of a frequency of 1,401 (statistically, 0.07%) would suggest that Africans, whether enslaved or not, and whether as a solution to the ongoing conflict or not, were far from his mind.

Returning to the Indigenous categories, of the 125 categories for Indigenous people, 37 could be described as openly negative (29.6%); 22 as openly positive (17.6%); and 66 as neutrally descriptive (52.8%) (fig. 1). Positive, in this case, refers to inclusive categories that indicate alliance, friendship, or closeness to the Spanish, the Jesuits, or their culture or cause. Negative categories can be understood as indicating the opposite. Negative categories were used 233 times (26%); positive categories 112 times (13%); and neutrally descriptive categories 526 times (61%) (fig. 1). Once again, the total frequency of use of these categories appears to map closely onto the type of categories used.

Negative categories can be further subdivided into those that demonstrated Valdivia's compassion for the Indigenous Mapuche such as "the sick," "the wretched," "the poor" (three subcategories: 8.1%), and those that demonstrated his perceived sense of superiority (six subcategories: 16.2%). Other negative subcategories included those that referred in different ways to captives, hostages, or Indigenous slaves: There were six of these categories (16.2%), all neutrally written without intended emotional or emotive meaning. Particularly shocking to modern sensibilities is the use of the category *"pieças,"* which literally translates as "pieces" or "chattel," meaning "slaves." Valdivia, here, is using a term in common usage at the time that demonstrates the absolute conversion of people into objects to be bought, sold, and disposed of at will. While there were laws governing the treatment of slaves, the term nonetheless highlights the stark reality of the trade.

It is important to note that in using this term, Valdivia was not writing in support of the enslavement of people, but rather describing what was happening as part of and which drove the conflict, as Spanish soldiers and settlers benefitted financially from capturing slaves and selling them. The legal proclamations that facilitated the enslavement of Indigenous people who rebelled against the king gave cover for slave raiding beyond the frontier.[22] This, in turn, entrenched Indigenous hostility toward the Spanish and made peace negotiations much more difficult.

There were also three negative, yet neutrally written, categories that referred to non-Christians (8.1%) and were all variants on the term "pagan;"[23] and, finally, the largest number of categories (nineteen, or 51.4%) referred to Indigenous enemies of the Spanish (fig. 1).[24] Particularly telling of these negative categories is that only 16.2% could be said to be deliberately disparaging. This subset that demonstrated perceived Indigenous inferiority (or Spanish superiority) included the categorizations of Indigenous Mapuche as "barbarians;" *"chusma,"* meaning "riff-raff;" *"gandules,"* meaning "lazy-ones;" *"viejos inútiles"* "useless old people;" *"ladroncillos,"* meaning "thieves;" and *"soldadillos,"* referring to young warriors. Even this subset should be placed in context, however, as they appear in Valdivia's letters to the king from 1612 to 1618 as part of a discourse to demonstrate how effective the defensive war policy had been, and how the threat from the Indigenous Mapuche south of the Biobío had largely ceased to exist. All that remained of the threat were "viejos inútiles," ladroncillos, and soldadillos. Valdivia's use of the diminutive "-cillo/-illo" appears patronizing but is intended to persuade the king that the young Indigenous Mapuche warriors, keen to enhance their reputation by raiding Spanish territory and stealing livestock, goods, and even taking slaves, were not worth worrying about. They could be easily controlled by punitive raids carried out by soldiers from the nearest fort and their Indigenous allies. As such, the defensive war strategy should be continued as it had brought (relative) peace to the frontier.

These deliberately disparaging categories were also used with relative infrequency. Their total frequency of use across the thirteen documents was 15 (only 6%). By comparison, the "negative due to compassion" categories had the smallest total frequency of four (2%); the negative categories referring to captivity or enslavement, thirty-eight (16%); the negative due to being non-Christian, nine (4%); and the negative due to enmity, 167 (72%) (fig. 1). The vast majority of Valdivia's use of negative categories to describe Indigenous people employed the observable fact of opposition to demonstrate difference rather than perceived inferiority and superiority. These categories tended to be neutrally written and included types such as "our enemies," "restless warriors," "people at war" (*"gente de guerra"*), "those who want war," "Indians at war," "Indians who have retreated [from the border]," etc. Worthy of note is the appearance in the last two letters (1617 and 1618) of two variations of this latter category, *"retirados"* ("[those who have] retreated") and *"yndios retirados"* ("Indians [who have] retreated"). In the letter of April 1617, "retirados" is used twice, while in the letter of January 1618, the term "retirados" is used seventeen times, and "yndios retirados," once.[25] Prior to

1617, the term is not used at all and is indicative of a new phenomenon in the course of the war—that of Indigenous Mapuche relocating as far south of the border as they could so as to remove themselves entirely from the threat of Spanish raids or, indeed, Spanish missionaries. Notwithstanding the fact that to this point the defensive war strategy was maintaining the peace, those who retreated, not surprisingly, wanted nothing whatsoever to do with the Spanish and remained deeply suspicious even of the Jesuits who were largely responsible for the negotiations and acted as mediators. Of course, this numerical observation does not say anything about the social impact of these migrations and, indeed, may be more a reflection of Valdivia's recent awareness of and growing preoccupation with the phenomenon. Nevertheless, it does suggest a shift in the Indigenous Mapuche response to the Spanish, and this numerical indication is one that might usefully be followed up with more research.

So far, we have dealt primarily with openly negative categories for Indigenous people used by Valdivia. These might be compared with the openly positive categories he also uses. The total frequency of "negative due to being non-Christian" categories (nine), for example, compares exactly with the total frequency of "positive due to being Christian" (also nine). The category of "almas," or "souls" (six out of the total of nine), has been included in this positive set as it is indicative of the Catholic belief in the universality of humankind. The fact that, of these Christian categories, two-thirds simply refer to Indigenous people as "souls" speaks volumes about Jesuit priorities and the way they perceived humanity. The total frequency of negative categories of enmity (167, or 62%, of the combined frequency of enmity vs. friendship categories), meanwhile, exceeds the total frequency of positive categories indicating friendship or alliance (101, or 38%) by about a third (fig. 2).

By far, however, the most important set of categories of Indigenous people is that which is neutrally descriptive, which, as mentioned above, covered 52.8% of all the categories used, with a total frequency of 61% (see figs. 1 and 2). This set can be further divided into those categories that referred to the Indigenous groups' (or person's) places of origin or lineage (i.e., where they were from, or their kinship group) and those that referred to social function (including rank or status, i.e., what they did, whether they were at war or at peace, whether they had a profession—essentially what their role was in

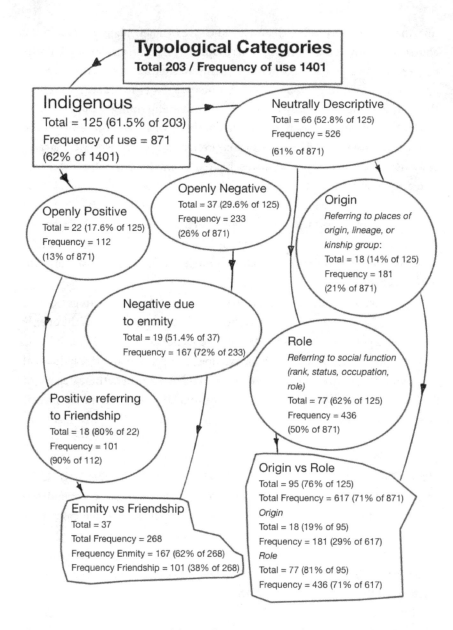

Typological Categories
Total 203 / Frequency of use 1401

Indigenous
Total = 125 (61.5% of 203)
Frequency of use = 871
(62% of 1401)

Neutrally Descriptive
Total = 66 (52.8% of 125)
Frequency = 526
(61% of 871)

Openly Negative
Total = 37 (29.6% of 125)
Frequency = 233
(26% of 871)

Origin
*Referring to places of
origin, lineage, or
kinship group:*
Total = 18 (14% of 125)
Frequency = 181
(21% of 871)

Openly Positive
Total = 22 (17.6% of 125)
Frequency = 112
(13% of 871)

**Negative due
to enmity**
Total = 19 (51.4% of 37)
Frequency = 167 (72% of 233)

Role
*Referring to social function
(rank, status, occupation,
role)*
Total = 77 (62% of 125)
Frequency = 436
(50% of 871)

**Positive referring
to Friendship**
Total = 18 (80% of 22)
Frequency = 101
(90% of 112)

Origin vs Role
Total = 95 (76% of 125)
Total Frequency = 617 (71% of 871)
Origin
Total = 18 (19% of 95)
Frequency = 181 (29% of 617)
Role
Total = 77 (81% of 95)
Frequency = 436 (71% of 617)

Enmity vs Friendship
Total = 37
Total Frequency = 268
Frequency Enmity = 167 (62% of 268)
Frequency Friendship = 101 (38% of 268)

Figure 2. Enmity versus Friendship and Origin versus Role. Courtesy of Andrew
Redden.

society). The former set included eighteen categories mentioned, with a total frequency of 181, while the latter included seventy-seven categories, mentioned with a total frequency of 436 (see fig. 2).

As we can see, the importance of categories indicating role or social function cannot be understated. Of the total number of Indigenous categories (125) mentioned with a total frequency of 871, seventy-seven referred to the role or social function, mentioned with a total frequency of 436. This equates to 62% of all Indigenous categories referring to role or social function, with a total frequency of 50%.

"Social function" itself can be subdivided into various classificatory types that appeared in the letters. Sixteen categories referred to societal rank and were mentioned a total of eighty-six times. Eighteen categories referred to family status (e.g. brother, daughter, son, children, wives etc) and was mentioned with a similar frequency of eighty four.[26] Twenty-three categories referred to (nonmilitary) occupation (things people did, rather than who they were) with a frequency of 117.[27] Not surprisingly, by far the biggest set (with some overlap with the previous categories of rank) was those that referred to military occupation, with forty-three categories and a total frequency of 289 (fig. 3).[28] Both the number of categories and frequency of mention correlate relatively closely and what is worthy of note is the clear predominance given to categories that denote occupation (whether military or otherwise): 66% number; 70% frequency.

The final typological set to be mentioned here (although there are more) is that of gender. Given the gendered nature of the Spanish language and also the gendered nature of war, only a minority of categories referred specifically to the female gender (whether Indigenous or Spanish). Nevertheless, women were profoundly affected by the frontier war, as they were the frequent victims of slave raids by both sides and, even though women are not Valdivia's prime focus (as might be expected from a celibate priest reporting on war), they do appear in the documentary record. Nine out of 125 categories for Indigenous people (7%) referred specifically to women with a total frequency of fifty-five out of 871, again showing a close correlation between number and frequency (fig. 3).

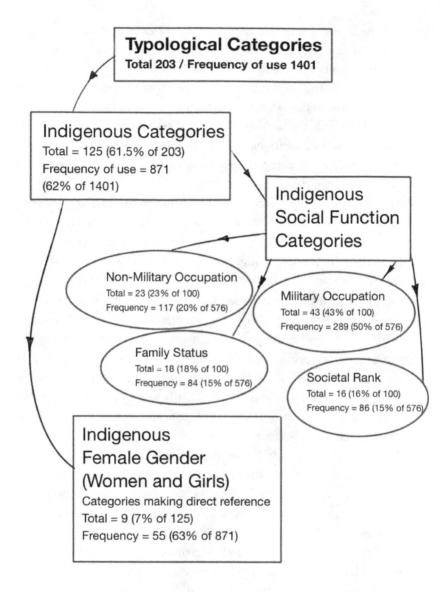

Figure 3. Indigenous Social Function and Gender. Courtesy of Andrew Redden.

Summary of Findings

From this quantitative analysis of typological categories used by Valdivia we can draw out three key findings. The first is that in these letters written over a period of fourteen years we see so many categories used with such frequency that in the messy reality of a conflict-riven frontier such as Chile in the early seventeenth century, the concept of "race" becomes relatively meaningless. Rather than helping us to better understand the complexities of colonial society or Jesuit thought and practices, arguably, it serves more to distract our attention from what contemporary society considered important in terms of the way it was structured and the injustices and conflicts that resulted. The fact that Valdivia did not use the collective term "race" (*raza*), or an equivalent synonym, once across the survey of thirteen documents over fourteen years reinforces this finding.

The second key finding is that the majority of categories or subcategories referring to Indigenous people, both in number and frequency, were neutrally descriptive and did not (openly at least) express sentiments of European superiority. Those categories that did were relatively few in number and were used specifically as part of a discourse to persuade the king that the Indigenous people they referred to were not worth concerning himself with and that he should continue his policy of defensive warfare that (according to Valdivia) had been so effective at bringing about peace on the frontier.

The third finding is that the majority of typological categories and subcategories used by Valdivia were based on various types of social function. Even the largest set of categories that marked difference between peoples was based on a dualistic opposition—enmity versus friendship—and was not explicitly dependent on vertical hierarchy for its criteria.

Nevertheless, these broad findings based on quantitative analysis certainly need to be qualified by the contemporary social circumstances mentioned at the beginning of this chapter together with a consideration of the ideological underpinnings of Jesuit thought at the time. The social context of Chile—a colonial society, established by conquest and sustained by the exploited labor of particular groups of largely Indigenous people—was overtly (and often brutally) hierarchical. Even if typological categories for the most part depended on social function, one's social function frequently determined one's status in the colonial hierarchy (and vice versa). Accident of birth (at the root of more modern racialized categorizations) certainly played a significant role in determining one's function and status within this society. The Society of Jesus, itself a hierarchical institution, also existed within these parameters and Jesuits like Valdivia had to make sense of the world accordingly.

The following section considers the writings of the Jesuit intellectual and missionary José de Acosta (1540–1600), a near contemporary of Valdivia's. Acosta was one of the most influential Jesuit thinkers of the time and left a tremendous imprint on the Jesuit missions in Spanish America, both through his leadership in the reform of evangelization after the Council of Trent (1545–1563) and its implementation in the Viceroyalty of Peru with the Third Council of Lima (1582–1583) as well as his wide-ranging studies of the world he encountered. These works, in which he tried to make sense of the diversity of world and its human population within the intellectual bounds of his own hierarchical worldview, became the points of reference for generations of Jesuit missionaries in the early modern period and provided important intellectual background for the writings of Valdivia in Chile. What will become clear in the following analysis, however, is his salvific rather than racialized framework for structuring human hierarchy within the "natural order."

The Salvific Ethnology of José de Acosta

By the seventeenth century, the Society of Jesus had become an integral part of Catholic European colonial enterprises both utilizing and being used by colonial powers (particularly Spain, Portugal, and France) to further particular interests. While these interests were not shared in their entirety (for example, the frequent disagreements between Jesuits and colonial officials and settlers with respect to the level and nature of exploitation of Indigenous labor), they were at least closely aligned (for example, with respect to belief in the dual necessity of the Christianization of Indigenous Americans and their integration as subjects of Christian monarchs). During this same period in the Spanish global empire, Jesuit missions and missionaries became an important strategic element in the pacification and incorporation of Indigenous groups who openly resisted direct colonization on the frontiers of the Spanish viceroyalties. It is true that many Jesuits (with varying degrees of success and failure) tried to defend Indigenous American peoples and African slaves (or those descended from them) from some of the worst excesses of colonial exaction and abuse but, as a rule, even the most ardent Jesuit defenders of these people did not question the legitimacy of the transatlantic slave trade or of colonial projects more generally. What is more, the Jesuit mission networks, which frequently became the envy of colonists for their efficiency and shared productive capacity, relied heavily on slave labor in the coastal areas of the Andean region (what is now Colombia, Venezuela, Ecuador, and Peru) and on that of their Indigenous neophytes in other frontier regions such as Paraguay and northern Mexico.[29]

In the meantime, Jesuits who were keen to evangelize newly trafficked slaves in the ports of Cartagena and Callao and the key urban centers used their own slaves as interpreters to mediate between the missionaries and the people from diverse ethnolinguistic groups from West Africa who had been violently sequestered and forcibly transported to the Americas. Two prominent examples were the Jesuits Alonso de Sandoval (1576–1652) and Pedro Claver (1580–1654), who Sandoval mentored. Both ministered to African slaves in the Caribbean port of Cartagena, the entry point for thousands of enslaved peoples forcibly transported to the Americas from West Africa during the sixteenth to eighteenth centuries.[30] Sandoval's contemporary, José de Acosta, had, in his blueprint for missionary evangelization, *De procuranda Indorum salute* (1576), vehemently criticized those missionaries who attempted to minister to Indigenous Americans without learning their languages to a high level.[31]

Notwithstanding this criticism, and despite the fact that Sandoval used Acosta's work as a model for his own, he recognized the logistical impossibility of so few missionaries being able to learn so many and such linguistically diverse languages at a sufficiently high standard. As such, he suggested that slaves owned and trained by the Jesuits be used as interpreters for catechesis and sacramental confession.[32] Sandoval's assistant, Pedro Claver, (canonized in 1888 for his life's ministry to enslaved Africans), also used slaves as interpreters, having learned this methodology from his mentor, even when called on to act as an interpreter for trials of Africans accused of witchcraft.[33] While both labored to improve the conditions of the captives they ministered to and were critical of the condition under which slaves were forcibly transported, neither condemned the institution of slavery itself, and Sandoval effectively limited himself to making recommendations to slave owners as to the way they treated their slaves, that they should "be few [in number]," and that the slaveholders should "give them a good example."[34]

If Jesuits did not question and even participated in the construction of hierarchical, colonial structures, that hierarchy nevertheless did not map seamlessly onto what we would understand as modern racialized typologies. The key to understanding this dissonance is the firm belief of early modern Catholics in a common origin for humankind. All humans were believed to be descended from Adam and Eve and, post-Flood, the lineage of Noah as recounted in the book of Genesis. All humans, therefore, were made in the likeness of God. As Colin Kidd points out, this "unity of the human race was fundamental to Christian theology. If mankind did not spring from a single racial origin, then theologians were confronted with a scenario that undermined the very essence of the Christian story."[35] He continues: "The sacred drama of Fall and redemption rests upon assumptions of mankind's common descent from Adam. Otherwise, the transmission of original sin from Adam would not have polluted the whole human race. In the second place, Christ's atonement—however limited the scope for election—would not apply to the whole of mankind."[36]

This universalism was as true for the Catholic world as it was for the Protestants. Shortly after the conquest of the Caribbean Islands, as a result of the demographic collapse caused by widespread abuse of the Indigenous islanders by colonists, theologians, intellectuals, and members of the colonial elite grappled with each other in protracted debates about the very nature of Indigenous American peoples. The outcome of these debates—the most famous being that between the Dominican friar Bartolomé de las Casas (d. 1566) and the secular cleric and humanist Juan Ginés de Sepúlveda (d. 1573) in the mid-sixteenth century—would determine whether and to what extent Indigenous Americans could legitimately (according to the laws of the time) be enslaved for the benefit of Spanish colonists.[37] Broadly speaking, the strength and vigor of the Spanish church's defense of Indigenous Americans (which, sadly, was never replicated with respect to enslaved Africans), was affirmed by the papal bull of Pope Paul III (r. 1534–1549), *Sublimis Deus* in 1537.[38] The bull condemned as diabolical the arguments of those who maintained that Indigenous Americans were less than human in order to justify their enslavement. The reason for this outspoken condemnation was the implication that if they were subhuman, they were thereby not capable of receiving God's grace or salvation: "Seeing and envying this, the enemy of mankind, who always opposes good men so that they might perish, devised a means, unheard of up to this time, by which the preaching of God's word to nations for their salvation would be prevented. And he inspired certain of his satellites who, in their desire to satisfy their greed, presume to assert here and there that the Indians of the south and west, and other nations who in these times have come to our knowledge, under the pretext that they are incapable of the Catholic faith, are brute animals who can be enslaved by us."[39]

The crucial statement that outlined the practical implications of this condemnation followed shortly after: "We command that the aforesaid Indians and all other nations which come to the knowledge of Christians in the future, must not be deprived of their freedom and the ownership of their property, even though they are outside the faith of Christ. Rather, they can use, increase, and enjoy this freedom and ownership freely and lawfully. They must not be enslaved. Furthermore, whatever else may be done, contrary to this command, shall be invalid and void."[40]

This universalism (and prohibition of the enslavement of Indigenous Americans) as underlined by Paul III was reiterated in April 1639 by Urban VIII in his bull *Commissum Nobis*, which stated: "No-one dare or presume to reduce the Indians to slavery, sell them, purchase them, exchange them or give them away, separate them from their wives and children, despoil them of their belongings and goods, move them to other places and displace them, or deprive them of their freedom in any manner whatsoever."[41] If any were to disobey this very clear proclamation and continue to participate in slaving expeditions against Indigenous Americans, then the slaveholders were to be excommunicated.[42] The former prohibition of the enslavement of Indigenous Americans caused riots in São Paulo, during which the Jesuit College was attacked. The *Paulistas*, whose wealth relied on regular slave expeditions that frequently attacked the Paraguayan missions, (rightly) considered the Jesuits responsible for either their excommunication or their loss of wealth.[43]

All this fed into the Catholic universalism of the Society of Jesus in the sixteenth and seventeenth centuries. Ignatius Loyola's maxim, *Ite, inflammate omnia,* meaning "Go and set the world aflame!" aptly summarized the evangelical mission of the Society of Jesus. The gospel should be carried to all peoples of the world just as Christ had commanded.[44] Yet this mission did not mean that colonial hierarchies should be necessarily questioned, especially if these hierarchies were perceived to facilitate evangelization. It was when colonial exploitation by Europeans who identified as Christian drove non-Christians or neophyte Christians to reject the Catholic Church and its teachings or made it difficult to administer the sacraments to those they had Christianized, that the Jesuit position diverged markedly from that of the colonial settlers. Such was the case of Jesuits like Luis de Valdivia, as we have seen, who were tasked with evangelization on the Chilean frontier. Their mission was to save souls, and this was nigh impossible to do if the communities that they wished to evangelize were in a state of war with the Spanish. For the most part, however, the Society was keen to maintain good relations with colonists, bearing in mind, of course, that Jesuits also ministered to them in the urban settlements, received financial support from them, taught their sons in schools and colleges, ministered to their wives and daughters, and recruited new members from their population. Just like the vast majority of colonists, they were also loyal subjects of the Spanish monarch who defended the Catholic faith at the head of a vast global empire. This was a hierarchical society that, in its ideal form, affirmed and defended the same cosmovision of the Society of Jesus which, in turn, taught that cosmovision to the people to whom it evangelized and ministered.

In order to teach this, however, it was necessary to try to understand more about the people they encountered. The paradox was that for this understanding to be coherent to the Jesuits (and Christian Europeans), it needed to fit within the universalist cosmovision that taught that all humans had descended from the progeny of Adam and Eve and then, subsequently, Noah. Indigenous American understanding of human origins, therefore, had to be documented and either contested or reworked. Origin stories such as the emergence and migration of the Toltec ancestors of the Central-Mesoamerican Nahua peoples from *Chicomotzoc* or "the place of the seven caves," or the Inca descent from the Ayar siblings who emerged from a cave by the shores of Lake Titicaca (while other Andean ethnic groups emerged from different caves) flew in the face of scriptural accounts of the common ancestry of humankind.[45] Indigenous typological differences had to be recategorized so that they could fit the dominant Judeo-Christian narrative. As mentioned above, one of the most influential Jesuit writers and missionaries to set out to do this was José de Acosta. Acosta was also responsible for drafting and overseeing the printing of approved trilingual catechisms and book of sermons in Spanish, Quechua, and Aymara, which were then used as a basis for subsequent translations for use in other regions of Spanish America, including Chile and the works in Mapundungun written by Luis de Valdivia.[46] These sermons and catechisms, designed to teach Indigenous peoples the fundamentals of the Catholic faith, did so by breaking down the Judeo-Christian (and then Catholic) cosmovision into digestible and chronological parts. It did not make sense to begin with a Christological narrative that talked about Christ's salvific mission, rather it was imperative to explain first the common origins of humanity and the reasons why Christ's salvation was necessary.[47] To this end, it was necessary to challenge absolutely the Indigenous origin histories that separated human lineages from each other and which recounted that humans had emerged spontaneously from different locations in the sacred earth or were fashioned by deities from ground maize-corn or other materials.[48] The universal narrative of Christianity required that the Indigenous histories of the universe be reconstructed from the very beginning; it was necessary to replace their entire hierarchies of being. As such, the structure of the catechism and thematic progression of the sermons began with the creation of the universe (the Genesis story), followed by the creation of spiritual beings (the angels), and then the fall of Lucifer and his fellow rebel angels. It then moved to the creation of the earth, animal and plant life, and then the creation of humankind via the fashioning of Adam and Eve. The next stage was to establish Adam and Eve's fall from grace and the beginning of Original Sin.[49] That was followed by the story of Noah and the common lineage of humankind (in all its sinfulness), which contextualized the coming of

Christ and his salvific mission. From the perspective of Acosta and other Catholic missionaries, anthropological typology and hierarchies of difference began with the creation of the universe itself starting with God, the hierarchies of the angels, and, subsequently, humankind, with its own internal hierarchies mirroring the celestial order.[50]

If this cosmological hierarchy was directed pedagogically toward Indigenous Americans within the Hispanic empire, Acosta also labored to understand how Indigenous Americans fitted within the hierarchy of human and material creation in order to present this to interested European readers. Both of these facets of his work, written for difference audiences, combined his understanding of human monogeneity in a single overarching worldview. With respect to his European readers, his seminal work, the *Historia natural y moral de las Indias*, which became the model for subsequent natural history surveys, examined the geography, flora, and fauna of the Americas as well as recounted and reworked the histories of the Aztec hegemony of Central Mesoamerica Nahua and the Inca Empire of the South American Andes.[51] His first task was to counter the arguments of classical and early Christian philosophers whose arguments about the Antipodes (as they referred to what they imagined the Americas to be) were necessarily speculative and wildly inaccurate. These early philosophers argued that the Antipodes—or New World, as Acosta referred to them—either did not exist or, if their existence was accepted, were fundamentally different from the Old World (for example, they had different skies).[52] By extension, Acosta was concerned to argue against any notion of difference of the inhabitants of the Antipodean New World (for example, they were somehow monstrous or less than human).[53]

If the basic premise was that all humankind was descended from Noah's lineage, the next task was to work out how it was that his descendants had reached the Americas and populated it, bearing in mind that Noah's ark was believed to have come to rest on Mount Ararat on the borderlands of what is now the eastern Anatolian region of Turkey, Armenia, and Iran. He categorically discounted "that there was another ark of Noah that brought men to the Indies; and [it was] even less likely that the first inhabitants of this [New] world might have been brought by some Angel dragging them by their hair like the prophet Habakkuk."[54] Importantly, he did not try to deny God's power to have brought humans over to the Americas supernaturally, but nonetheless argued for a natural explanation, "rather, [one which] is reasonable."[55] He pled with the reader to allow him to follow the "thin thread of reason" for "lack of eye-witnesses" and argued that the first inhabitants of Peru must have come there by one of three ways: either deliberately by sea, or accidentally by sea (blown there in a storm), or by land. He entertained the possibility of the sea routes but discarded the deliberate sea crossing due to the ancients not having known the magnetic compass for open ocean navigation. The accidental crossing was more likely he contended, but then disregarded this second option due to the difficulty of understanding how so many people could have come to the Americas with so many animals (bearing in mind that all came originally from Noah's ark). One small shipwreck, even if it did carry animals, would be unlikely to have been the origin of so many people and such rich fauna, and they certainly could not have reached there by swimming.[56] With that, he reasoned, the most likely possibility was a land bridge that joined the New World to the Old: "It is for me a great conjecture, to think that the new world, which we call the Indies, is not entirely divided and separated from the other world. And, to offer my opinion, I sometimes think that the one land and the other at some point join up and connect, or at least come close together. To the present there is no certainty that the opposite is true because to the Arctic Pole, which they call North, the entire longitude of the earth has not been discovered or known."[57]

Acosta's process of reasoning is impressive in that it successfully anticipated the main theories of human and animal migration to the Americas still in common currency today. For the purposes of this discussion, however, what is important is that his detailed reasoning follows a logical progression from the universalist starting point that all humans, including Indigenous Americans (and the Papal bull of 1537 put that matter beyond dispute) were descended from the lineage of Noah and thus had the same origins. Acosta continued by challenging the theories that tapped into European myths of Atlantis or that Indigenous Americans were somehow one of the lost tribes of Israel before concluding with the somewhat frustrating but eminently reasonable (and scientific) argument that we just cannot know for sure.[58] He concluded the first book with a chapter that, again, we might reasonably think considers "what it is that Indians tend to recount about their origins" and focused on the origin stories of the central and southern Andean peoples.[59] This was by no means an exercise in anthropological relativism; however, nor was it any acknowledgement that even if Europeans could not know for sure how humans reached and populated the Americas, Indigenous explanations of their own origins were as valid as European—quite the opposite. He gave a very brief summary of the Andean origin story of the birth of "a Viracocha" from Lake Titicaca who then founded his capital "in Tiaguanaco [Tiwanaku], where today you can see ruins and pieces of ancient and very strange buildings and that from there they came to Cuzco."[60] The origin story of the Ayar siblings (mentioned above) he glossed as "others tell how six, or I don't know how many, men came out of a cave via an opening and that these began the propagation of mankind. . . . From them, they say that Manco Capac originated, whom they recognize as the founder and head of the Incas."[61] His point, however, was not to affirm these origin stories as possibilities—as this would have been an admission that Indigenous Americans (in this case Andeans) were not human (i.e., that they had different origins than Europeans, Asians, and Africans) and would have laid him open to charges of heresy. More to the point, he simply did not accept this as a possibility, writing, "All this is full of lies and beyond reason."[62] His counterpoint to these origin stories, of course, was to cite scripture, arguing that Indigenous Americans were disabused of any notion that their ancestors originated in the New World, "with our Faith, which teaches us, that all men [humans] come from one first man."[63]

One final argument he made anticipated more modern historical debates about the legitimacy of certain types of sources—in this case reliance on oral tradition rather than written sources. He wrote: "All that exists that refers to the memory and relationship of the Indians goes back [no further than] four hundred years, and that everything before then is pure confusion and shadows, without it being possible to find anything that is certain."[64] He stated that even the *quipucamayoc*—those charged with the task of keeping, recording, and interpreting the knotted strings known as *quipus* that circulated in the Andes and served as mnemonic aids for recording different types of information—could not help, and the issue here, he wrote, was their "lack of books and writing."[65] It is at this point we gain an insight into another of his academic goals, which was the criteria for his attempt to classify and rank human civilizations according to their perceived intellectual achievement.

In book six of the *Historia natural*, Acosta took issue with "those [Europeans] who consider the Indians to lack understanding" and compared the Mexican and Inca civilizations with those of the republics of Athens and Rome. Both, notwithstanding the philosophy and learning of these ancient republics, followed teachings that were erroneous just like the "Republics of the Mexicans and of the Incas."[66] In a rather paternalistic apologia, which was more a defense of the project to evangelize than it was a defense of Indigenous intellect; he argued, "Even though they had many things [customs] that were barbarian, and without basis, they also had many other things that were worthy of admiration, which clearly shows that they have a natural capacity to be well taught."[67] As examples of things "worthy of admiration," he went on to discuss (in a cursory way) the complex calendar systems that were used by the Mesoamerican and Andean peoples.[68] The issue that, for Acosta, affected where Indigenous American civilizations ranked in the hierarchy of human civilization, was that they had never discovered or used writing, which he narrowly defined as being invented "to refer to and mean immediately the words which we pronounce."[69] He distinguished images or pictographs from writing because the former "serve only for the memory."[70] His distinction was a nuanced one that arguably anticipated much later development of the theory of semiotics, as he wrote that "the one who invented them, did not do so to signify words, rather to denote that [a particular] thing." As such, he continued, "they are not strictly letters nor writing, but characters, or memory aids."[71] Using this very fine distinction, he placed European civilization higher than those not only of the Indigenous American civilizations of Mexico and Peru, but also of the Japanese and the Chinese. The chapters that follow go on to express his admiration for the level of learning in Japan and China, praising their universities, philosophy, and study of the natural sciences. Before he does this, however, he proved to doubters that Chinese and Japanese writing does not involve letters, as is commonly believed, but characters that signify things, rather than being immediate signifiers of the words that are pronounced. How else, he argued, would the same characters be understood across so many mutually unintelligible languages?[72] He then turned to

Mesoamerican civilization and discussed their pictographic writing systems, appreciating their ability to record information, "even though they are not as curious or as delicate as those of the Chinese and Japanese." Significantly, he refuted the arguments of those Europeans who dismissed Mexican manuscripts as "superstition" and "sorcery."[73] Following this, he discussed the Andean method of recording information using quipus or knotted string and beads as mnemonic aids, and talked about their continued usefulness in contemporary sixteenth-century Peru: "If this is not ingenious, and if these men are beasts," he argued, "then let whosoever be the judge, because what I judge to be certain is, that when this [method] is used, it is greatly advantageous to us."[74]

Ultimately, Acosta's work served as a double-edged sword that both defended the universality of humankind and the rationality and civilization of Indigenous Americans whilst simultaneously ranking the civilizations of the world hierarchically. Not surprisingly, perhaps, he placed Europeans at the top, closely followed by the Chinese and Japanese and, only then, by the Indigenous Americans. Aside from the fact that this rather cursory overview completely ignored ancient and contemporary civilizations from South Asia and Africa, it set the frame for intellectual justifications of European superiority in the years to come and became a model approach to the study of non-European cultures and peoples for fellow Jesuits.

Conclusion

This chapter began with a dual premise: first, that seeking to superimpose modern, primarily phenotypical racial hierarchies on the reality of seventeenth-century Jesuits would be at best ahistorical and, at worst, a distortion of what was lived and understood at the time. Second, the Jesuits, in seeking to describe contemporary events with a particular salvific agenda, did nevertheless classify groups of people according to particular criteria. As part of this premise, the chapter sought to test the assertion by Peter Wade that "ideas about human difference, while they may have involved a concept of race that was diverse, contested and even not very central, were certainly powerfully structured by ideas of European superiority."[75]

The plethora of typological categories that Luis de Valdivia used, writing from Chile in the early seventeenth century, reflected a strong preoccupation with opposition. In a survey of thirteen letters written over fourteen years, roughly twice as many categories referred to enmity as they did to friendship or alliance. Arguably, this is not surprising in a series of letters that were written to recount the progress of a war. It might be argued that in this could be seen the growth of "a concept of race structured by European superiority," but in Valdivia's letters to the king and his counsel, traces of modern concepts of race were ultimately so faint as to be barely noticeable. Role or social function seemed to be the principal method of classification that Valdivia used to refer to people. When this is placed in a colonial context, however, hierarchy takes sharper form. Hierarchical classification of human typology becomes clearer when we view the letters and their context through the lens of salvific cosmology, typified by the works of José de Acosta.

José de Acosta, the most influential Jesuit writer with respect to the Americas, without a doubt sought to classify humankind in terms of a civilizational hierarchy. Notwithstanding his powerful use of reason, or, arguably, because he was using his reason from within a particular (European) cosmovision, this hierarchy not surprisingly placed European civilization at the top of the quite limited number of contemporary civilizations that he considered. An important nuance, however, was the universalist nature of the Catholic cosmovision that Acosta was a part of and through which he understood the world. All humans were rational beings, with souls, and all were descended from common ancestry. All were entitled to receive God's grace, and all were entitled to salvation; place of origin, cultural differences, phenotypical variations—none of these mattered when it came to the capacity to receive Christ's saving grace. Nevertheless, Acosta's preoccupation was to try to understand the complexity of the lands and peoples he had encountered in the Americas whilst condensing that complexity into a simplified and coherent structure. This structure necessarily affirmed his cosmological reality in which the social hierarchy reflected the celestial and provided a blueprint for exporting that reality and bringing in those who were outside of it. In seeking to defend the Indigenous Mapuche from the worst of colonial exactions and in his attempts to bring peace to the frontier in order to better evangelize, Luis de Valdivia's own cosmovision replicated that of Acosta's. The complexity of his typological categorizations, however, should serve as a reminder of the complexity of colonial life as understood and represented by members of the Society of Jesus.

Notes

1.   My thanks are due to Luke Clossey, Jack Leung, Charles Parker, and Nathaniel Millett for their careful reading of previous drafts of this chapter and their helpful comments and suggestions.

2.   Critique of Michael Banton, *Racial Theories* (Cambridge: Cambridge University Press, 1987), in Peter Wade, *Race and Ethnicity in Latin America*, 2nd ed. (London: Pluto Press, 2010), 6.

3.   Wade, *Race and Ethnicity*, 8.

4.   For Luis de Valdivia's biographical details, see Andrés Ignacio Prieto, "Valdivia, Luis de, SJ (1561–1642)," in *The Cambridge Encyclopedia of the Jesuits*, ed. Thomas Worcester (Cambridge: Cambridge University Press, 2017), 813.

5.   Sergio Villalobos refers to Santa Cruz as "Santa Cruz de Óñez." Villalobos, *La vida fronteriza en Chile* (Madrid: Editorial Mapfre, 1992), 237. See also Alonso de Ovalle, *Histórica relación del Reino de Chile y de las misiones y ministerios que ejercita en él la Compañía de Jesús* [1646] (Santiago: Pehuén Editores, 2003), 365. Rather than Osorno, Ovalle names Chillán as the one of the six destroyed cities.

6.   Eugene Korth, *Spanish Policy in Colonial Chile: The Struggle for Social Justice, 1535–1700* (Stanford: Stanford University Press, 1968), 111.

7.   José Manuel Díaz Blanco, ed., *El Alma en la palabra: escritos inéditos del P. Luis de Valdivia* (Santiago: Ediciones Universidad Alberto Hurtado / Pontificia Universidad Católica de Chile, 2011), 30. See also Andrew Redden, "The Best Laid Plans . . . : Jesuit Counsel, Peacebuilding, and Disaster on the Chilean Frontier; The Martyrs of Elicura, 1612," *Journal of Jesuit Studies*, 4, no. 2 (2017): 250–69.

8.   Díaz Blanco, *El alma en la palabra*, 31–32.

9.   Luis de Velasco was named viceroy by Philip II on June 7, 1595 but reached Lima and took office over a year later on July 24, 1596. He also served as the viceroy of New Spain, during the years 1589–1595 and again in 1607–1611. Gaspar de Zúñiga Acevedo y Fonseca was named viceroy of Peru by Philip III on May 19, 1603 and entered Lima and took office on November 28, 1604. He died in office in 1606. Like his predecessor, Zúñiga also served as viceroy of New Spain immediately prior to being named as viceroy of Peru (1595–1603), For biographical information about respective viceroys of Peru, see Manuel de Mendíburu, *Diccionario histórico-biográfico del Perú*, vols.1–8 (Lima: Imprenta de J. Francisco Solis, 1874–1890), http://www.cervantesvirtual.com/obras/autor/mendiburu-manuel-de-1805–1885–6133. For Luis de Velasco and Gaspar de Zúñiga Acevedo y Fonseca, see vol. 8, 285–94 and 383–85. The jointly addressed letter by Luis de Valdivia can be read as "Memorial a Luis de Velasco y el Conde de

Monterrey, Lima 1604," in *El Alma en la palabra*, ed. Díaz Blanco (Santiago: Universidad Alberto Hurtado, 2011), 85–104.

10. John Padberg, ed., *The Constitutions of the Society of Jesus and their Complementary Norms: A Complete English Translation of the Official Latin Texts* (St. Louis, MO: Institute of Jesuit Sources, 1996), part vi, no. 591, 258.

11. Redden, "The Best Laid Plans," 253. See also Díaz Blanco, *El alma en la palabra*, 39–44. See also Korth, *Spanish Policy in Colonial Chile*, 123–5.

12. Valdivia specifically requested Ribera's appointment.

13. Redden, "The Best Laid Plans," 263–7.

14. Díaz Blanco, *El alma en la palabra*, 43–44.

15. Contemporary copies of all the documents analyzed can be found in various archives in Chile, Spain, and Italy, particularly the Archivum Romanum Societatis Iesu (ARSI) in Rome, the Archivo General de Indias (AGI) in Seville, the Archivo Nacional Histórico de Chile (ANH), and the Biblioteca Nacional de Chile (BNC) in Santiago, Chile. This chapter uses the transcripts compiled in the critical edition by José Manuel Díaz Blanco, ed., *El Alma en la palabra*.

16. Luis de Valdivia, "Impreso propagandístico de la guerra defensiva, Lima 1611," in *El Alma en la palabra*, 125–34.

17. Total frequency refers to the number of times that categories were mentioned over the thirteen letters.

18. Luis de Valdivia, "Memorial a Luis de Velasco y al Conde de Monterrey, Lima, 1604," in *El alma de la palabra*, 96.

19. Ibid.

20. Valdivia, "Carta a Felipe III, Concepción, 20 de Febrero de 1614," in *El alma de la palabra*, 298.

21. Ibid. This and, unless otherwise stated, all subsequent translations are by me.

22. The longer the conflict continued, transcending generations, the harder it became to talk in terms of a "rebellion," as Spanish dominion did not reach the Mapuche with whom they were in conflict. This, of course, undermined the legal justification for the war and, ultimately, for Spanish rule.

23. The literal translation of the word "*infiel*" would be "infidel" or, more literally, "unfaithful." In this context it means "un-baptised" or "pagan."

24. Negative, yet neutrally written, means categories that "other" the Indigenous person or group and separate them from the Spanish, but not in a disparaging way.

25. Luis de Valdivia, "Carta a Felipe III, Concepción, 12 de Abril de 1617" and "Carta a Felipe III, Concepción 31 de Enero de 1618," in *El alma en la palabra*, 396–402, 405–14.

26. These categories also include those that refer to age such as *viejos* (old people) or *moços* or *muchachos*, meaning youths.

27. It should be noted that there is some overlap here as the four categories of *cacique* or community leader were indicative of social status but also referred to what people did.

28. Thirty-three categories overlap here between military occupation and societal rank, which creates a discrepancy between the total number (77) of social function categories (fig. 2) and the number (100) of social function categories when they are subdivided (fig. 3).

29. See for example, Jaime Torres Sánchez, *Haciendas y posesiones de la Compañía de Jesús en Venezuela: el Colegio de Caracas en el Siglo XVIII* (Seville: Consejo Superior de Investigaciones Científicas, Escuela de Estudios Hispano-Americanos, 2001), see particularly 103–32.

30. Estimates provided by the *Slave Voyages Database* suggest that between the years 1526 and 1825, 167,987 captives embarked for the Spanish circum-Caribbean, of which the principal port was Cartagena, while 119,153 were disembarked. During the first quarter of the seventeenth century, which is the period this chapter is primarily concerned with, 75,564 captives embarked, while 52,892 disembarked, https://www.slavevoyages.org/assessment/estimates. Even factoring in smuggling, which would reduce the numbers officially registered as disembarked by 22,672, is testament to the horror and sheer waste of life of the transatlantic slave trade.

31. José de Acosta, *De Procuranda Indorum Salute [1576]: Educación y Evangeli-zación*, ed. Luciano Pereña (Madrid: Consejo Superior de Investigaciones Científicas, 1984), 47–83. For other editions, see book 4, ch. 6–9.

32. Margaret Olsen, *Slavery and Salvation in Colonial Cartagena de Indias* (Gainesville: University Press of Florida, 2004), 68–70. For Sandoval's work, see Alonso de Sandoval, *De Instauranda Aethiopum Salute: Historia de Aethiopia, naturaleça, policia sagrada y profana, costumbres ritos y cathecismo evangélico de todos los Aethopes con que se restaura la salud de sus almas* (Madrid: Alonso de Paredes, 1647). This was first published in 1627 in Seville.

33. Despite the fact that the Society of Jesus had an uneasy relationship with the Inquisition, Jesuits did act as theological advisers (such as José de Acosta) and interpreters (such as Pedro Claver). A request such as this could not easily be turned down even if those called on had wanted to. For an analysis of Claver's role in the witchcraft trials, see Andrew Redden, "The Problem of Witchcraft, Slavery and Jesuits in Seventeenth-Century New Granada," *Bulletin of Hispanic Studies*, 90, no. 2 (2013): 223–50.

34. Sandoval, *De Instauranda*, part 1, book 1, ch. 26, 114. See Olsen, *Slavery and Salvation*, for an in-depth discussion of Sandoval's position.

35. Colin Kidd, *The Forging of Races: Race and Scripture in the Protestant Atlantic World 1600–2000* (Cambridge: Cambridge University Press, 2006), 25.

36. Ibid.

37. The historiography on Las Casas and what became known as the Great Debate is wide-ranging, but key works might include: Bartolomé de las Casas, *Apología o declaración y defensa universal de los derechos del hombre y de los pueblos* [1551], ed. Vidal Abril Castelló (Salamanca: Junta de Castilla y León, 2000); Bartolomé de las Casas, *De Regia Potestate: o derecho de autodeterminación* [1559/1571] ed. Luciano Pereña et al. (Madrid: Consejo Superior de Investigaciones Científicas, 1984); Juan

Ginés de Sepúlveda, *Apologia Ioannis Genesii Sepulvedae Cordubensis pro libro De iustis bellis causis* (Rome: S.P., 1550); Lawrence Clayton, *Bartolomé de las Casas: A Biography* (Cambridge: Cambridge University Press, 2012); Lewis Hanke, *Bartolomé de las Casas: An Interpretation of His Life and Writings* (The Hague: Nijhoff, 1951). For an analysis of the debate between Las Casas and Sepúlveda, see Anthony Pagden, *The Fall of Natural Man: The American Indian and the Origins of Comparative Ethnology* (Cambridge: Cambridge University Press, 1982), 27–148. See also David Brading, *The First America: The Spanish Monarchy, Creole Patriots and the Liberal State: 1492–1867* (Cambridge: Cambridge University Press, 1991), 79–101.

    38. The bull is sometimes incorrectly referred to as *Sublimis Dei* and other variations. Cited in Clayton, *Bartolomé de las Casas*, 102 and Gustavo Gutiérrez, *Las Casas: In Search of the Poor of Jesus Christ*, trans. Robert Barr (New York: Orbis, 1993), 324. The content of *Sublimis Dei* is confirmed by the bull *Veritas Ipsa*, "Indos in Servitutem Redigere Prohibetur" ["Prohibition of the Enslavement of Indians"] issued on June 2, 1537. The full text of *Veritas Ipsa* can be found in Josef Metzler, ed., *America Pontificia: Primi Saeculi Evangelizationis 1493–1592*, vol. 1 (Vatican City: Librerria Editrice Vaticana, 1991), 364–66. In 1516, Las Casas infamously proposed the importation of "blacks or other slaves" as a substitute and solution to the need for Indigenous labor. An important and often forgotten nuance, highlighted by these authors, is that he was not proposing the massive, systematic, and genocidal institution directed against African peoples that the transatlantic slave trade became. Rather, he was referring to the already existing institution whereby relatively small numbers of people had been enslaved regardless of race or skin color. By the mid-sixteenth century he had regretted this so-called solution and wrote to condemn the traffic of enslaved peoples more broadly. Cf. Gutiérrez, *Las Casas*, 326–30. One other polemicist in the late seventeenth century who stood out for his condemnation of the institution of the transatlantic slave trade was the Capuchin friar Francisco José Jaca de Aragón (1645–1689). Cf. Gutiérrez, *Las Casas*, 323; Miguel Anxo Peña González, "Francisco José de Jaca, primer antiesclavista de la historia," *Rolde: Revista de cultura aragonesa*, 116 (2006): 4–15.

    39. Pope Paul III, "Sublimus Deus: On the Enslavement and Evangelization of Indians, 29 May 1537," cited in Bartolomé de las Casas, *In Defense of the Indians*, trans. Stafford Poole (DeKalb: Northern Illinois University Press, 1992), 100–1.

    40. Ibid, 101.

    41. Cited in Gutiérrez, *Las Casas*, 311–12. A contemporary (seventeenth-century) translation into Portuguese of the bull, has been reprinted in: Serafim Leite, "Apêndice B: Breve do Papa Urbano VIII, <<Commissum Nobis>>, de 22 de Abril de 1639, sôbre a Liberdade dos Índios da América," *História da Companhia de Jesus no Brasil*, vol VI (Lisbon: Livraria Portugália, 1945), 569–71. The excerpt reads: "daqui por diante naõ ouzem ou presumaõ cativar os sobredittos Indios, vendellos, compralos, trocarlos, dalos, apartalos de suas molheres e filhos, privalos de seus bens, e fazenda, levalos e mandalos para outros lugares, privalos de qualquer modo da liberdade" (570).

    42. "com pena de excomunhaõ *latae sententiae* que se incorra *eo ipso* pellos

Transgressores da qual naõ possaõ ser absolutos senaõ por nos ou pello Romano Pontifice que entaõ for salvo estando em artigo de morte." ("Trangressors will automatically incur the penalty of excommunication after which they cannot be absolved if not
by us or by the Roman Pontifice of the moment excepting when they are about to die").
Leite, "Apêndice B: Breve do Papa Urbano VIII," 570.

43.   See Andrew Redden, "Priestly Violence, Martyrdom and Jesuits: The Case of
Diego de Alfaro," in *Exploring Jesuit Distinctiveness: Interdisciplinary Perspectives on
Ways of Proceeding within the Society of Jesus*, ed. Robert Maryks (Leiden: Brill, 2016),
83–84, 90. See also Leite, *História da Companhia de Jesus no Brasil*, vol. VI, 253–55.

44.   "Therefore go and make disciples of all nations, baptizing them in the name of
the Father, the Son and the Holy Spirit," Matt. 28:19.

45.   For *Chicomotzoc* see the manuscript illustration in the *Historia Tolteca Chichimeca*, fol. 29. The manuscript is held in the Bibliothèque Nationale de France
(Département des Manuscrits, Mexicain 46–58 Historia Tolteca-Chichimeca), but the
illustration is widely available online. See, for example, "Historia Tolteca Chichimeca,
Chicomoztoc [1545–1565]," *Vistas: Visual Culture in Spanish America*, https://vistasgallery.
ace.fordham.edu/exhibits/show/otherworldly-visions/item/1738. For the Ayar siblings
(albeit not mentioned by this name), see Juan de Betanzos, *Suma y narración de los Incas
[1542]* ed. María del Carmen Martín Rubio (Madrid: Ediciones Polifermo, 2004), 53. For
different editions, the narration can be found in chapter 2.

46.   Luis de Valdivia's own grammar of Mapundungun (written to enable other missionaries to be able to minister to the Indigenous Mapuche in Chile and first published
in 1606) contained a guide to hearing confession and catechism. He followed this with
a book of nine sermons in Mapundungun to facilitate preaching the Christian faith.
Both of these works were based on the model developed by Acosta as part of his contribution to the Third Council of Lima. See: Luis de Valdivia, *Arte y gramática general
de la lengua que corre en todo el Reyno de Chile, con un vocabulario, y un confessionario
. . . Juntamente con la Doctrina Christiana, y catechism del Concilio de Lima en español,
y dos traduciones del en la lengua de Chile* (Lima: Francisco del Canto, 1606); See also,
Luis de Valdivia, *Sermon en lengua de Chile, de los mysterios de nuestra santa fe cath-
olica, para predicarla a los indios infieles del Reyno de Chile, dividido en nueve partes
pequeñas acomodades a su capacidad* (Valladolid: S.P., 1621).

47.   Eduardo Valenzuela Avaca refers to the theological term *kerygma* meaning
"proclamation" to refer to this first stage of evangelization and argues that "everything
that is proclaimed in the *kerygma* has the goal of substituting previous realities [for
new ones]." Eduardo Valenzuela Avaca, "Los ángeles caídos en el nuevo mundo: uni-
versalismo y demonología en la conquista ontológica de los cultos americanos (siglo
XVI)," (PhD thesis, Universidad de Chile, Facultad de Filosofía y Humanidades, 2016),
7. For a full explanation of the term and concept of kerygma, see pp. 23–40.

48.   The K'iché Mayan tradition is that their ancestors were created from paste
made from maize, ground by the immortal grandmother Xmucane on the instructions
of the deity Sovereign Plumed Serpent. Once she had ground the maize nine times,

the god fashioned it and breathed life into it with an incantation. See Dennis Tedlock, trans. and ed., *Popol Vuh: The Mayan Book of the Dawn of Life* (New York: Simon & Schuster, 1996), 145–6.

49. Concilio Provincial, *Doctrina Christiana y catecismo para instruccion de los Indios, y de las demas personas que han de ser ensenadas en nuestra santa Fe con vn confessionario, y otras cosas necesarias para los que doctrinan,* . . . (Lima: Antonio Ricardo, 1584). See the facsimile edition by Luciano Pereña (Madrid: Consejo Superior de Investigaciones Científicas, 1985).

50. See Ramón Mujica Pinilla, "Angels and Demons in the Conquest of Peru," in *Angels, Demons and the New World*, ed. Fernando Cervantes and Andrew Redden (Cambridge: Cambridge University Press, 2013), 179–85.

51. José de Acosta, *Historia natural y moral de las Indias* (Seville: Casa de Iuan de Leon, 1590). See the facsimile edition edited by Antonio Quilis (Madrid: Ediciones de Cultural Hispánica, 1998). For a study of Acosta's work as a "programme for comparative ethnology," see Pagden, *The Fall of Natural Man*, 146–97. The structure of Sandoval's *De Instauranda* was based on Acosta's *Historia natural y moral.*

52. The very name "Antipodes" refers to opposition.

53. See Acosta, *Historia natural y moral*, book 1 ch. 2 and 4, "Que el cielo es redondo por todas partes y se mueue en torno de si mismo" ("that the sky is round in its entirety and it moves about itself"), 16–19 and "En que se responde, a lo que se alega de la escritura a la redondez del cielo" ("the reply to [arguments] drawn from scripture against the roundness of the sky"), 24–25.

54. Acosta, *Historia natural y moral*, book 1, ch. 16, 57. This is a reference to the Book of Daniel, in which, after Daniel has been thrown to the lions in Babylon, an angel appeared to Habakkuk in Judea and tells him to take a stew to Daniel, which he had prepared for some field laborers. When Habakkuk replied that he did not know where Babylon was, the angel seized him by the hair and carried him to Babylon, where he delivered the food to Daniel. Once delivered, the angel carried him back to Judea. Dan. 14:33–39.

55. Acosta, *Historia natural y moral*, book 1, ch. 16, 57.

56. Ibid., ch. 20, 69–71.

57. Ibid., 71.

58. Ibid., ch. 22–24, 75–82.

59. Ibid., ch. 25, 82–84.

60. Ibid., 82. Tiwanaku is found in present day Bolivia, approximately 20 kilometers from the shores of Lake Titicaca. This particular origin story links to rise and apogee of the Tiwanaku civilization, which controlled the southern to central Andean region during the years AD 500–1000.

61. Ibid., 83.

62. Ibid.

63. Ibid.

64. Ibid.

65.   Ibid.

66.   Ibid., book 6, ch. 1, 396. It is worth noting that neither the Mexica-led Triple Alliance (frequently known as the hegemonic Aztec Empire) nor the Inca empire were republics.

67.   Ibid., 396. For a discussion of the use of the term "barbarian" in the European intellectual tradition, see Pagden, *The Fall of Natural Man*, 15–26.

68.   Ibid., ch. 2 and 3, 397–400.

69.   Ibid., ch. 4, 401.

70.   Ibid.

71.   Ibid.

72.   Ibid., ch. 5, 403. Acosta is correct in this regard, but not in the value judgement that places "letters/words" as immediate signifiers as indicative of a higher level of civilization than writing systems based on symbolic characters.

73.   Ibid., ch. 7, 407.

74.   Ibid., ch. 8, 412.

75.   Wade, *Race and Ethnicity*, 8.

CHAPTER FIVE

How to Be a Country Jesuit

Practices of Continence, Care, and Containment in a Racializing Religiosity

J. MICHELLE MOLINA

No han de ser tan campistas los Administradores que por andar todo el día en el campo / The Administrators ought not be on an excursion, roaming all day in the countryside.[1]

THIS ESSAY OFFERS A close reading of a set of eighteenth-century guidelines written for a Mexican Jesuit who found himself tasked with overseeing the smooth operation of a hacienda.[2] The anonymous manuscript, titled the "Instructions that the Brothers Administrators of the Haciendas Must Observe," held in the Archivo General de la Nación in Mexico City, was written for an administrator who had little to no experience running a hacienda.[3] The "hermanos" in the title refers to the special grade of Jesuit called "temporal coadjutor." Known as brothers, these members of the Society of Jesus did not take final vows but could teach and perform a variety of other functions. Jesuit brothers primarily ranked among those most often tasked with keeping the occupations of cook, nurse, or doorman. In New Spain, *hermanos* were frequently hacienda administrators. The *Instrucción* covers all aspects of hacienda life, beginning with how the Jesuit ought to manage himself, then filling almost half the pages to describe how he ought to manage servants and slaves. From there the manuscript turns to instructions on planting and harvesting, the care of animals and farm implements, as well as how to care for the house and the adornments in the chapel. Because of the careful attention given to servants and slaves, the *Instrucción* affords a unique vantage point to explore the racializing aspects of the Jesuit mission "to console souls" and provides an opportunity to engage in conversation with recent scholarship on the intertwining of religion and race in colonial Latin America.[4]

In structuring daily life around devotional practice, the *Instrucción* presents the hacienda as an ideal, quasi-monasticized community comprised of Christians who, quite literally, know their place. The anonymous *Instrucción* pays careful attention to the places and spaces where servants and slaves ought to be, but also instructs the Jesuit Administrator to be attentive to his own space-making practices. The Jesuit administrator was to facilitate daily living and working conditions such that life on the hacienda was conducive to Christian virtue in accordance with the status of each member. Importantly, to keep people "in their place," he must control his own passions. What all of these subjects share (ideally) was a disciplined collective spiritual life centered around the hacienda chapel as the site of sacramental practices. Prominent in the *Instrucción* is how the hacienda, an extractive economic institution, was tied to an individual Jesuit's devotional life. That hacienda-produced commodities funded Jesuit education, remote missions, and urban evangelical undertakings is well-known. Less understood is the extent to which the *Instrucción* provides a vantage point to examine how the Jesuit who governed hacienda servants and slaves was to think about his vocation as a consoler of souls.

In other words, the *Instrucción* offers the opportunity to explore how the Jesuit administrator's devotional life was intertwined within everyday forms of racialization in New Spain. Following Daniel Nemser's call to give greater attention to "the structures of care that shaped the practice of colonial governance,"[5] this study looks to the Jesuit hacienda as a key component of an integrated Jesuit evangelical infrastructure. On the hacienda, patriarchal management took the shape of an enforced devotional life structured around the sacraments, primarily penance, and the eucharist. This sacramental logic shaped an everyday form of governance that wove together the care of self, the care of servants, and the care of slaves.

The unarticulated assumption in the *Instrucción* was that people were on the move. The order it attempted to create was, in large part, a response to the fact that Jesuit haciendas in New Spain were situated at the crossroads of Jesuit mobility and labor mobility. For all parties, the *Instrucción* worked to anchor moving subjects in virtuous practice. Accordingly, the manual emphasized physical and moral containment. As captured in the epigraph, the *Instrucción* reminded Jesuits that they were not to range over the countryside and forget their duties back at the main house. Containment—moral and physical—was important precisely because there is a great deal of mobility among laborers, both slave and free, but also because the countryside is a place where the Jesuit is "free" from his usual constraints at the college. In this essay, the concept of "continence" is deployed to capture the spiritual work that the Jesuit administrator undertook to maintain himself as a virtuous subject absent the routines normally provided by the Jesuit college.[6] By paying particularly close attention to the first half of the *Instrucción*, this essay studies the idealized view of how everyday life is to be structured to best ensure that the Jesuit, servants, and slaves develop habits conducive to virtuous living. Accordingly, this single site enables an interrogation of Ignatian devotional practices in an extractive labor setting in which "care" and "containment" constituted one another.

Explicit racial terminology is notably not deployed in the *Instrucción*. While we hear about "slaves" and "Indians," there is no discussion of "blackness" or "Indianness" to justify assumptions about proper emplacement. Yet the terms *indio* or *negro* contain within them a reference to a perceived limited or contingent capacity for virtuous living, underwritten by assumptions that tutelage was required to enable "the Indian" to leave his childlike state, or to teach "the Black" to control his passions. The virtue discourse utilized here marks both the universal standards of virtue and the different perceived capacities of various peoples to achieve them. All can aspire to Christian virtue, yet some have issues of *calidad*, a term that refers to one's social status or "quality." Its deployment in New Spain captures the complex ethnoreligious-social factors that figure into colonial status marking. One's calidad could signal a requirement for more work—more tutelage, more humility, more punishment—all conceived as the necessary "care" to bridge a perceived divide.

Yet in its ambiguity, calidad both constrained and enabled social mobility. The history of freedom-making in colonial Mexico has shown that virtue practices—such as seeking out Catholic marriage for oneself or one's children—enabled individuals to make shifts in calidad over a lifetime or across generations. Pablo Silva's recent study of urban slavery in New Spain demonstrates how *Poblano* slaves made use of social networks to contest their bondage, arguing that "Afro-indigenous interactions notably eroded the foundations of slavery" in a society in which familial and religious bonds "paved the way for generations of freeborn children."[7] This explains an oft-repeated line in the *Instrucción*: "Slaves, where there are any . . ." Ursula Ewald confirms that the number of slaves on the Jesuit haciendas in the area surrounding Puebla de los Angeles was consistently on the decline in the eighteenth century.[8] Slavery in Mexico was dying out, in large part due to the active work that slaves and freed Afro-descended peoples were undertaking, often with the assistance of Indians, to utilize both legal and ecclesiastical systems to establish themselves as free and virtuous Catholic subjects.[9] Rich scholarship on race in the Americas demonstrates how religious and legal processes of racialization were built upon the shifting terrain of mobile historical actors who worked the fissures of sacramental and legal domains to claim land, rights, and freedom for themselves, their children, or others in their social and kinship networks.[10]

This body of literature makes plain how "race" is, indeed, a contested category, as evidenced by the cascade of qualifications that ensue once the term is deployed to describe what were very fluid practices of differentiation in colonial Latin America.[11] But the term "religion" similarly abbreviates a dizzying array of institutions, beliefs, and practices that change according to time and place. "Race" and "religion" may be scholarly shorthand, but both categories are inadequate to the historian's task of following in the wake of complex human actors on the move, as their worldviews and practices shift according to context and change over time. Through the *Instrucción*, one sees the efforts a Jesuit administrator makes to root himself in place and practice, as well as the demanding daily devotional rituals intended to shape Christians who know their "proper place." Indeed, as Stephen Greenblatt notes in his "mobility manifesto," this "sensation of rootedness" can be experienced—imposed—as a "glacial weight."[12] But in foregrounding "mobility and containment" as a twinned problem that, in colonial Mexico, encompasses labor, ethnicity, and devotion, what emerges is a view of calidad as a form of place-making and place-breaking practices.

Jesuit Haciendas

Haciendas were essential economic institutions that were established to support much of the Society's better-known foundations in the Americas, notably colleges and missions. While the term refers to a landed rural estate, the primary aim of Jesuit hacienda production was cash revenues. Accordingly, it is useful to bear in mind its Latin root "*facer*"—to make or to do. Across the Americas, Jesuits produced important staples, among them were maize, barley, cattle, sheep, sugar, goats, hogs, horses, wool cloth, and "Jesuit tea" (yerba mate). Haciendas provided a range of occupations from cowboys and sheep-herders to textile workers and tortilla-makers, all of these tasks performed by both slave and free labor, the latter being Afro-descended, Indian, and Spanish.

The Jesuit haciendas also differed from neighboring haciendas in that they had chapels—sometimes very finely decorated spaces like the chapel on the main hacienda outside Puebla that was sumptuously remodeled in the eighteenth century. The day began with the Mass (mandatory for slaves and house servants), and some religious instruction was provided for children of workers, both slave and free (and in Native languages for Otomí and Nahua speakers); religious instruction on Sundays and holidays was conducted in Spanish. Workers lived on site, in small farmhouses, which has been attributed to the desire to keep workers close to the worksites.[13] The onsite housing also kept them close to the hacienda chapel, which made possible the daily devotional practices that were central to structuring spiritual containment on the hacienda.

Put on Your Own Oxygen Mask First: *Campista* Continence

The opening chapter of the *Instrucción* makes clear that Jesuit care of self is of primary importance. Only slowly does one see how deeply intertwined his self-management is with the physical and moral disciplining of slaves and

Indigenous laborers. The guide contains information about the economics of hacienda life, reminding the Jesuit that the "economy" of all things related to agriculture must be ordered toward the "successful multiplication of the fruits of the land." We find these fundamental agricultural directions beginning in chapter six, a little over halfway into the document.[14] Why wait so long to talk about production? We judge this crucial information about production "delayed" only if we consider cultivating and extracting the "fruits" of the land to be the Jesuit author's first concern. Yes, clearly, the author of the manual understands the import of hacienda production and a good part of the manual pertains to the efficient management of crops and livestock. But, in contrast to predominant trends in Latin American historiography, the Jesuit author does not see the hacienda only as an economic institution. Rather, he recognizes that the hacienda is a unique or possibly even a strange place for a Jesuit to carry out his religious life.

His audience, then, is a Jesuit who has no training in running a hacienda *as a part of his vocation*. Accordingly, the first line of the first chapter of the *Instrucción* reminds the reader that he is living on the hacienda *por obediencia*, that is, the Jesuit administrator has been assigned this post by his superior, and this work is vitally concerned with religious observance.[15] Although he is likely the only Jesuit at the hacienda, he must imagine himself among his Jesuit brethren and engaged in their shared mission. The vow of obedience is amplified: he is to obey not only the padre rector, but he is to accept the orders from the procurator, who was key to maintaining the flow of goods and things, both local and trans-oceanic.[16] Accordingly, "nothing should be disposed of the things belonging to the hacienda against his [the procurator's] will."[17]

At the hacienda—and "there more than in other places"—administrators need to demonstrate that they are "true religious men in the fervor of their spirits and in their observances."[18] The *Instrucción* singles out the task of running a hacienda as unlike any of the would-be administrator's past experiences at a Jesuit college. On the hacienda, there is no superior to keep a watchful eye, no bell to call him, no visitor to keep a record, no eyes that observe, nor censors that note the life of "un religioso campista"—a country Jesuit who must (in a small twist on the Jesuit phrase "God in all things") demonstrate that God is present everywhere (*en todo lugar*).[19]

The hacienda administrator lives, the author warns, in liberty in the solitude of the countryside. These are problematic conditions. "Liberty" indicates that he is in charge of his own schedule; and "solitude" his lack of Jesuit companionship. Combined, liberty and solitude mean that there are "occasions in which he is surrounded by the devil, who offers temptations of the flesh, the problem of idleness, the difficulties of dealing with lay people attached to the hacienda." The Jesuit administrator is presented as stranded because distant from the center of gravity, the Jesuit college, and therefore "lacking in the abundant spiritual methods one can take advantage of in the Colleges."[20] He is to be obedient to his distant superior and must be able to lead a disciplined life to stabilize his vocation in this locale. The administrator is reminded that he has been selected because his virtue is solid and he has been tested. The author is not complimenting the administrator, but rather, is putting him on notice: This confidence is a trust that must not be abused.[21] Absent these supports, the administrator risks going "unaware of the cooling of the fervor, the distracting of the spirit, the diminishment of the fear of God, and the relaxing of the conscience."[22] These initial instructions are telling about the place of the college as the center of Jesuit spiritual life. The *Instrucción*, thus, pertains to sustaining one's devotional life when not informed by the rhythms of the college.

How should one maintain his spirit? He should pray each day "as one does in the Colleges." The morning prayer should address the work that he needs to do that day. But unlike life at the college, the rhythms of his daily life are dictated by a schedule that makes possible agricultural production and the requirement that the lone Jesuit project leadership. Accordingly, he is advised to avoid praying at night because this might tire him, making it difficult to get up before daybreak, which is important because "the administrator who sleeps late will be disdained by many."[23] When possible, he should hear Mass each day. The temporal coadjutor ("Hermano")—was not ordained, so he could not say the Mass himself and could not hear confessions.[24] If Mass is not being said, he should engage in spiritual reading, and make the examination of conscience each and every day, once at midday and again at night. He should make a schedule that marks his devotional labor as distinct from the daily work of managing the house and fields.[25] There are also guidelines for the Jesuit's penitential habits:

When there is a chaplain at the hacienda, confess with him and none other. If not a chaplain, you can confess with a confessor from *la Compañía* if there is one there. If you have none of these, confess with some other confessor of the local parish, or with another who is passing through the hacienda.[26]

To maintain the vow of chastity, he is to be always accompanied by a servant, and he should limit his engagement with women. Only single men sleep in the house.[27]

These instructions appear to be about reducing temptation, but also serve to maintain his reputation by ensuring witnesses to an irrefutable chastity. The overall impression is a monasticization of the hacienda, shaped around prayer and labor, with only single men sleeping in the house.

"If he has not finished his formation, he should travel twice a year to his college to renew his vows within the community and, before returning to his duties on the hacienda, he is to give an account of his conscience to the Father Superior."[28] But the rhythms of hacienda life might conflict with this ritual, in which case he can be given dispensation from returning to renew his vows and instead have his "triduo" at the hacienda, "as his country duties permit, adding to this schedule more prayers, more spiritual reading, more devotions, and increased mortifications. And on the day of the renewal of the vows, he will make his renewal secretly in the chapel after taking communion."[29] Likewise, every administrator must return to the College once each year to make the eight-day version of the Ignatian Spiritual Exercises. "For this choose a time of the year clear of the occupations of the country, when you can leave things to the Mayordomo and other servants."[30] There is no substitution offered for this annual retreat. "And either before or after making the exercises, he is to give the father rector an account of everything pertaining to the hacienda in which his records are to be checked against the records of the Padre Procurator."[31] His accounting of self and the accounting of the hacienda records run in tandem.

In the next two sections, it will become clearer that containment practices, that is, the management of segregation and congregation, emerge from the administrator's labor to maintain himself as a virtuous subject. To keep himself and others in their proper place entails fashioning himself as an authority of a particular type: the father figure.[32] To harvest souls and worldly fruits, Jesuits are advised to care for servants as if they are "fathers" in a family. Many laborers, indeed, were born and raised on the hacienda.[33] The language in the *Instrucción* slips back and forth between "servants" and "Indians," implying that most hacienda workers were Native people. Notably, the terms "*mestizo*" and "mulatto" are absent in this text.[34]

The Jesuit administrator is instructed that "just as there are seasons for sowing, so one must put great care in the cultivation of souls and the good education of the servants and their families . . . God has promised abundant harvests of worldly fruits to those who keep the holy Law." The Jesuit administrators are admonished to manage the spiritual lives of the workers on the haciendas, just as any good father would do, reminding them that Saint Paul railed against fathers who neglected the education of their servants as "worse than infidels."[35] Meditating upon his role as a father of a family, the administrator is instructed to consult and reread every year "*plática* 36 of Padre Parra's work." He is referring to Juan Martínez de la Parra, S.J., who wrote the three-volume work titled *Luz de verdades católicas y explicación de la doctrina christiana*. The sermon that the *Instrucción* mentions is titled "On the Obligations that Masters and Slaves must Observe."[36] Parra begins by pointing out that the Latin root—*famel*—links slaves (*famulus, famuli*) with the Spanish term "*família*." Slaves and owners have obligations to one another, and the master is obliged to enforce his dominance ethically. The father of a family ought to be a father to his slaves.[37] Parra refers his reader to "the genius" of Seneca, and in particular to his Letter 17, where he taught that "neither should masters become hateful through the tone of their domination, nor should slaves always be face to face with their powerlessness." But the sermon also stipulates that slaves ought to consider salvation in the afterlife, where "souls have no color"[38] and consider the commands of the slave master as an opportunity to turn tribulaton and fatigue into merit and glory. "Pues haced todo quanto os mandan, considerando que es el mismo Dios quien lo manda," that is, through obedience to the master, the slave is rendering service to God.[39] The *Instrucción* indicates that this advice is best read not only with the care of slaves in mind, but Parra's sermon should structure the Jesuit Administrator's fatherly attitude toward his domestic servants.

The parish priest, while he may have been called "father," was not this kind of figure. The *Instrucción* states this is not only because parish priests widely neglect the haciendas, but truly because the Jesuit administrator cannot expect the local priest to minister to the wide-ranging spiritual needs of the hacienda servants. Rather, the patriarch is obligated to provide his family with this more intimate and immediate form of care.[40] Thus, even if the hacienda has a chaplain in residence, his duties are merely to say Mass, offer the sacrament of penance, and preach to the residents.

A large portion of the Jesuit's paternal responsibilities are related to structuring and monitoring devotional life. Each night, after doing the bookkeeping and giving orders to the *mayordomo* about the next day's tasks, he is to ring a little bell to call to the chapel the servants who live at the hacienda, "and the slaves, if there are any." The residents of the hacienda all come together, congregating to pray a "chorus" of the rosary in unison, and then, on their own they can pray from a devotional guide (*algún librito manual*). The prayers should finish with a litany to the Virgin. The Jesuit is advised to limit evening prayers to this simple devotion, remarking that inhabitants can pray on their own and that communal prayer should not be an onerous aspect of the schedule of daily devotions.[41]

Sundays, however, are quite full. Every Sunday of the year, the administrator is to ensure that everyone living on the hacienda takes communion. Sundays are for accounting: the betterment of souls, payment of wages, and distribution of rations go hand in hand. On Sundays and feast days, the administrator is to ring the bell three times at thirty minutes prior to the start of Mass, and once more at the start of the services. He is to make certain that everyone attends Mass weekly and on feast days and ensures the inculcation of punctuality.[42] Their attendance at Mass is taken as they depart. "Have written on a chart [*tabla*] the names of the Indians of the hacienda along with their women and children. When the Mass is ending, leave by the door of the chapel, along with the mayordomo, *ayudante*, and *fiscal* (assistant to the priest/chaplain). As you call out the names in a loud voice, they are to answer *Ave María Santísima*." The administrator is to note who failed to attend and make inquiries the following Sunday. If no "rational excuse" is offered, the fiscal will be instructed to give them six to eight lashes. The same is to be practiced with slaves "on haciendas that have them."[43] "But it is the father of a family who must subject them [to punishment] when they live badly, because as the one who feeds them, he is respected."[44] More on this topic of punishment follows below, where it becomes clear that while the administrator decides who deserves punishment, he never delivers it himself.

All of the Native people at the hacienda are required to arrive one half-hour prior to the Mass to pray the *doctrina Cristiana* "en mexicano," that is, in Nahuatl. "For this, find a blind Indian to teach it, and give him a donation (*limosna*) on that day for his work." If it is not possible to pray together before Mass, then they can do so after, in which case attendance would take place after the *doctrina* instead of immediately after the Mass.[45] Later on Sunday afternoons, from three o'clock onwards, the Indians on the hacienda "will gather once again at the ringing of the bell to pray a chorus of the Crown of María Santísima, and the end of their Litanies to pray again in the doctrina Cristiana, but this time in Spanish, which should conclude with a reading from the short Catechism of Padre Castaño."[46]

If the hacienda has a chaplain, he is an important support to the running and regulation of devotional practices. The administrator should procure the cooperation of the padre capellán, to make sure the servants in his charge go punctually to the chapel, and that they attend the *pláticas de Doctrina Cristiana* prior to the Mass, and remain until the end of the Gospel. The Mass is described as "an important means [*un medio*] to attain the well-being of their souls; as is the frequent reception of the sacraments during the major fiestas of the year."[47] A similar schedule holds for feast days, but only if Mass can be said at the hacienda. In other words, when feast days land on workdays, the laborers will not be trekking into town to attend Mass. The Jesuit administrator is to keep track of the required communion days (*comuniones de regla*) and he is to pin it to his wall so that he will not forget.[48]

More generally, the administrator is to ensure moral order on the hacienda and invest great care that the servants and workers on the hacienda "live well." Here quality of life is measured in terms of drunken brawls, lawsuits, and couples living together outside of marriage: there should be none. "Hatreds and scandals" are to be avoided. The administrator can rely upon the mayordomo as well as the captain of temporary Indian laborers (*la quadrilla*) to take care that any disorder is stopped at the outset.[49] Persons known to be troublesome (*de mala fama*) should never be admitted to the hacienda. If any employee develops bad habits, they should be given two warnings, but then they are to be paid and dismissed from the hacienda.[50]

Great suspicion is cast upon men who do not work on the hacienda but live there with their wives. They "must be examined with diligence." These *indios forasteros* are suspect, the author writes, because the couple is "usually living together under the guise of being married." If this is the case, the administrator should send them to the parish priest if they wish to be married, and if not, they are to be separated. The other problem is men who come to the hacienda "when they owe money elsewhere in order to hide out under a false name."[51] Labor mobility means that the administrator must police the moral boundaries of his idealized community. But for the most part, "fathering" servants entails the labor of what today one might dub a devotional "soccer mom," that is, one who keeps on top of the schedule, utilizing lists and charts to maintain devotional order.

As we have begun to see, among the primary tasks of the administrator was to ensure that servants and slaves had well-regulated devotional lives built around the sacraments, making the Mass and the Eucharist central to the mechanics of everyday governance of servants and slaves. If we probe a little deeper, we see that the importance of penance, but especially the advocacy of frequent communion, meaning that hacienda inhabitants were trained to practice a Catholicism that bore a distinctly Jesuit stamp.[52]

The Jesuit advocacy of frequent communion on the hacienda needs to be understood against the backdrop of a Catholic sacramental culture that placed the minimum requirement that all Catholics make the sacrament of penance and receive the Eucharist once per year during the Easter season. No matter how many times hacienda residents had taken communion, the annual requirement was not to be taken lightly by the Jesuit Administrator, who was tasked with ensuring that his charges complied with the *precepto anual* at their own parishes, where the communicant ordinarily received a receipt or certificate of confirmation. William Taylor has documented how the *precepto anual* could pit lay hacienda owners against parish priests, with *hacendados* engaging in a paternalistic turf war, and balking at the intrusion of the parish priest.[53] Perhaps not unlike a Jesuit administrator, patriarchal *hacendados* claimed to better know and control their "own."[54] But the *Instrucción* is clear that the Jesuit administrator should not be accused of the same refusal to comply, that the annual precept is the domain of the parish clergy, and that the Jesuit administrator's only duty is to ensure that everyone fulfills the obligation.

Hacienda residents could obtain a special license to meet the obligation at the hacienda chapel or could ask their parish priest to come to the hacienda. If this could not be arranged, the administrator was compelled to ensure that residents confess and take communion in their own parish. "And if the parish gives communion receipts [*cedulitas de comunión*] but after do not come to collect them, you must collect them. If there is no custom of giving receipts, give them a hand written receipt, and after collect them to know who has missed, and urge them to commune, and if someone holds fast in their resistance, dismiss them from the hacienda."[55] The Jesuit patriarchical claims over a hacienda's subjects make a show of yielding to ecclesiastical demands, but in reality these two domains of church power comprise overlapping spheres of governance, both concerned with the formation of good Christian subjects.

Occasionally, the formation of good servants and slaves was less concerned with containment, but rather, sought to elicit some collective effervescence. The case in point is the popular mission, akin to an evangelical revival. "Every third year, write to the Padre Rector, asking that he solicit the Padre Provincial to send two Padres *sacerdotes* to make a mission for the servants at the hacienda, and from there to pass to our other haciendas." This is of utmost importance for the reformation of customs, and is even more necessary on those haciendas where in the whole year they do not hear the word of God, when there is no conscientious chaplain to do so.[56] To that end, the mission's raucous preaching and self-searching devotional exercises can take place at night, in the chapel, while during the day, the administrator is to assist the visiting priests in hearing confessions.[57] In the quiet of the day, the emotion produced by the previous night's preaching could be harnessed and turned toward a searching evaluation of self as sinner. But note that the mission is to be conducted in a way that does not impinge greatly upon hacienda production.[58]

"On the good governance of Slaves, where there are any"

In turning his attention to the management of slaves, the author indicates that all instructions pertaining to servants should also be applied to the *la crianza y buena educación de los esclavos* (the raising and good education of slaves), except for the things that would pertain only to free servants. He recognizes that Jesuits have relied upon slave labor in *ingenios* (refineries), *obrajes* (textile mills), and *trapiches* (sugar mills). "This is a numerous community with many and different *gremios* (guilds), who thus require a special mode of economic and Christian governance, upon one and the other hangs the spiritual and temporal well-being of the hacienda, and from its lack follow notable *atrasos* [backlog, delays] and sometimes also total ruin [of the hacienda]."[59] Even more than the proper management of servants, such damage can be averted if the administrator keeps in mind the following: "To contain such damage, more than what is said in the last chapter [about servants], the Administrators will keep well the following advice, the first of which pertains to the physical containment of slave laborers."[60]

The administrator is to be certain that the slave barracks (*el real*) is securely fenced, and always locked at night, to be reopened in the morning. The secured door is to be visible from the main house. A bell is to be hung over the door, which can be used to call the slaves to work in the morning, and to pray the rosary at night, and at other times of the day when they are required for different tasks.[61] Here one sees that slaves were physically restrained, kept segregated from other workers on the hacienda, and that their movements were to be visible from the house. Unspoken is that fact that slaves affiliated with the haciendas that supported the *Colegio de Espíritu Santo* were assigned as foremen, shepherds, or in the *recuas* [pack-mule trains] carrying goods to the college. This liberty of movement is not mentioned directly in the *Instrucción*.[62] Clearly, slave mobility is a source of anxiety.

As with servants on Sundays and after working hours, the ordering of slaves' time takes a devotional shape on a daily basis. Young slaves undergo training; first, in the prayers and Christian doctrine, and second, in the modes of physical labor in which they are intended to one day fully participate. Both modes equate regular physical labor and structured devotional practice as key to the inculcation of moral values.

Do not have laziness among the young slaves, give them some work from the time they are *niños* up to the age of eight, occupying them in some work proportionate to their strength. To help them, designate an old female slave who can no longer work, who will bring them to the morning mass every day. But before mass, have them pray in the cemetery of the church, and seated on one side the boys, and the other the girls, where they pray the Doctrina Cristiana, the old slave who cares for them teaching them, or a young man who knows it well; if there is Mass, they go in to hear it with devotion, keeping the above stated separation; if there is no Mass, they will sing *el Alabado* at the end of the Doctrina and then they go to have breakfast. After this she will bring them to the fields where they have tasks like gathering stones, cleaning roads, hoeing seedlings, sweeping away trash, and similar things, following what the *mandador* or the mayordomo orders, and, when the big slaves finish their work, they should return the young men with their mothers to the barracks.[63]

The youngest, ages five to eight, do not need to go with the others, but can stay with their mothers in the field to carry the babies who are still breastfeeding. The small children, ostensibly the weaned children who are under five years old, remain in the house while their mothers go to the field. They should be in the care of another old woman retired from work, who can care for them and teach them to cross themselves and to say their prayers.[64]

Containment and continence coincide in managing the lives of girls who are over twelve. Due to "grave problems" that are always experienced when young women—he calls them *doncellas* or "maidens"—are separated one from the other, the administrators should gather all girls who are twelve years old (and older) in a capacious room that is separated from the slave barracks. "This should serve as a school for the doncellas, where they will live and from which they do not leave until they marry, in order to conserve, by this road, their virtue and integrity. They should be housed with a slave, a widow of good judgment, who will be a teacher who lives with them, and takes them out to the field, and works with them, and cares for them in everything, and who gives an account to the Administrator if there is any disorder."[65] This is a makeshift *recogimiento*—a withdrawal from public view that, as Jessica Delgado has argued, is a complex mode of virtue marking that confers spiritual status.[66] Here modesty, chastity, and obedience are enforced via segregation, which enables the author to paint an idealized portrait in which young slave woman earn the honorific "doncella" for living an enslaved life, *muy recogida*.

Just as the administrator is to police morality among the servants, he is similarly to oversee the moral conduct of slaves. Slaves should not go to the nearby towns, even on fiesta days, because "there are ordinarily thefts, drunkenness, and other bad things." Among actions with unforeseen consequences is ethnic mixing: "Do not consent to Indians entering into the slave barracks, neither merchants nor gamblers nor other *forasteros*, because in all of this there are grave problems."[67] Hacienda Indians and slaves should congregate only in the hacienda's chapel.

One can see devotional practice as disciplinary in the micromanagement of the consumption of food. Distribution of rations is to be done in an orderly fashion, but in an order that enforces norms about refraining from eating meat on Fridays. The administrator was instructed to:

> Each week, provide the slaves with necessary sustenance, distributing a ration of maize, meat, salt, chile, and tobacco, and a bit of honey when there is any. These are for meat days; for Fridays and Saturdays, vigils, and Lent, you must give them fish in place of meat, or broad beans or beans, or something similar.[68] Do not distribute together the ration for Fridays with the ration for meat days, because they usually eat the latter prior, saving the meat for Friday and Saturday; give it to them on Thursdays in the afternoon, and this opportunity will be removed.[69]

As such, compliance with the Catholic devotional norms is enforced. The only food to eat on Friday is fish or broadbeans.[70] This is a hands-on job for the administrators, who should assist the mayordomo and other slaves who divide and distribute the food. "The quantity signaled in the *tabla* should not be altered, neither augmenting or diminishing. The proper amount is to be discussed with the Procurador and the Padre Rector, and once set, not to be altered."[71]

The *Instrucción* expresses concern about the presentation of slaves at Mass, especially on religious holidays. Clothes are distributed in a similar fashion, and once again, the *Instrucción* pertains to proper participation in devotional life. "Once a year, on the accustomed day, distribute new clothing to all the slaves, including hats and blankets. Make the request to the Procurator with enough time to provide the necessary things, and see to it in advance that a tailor comes to the hacienda to cut and sew the clothing." These are distributed to family units, with the warning that they will be punished "if in the next year they do not wear their new clothing, principally in the days of fiesta. This is to close the door to disorder of the many who will later sell their new clothing, and remain all of the year wearing their tattered rags."[72] This reference to the appropriate presentation of slaves at Mass, especially on religious holidays leads to questions about audience: Who, in this Jesuit author's mind, will bear witness to the slaves' new clothing—other slaves? Indians? Visiting Jesuits who are meant to be impressed by the order and discipline of the well-dressed devotionally minded slaves? Are the slaves meant to admire themselves and be appreciative of the new clothing? This remains unclear. What is certain is that slaves had access to and made use of informal markets to sell such items.

In these instructions about the distribution of goods and elsewhere in the *Instrucción*, the figure of the *mandadero* (slave foreman) assumes a certain prominence, emerging as among the Jesuit's daily companions. The administrator is advised to choose a slave foreman who is faithful, of sound judgment, and of mature age, who can serve as the "instrument" for giving orders for everything that is to be done on the hacienda. This overseer assists in the operations of the country and the house. The foreman is to accompany the administrator when he assigns work, or when he distributes food rations. He is expected to warn the administrator about any disorder whatsoever, move to contain it, and then remediate it. Each night after the *rayada*, he is obligated to go over the day's operations as well as the orders to be executed on the following day.[73] The administrator is also advised to select a *mandadera*, a female slave "who is of sound judgment and mature age." She is to monitor the women and be "zealous" about curtailing fights, arguments, and any other kind of disorder or dissension. She is to promptly advise the administrator when a punishment is required. Any imprisonment or punishment is the mandate of the administrator, and while the punishment is executed in his presence, he is never to administer it, rather, the free servants or the *mandadores* serve as executors of his will.[74] There is an added instruction that if women "distribute lashes to any man, it cannot be in a public place, but the mandadera must retire from view, assisted by some women singled out for this."[75] Yet servants and slaves are never to be empowered to take it upon themselves to respond in the moment. Rather, all punishment follows from the explicit authorization of the father figure.

Paternal Self-Mastery and the Fugitive Slave

The most detailed instructions about punishment pertain to slaves. The advice is framed around a perception that slaves run away to avoid corporal punishment, but now the *Instrucción* circles back more explicitly to the issue of Jesuit continence. That is, the administrator is offered some simple advice about the physical containment of slaves, as well as techniques to assert his authority through mastery of his passions by appealing to what is now the Jesuit's increasing self-understanding of his role as patriarch of a family.[76] Accordingly, the administrator is instructed "to comport himself with great moderation and repose in the punishment of those who are guilty." To appear angry or out of control is counterproductive, as the slaves will then "be discontent, feeling themselves forced and their service subsequently violent and poorly executed."[77] A good father will tell his child that the punishment is no more than what is necessary, but he should be willing to give a hearing to those who beg for leniency, and be ready to "forgive everything."[78]

But administrators should avoid becoming friendly and familiar with slaves: "You are not a friend who always echoes the noise of fetters, stocks and chains."[79] The *Instrucción* does not elaborate on these worries about becoming "fettered" by friendship with a slave, but the need to inflict punishment is likely the cause, as the very next statement indicates that it may become necessary to imprison slaves "when a more serious crime" is committed. The Jesuit is to ensure that imprisonment is short, and most curious is the advice that the administrator secretly seek out the godparents who can come to beg for them to be released. "Show a bit of resistance to the plea in front of the guilty, pondering the gravity of his crime that does not merit pardon, but by the end give them liberty, doing so, that they are left thankful for the pardon and together intimidated by the threat of a worse punishment if they relapse."[80] Jesuit theater, always about instruction in virtuous living, relied upon rhetoric's ability to evoke, harness, and shape bodily action.[81] The hacienda administrator's role-playing shapes a tense pedagogical moment in which the slave can take center stage by "putting on virtue."[82] Simultaneously, this moment of paternal justice cements his role as father-judge and father-caregiver, with the family—extended through religious kinship—serving as the foundation of a disciplined community.

Of course he can only maintain his authority, the author warns, if the administrator refrains from punishing slaves "in fits of anger." Rather, he should "take the time to first quiet his spirit and only later, with repose and serenity, announce the crime, the just punishment to amend the crime, and that this be a lesson to others." Further, he is to refrain from long discussions that linger upon disgrace, or levy insults, because these will merely "exasperate the spirits of everyone, and, instead of causing the blamed to make emends, in fact makes things worse." Most of all, he should not imitate "the tyrannies" deployed by administrators on other haciendas or *ingenious*. Here the *Instrucción* refers to prolonged imprisonment and excessive whipping that he describes as "distributed like a novena with fifty lashes every day." This is a grave fault, against charity, and "so as not to err, take council and advice from the Padre Rector and the Procurator of the College, and also of the Padre Capellán where there is one."[83] There are many "fathers" to consult!

To be a good father, the administrator is instructed to be very lenient with first-time runaways, especially if fugitives return "to ask pardon and mercy" and are supported by "an honorable *padrino* who pleads on their behalf." The logic is clearly stated: they will owe something to the person who intervenes for them, while offering a vivid example to other slaves. But the *Instrucción* is dismissive of those slaves who do not return: "There are some that merit neither humility or patronage, once fled, will not return again to the hacienda, but will give over to thievery and will be lost."[84] The terms used here give a stronger sense of what the *Instrucción* values in the smooth running of hacienda life: humility and patronage. These are the foundational values of this hierarchically based social structure that we see, in the next line, has the added benefit of keeping at bay the extra cost of involving the authorities. "But if they return having been captured by the authorities

[*Justícia*], this is expensive. Receive and pardon them this one time, but warn them that if they flee again, they will pay double."[85]

When more than one person is involved in "crimes," the administrator ought not punish everyone, because this leads to flight, or commotion. "In such cases, dissimulate, as if you do not know, or punish only one or another of the heads who were most culpable, and pardon the rest, and give to everyone in common a convenient a rebuke."[86] Never give mere threats, or threaten with a punishment to be deferred "because with this you give them occasion and time to flee. What you can do is dissimulate, then, or if dissimulation is impossible, reprimand them mildly, without threats, and when then unsuspecting, you can deal with them later."[87] To remove the temptation to flee, the administrator can support slaves with little offerings [limosnas] for daily necessities. "Do not make it a set thing that you have to give in common to everyone. Rather, distribute these little gifts now to one, now to another, and principally to the most hardworking and faithful, either of *reales* (coins) or other little things, necessary trifles: of these [administrators] will always have a provision precisely for this aim.[88]

The Catholic sacraments were an important part of slave life on the hacienda. The Jesuit administrator was advised to prepare for the sudden and urgent requirements for the sacraments of baptism and penance when death was imminent. The *Instrucción* clearly spells out that to assist slaves in giving birth requires "an intelligent midwife," her value explained in both medical and sacramental terms. "Be sure that the *partera* is instructed by the Padre Capellán (and if there is not one, then by the parish priest) in the manner of baptizing in case that the necessity arises by the urgency of imminent danger, and there is no time to call for a confessor."[89] In other words, the slave midwife is to be prepared for the responsibility of baptizing the child and hearing the last words of the dying mother. The *Instrucción* recommends that preparedness is always the best practice, and whether midwife or nurse, she is expected to give ample warning when someone is very ill, or when a woman nearing the time of delivery, so the "assistance and remedy" provided by the confessor will be at hand.

For slaves, the sacraments of marriage and baptism were to be marked and celebrated. The administrator is to make another "tariff" (*arancel*), marking what has been distributed to slaves when they marry, when a child is born, and when the child is baptized. There are also gifts made at Easter and Christmas. "Keep this list on the wall of your room and refer to this always when these occasions present themselves, so that the slaves do not take it upon themselves to introduce new impositions, especially when a new Administrator enters, but that all conforms to the *arancel* that has been checked prior with the Procurador, and approved by the Superior."[90]

The sacramental logics of baptism afforded a broadened definition of kinship. The recommendations about godparents for the baptized children offer important clues for thinking about the importance of family and the expanded kinship network afforded by the selection of godparents at the time of baptism. "Be advised that slaves should not choose free stepparents (*padrinos libres*) because with that comes some difficulties. Also, see that they choose a stepfather or stepmother from among their kin to avoid blocking some later marriage with spiritual kinship."[91]

As the author brings the section on slaves to a close, his remarks make clear that in the Jesuit view, care has devotional aims. Be sure, he writes, to foment devotion among them, the frequent reception of the sacraments, and the *pláticas* (spiritual talks) and examples from the novenas of the Virgin, at night where there is a chaplain, more when there is not one to make up for this with reading, on these nights, some examples from the *Año Virgíneo*, or another book that treats devotion to the Virgin.[92] Read to them on Sundays, after the Mass, "from the Catechism of Padre Belarmino or the Roman Catechism of Padre Eusebio and during Lent give some spiritual talks from Padre Parra, who treats the topics of confession and communion, and in the case of the *Doctrina Cristiana*, they will pray it before the Mass."[93] These were very popular Jesuit writers, a sign that slaves and servants were spiritually groomed in a Jesuit style.

> Finally, remember to do well for the souls of the slaves who have died; for each one who dies, everyone is charged with praying the Rosary for eight days, and the Mass on the first Sunday following, and command that Masses be said in the Parish, giving an offering of one peso (whether there is or is not a Chaplain); take out an announcement of the dead (*una bula de difuntos*) and apply in writing the [slave's] name, and give this to the living whenever there is new publication of bulls, distributed to all

who are twelve years old and up. All this can be obtained by the Administrators as they wish. Make good Christians of the slaves, and they will
be good servants, and God will cast upon all his blessing.[94]

Practices of containment, whether segregational or congregational,
should bear devotional fruit, but not only for the enslaved. In closing the
comments on slave management, the administrator is asked to look back at
himself, to evaluate the care he is giving to the slaves, especially because they
"have no other superior to care for them."[95] As the father of a family, "the
Administrator must give a tight account to God, of the harm he does out of
carelessness, and of the good he has omitted to do."

Conclusion

For the Jesuit administrator on a Mexican hacienda, the governance of
servants, slaves, and self was, ideally, a habituated practice of orderly self-
management. Much of this ordering was embodied—he was to master his
passions and adopt the patriarchal norms of fatherhood modeled in
classical literature. But the littered room of the Jesuit administrator
indicates that note-taking was key—how many charts, tables, and lists was
he required to keep or pin to his wall? This mode of management runs
parallel to his spiritual management and his training, via the spiritual
exercises, to make marks in a notebook to indicate how he was progressing
spiritually, a practice that entailed breaking up the day and evaluating what
one needed to do/change/think about before noon that day or before the
evening meal. In other words, the Jesuit was well trained to mark up the
page in management exercises, both of self and of others. For the Jesuit
administrator, hacienda life was shaped by, but also often in competition
with, the distant college. The liturgical calendar, the stages of the Jesuit's
vocation, and the seasons for planting and harvesting dictate the way in
which the Jesuit administrator structured both the agricultural and
devotional labor of those affiliated with the hacienda, whether slave,
Indian, or the Jesuit himself.

But what does Jesuit virtue marking have to do with slavery? He is the
virtuous father who constructs the ideal devotional world of the hacienda's

servants. If the Jesuit administrator reread Parra's "On the Obligations of Masters and Slaves" every year, as instructed, what would he think of the advice to the slave to take the command of his master as a command from God? Perhaps this resonates because it is in keeping with his own hierarchically structured world: he is obedient to his own superior, instructed to be as if a cane in the superior's hand, a mere tool. This was especially so for the "brothers," whose obituaries laud their humble adoption of a servile demeanor.[96] The Jesuit's spiritual training at the college is replicated here, with a quasi-monastic inner core of single, obedient men. But does the wise Seneca authorize role-reversal in which the lowly coadjutor rises to become the patriarch among the largely Indigenous familial units that circle the hacienda? Indeed, there are echoes here of the closed utopian Christian world aimed at in the Jesuit missions of Paraguay. But the reality of hacienda living in the central valley of Mexico is that its inhabitants had much tighter material and spiritual connections to other nonhacienda wage laborers, markets, the parish system, as well as connections to religious and market cultures of not-so-distant urban centers.

These unarticulated local networks vitally inform the way in which the *Instrucción* proffers paternalistic care in order to anchor subjects in devotional life *and* in extractive labor, simultaneously. Correct living leads to a productive estate, whose managerial center is the hacienda chapel. The Catholic God, present in the sacrament of the Eucharist, celebrated at the Mass, authorizes this hierarchy, with the lowly brother, now Jesuit administrator, at the top of the pecking order, charged with overseeing how slaves and servants work, eat, sleep, and pray.

Although the administrator's management practices concerned segregation *and* congregation, explicit racial terminology is not deployed in this document. The author does not have to: It is "doxa," that is, it goes without saying because it comes without saying,[97] that slaves were black and that the majority of low-level laborers were Indigenous. But these are not fixed categories. This is worth reiterating: all Afro-descended people were not slaves, despite the fact that by the first decade of the seventeenth century the slave trade had brought at least six thousand Africans to New Spain in chains. In colonial Latin America, mobile actors are subject to racializing practices and categories, but this is not the racial *fixity* that is the hallmark of racializing practices in the United States.[98] The document itself acknowledges this with the words "slaves, where there are any."

This study, then, shows us how racialization, economic, and sacramental practices were intertwined in the Jesuit evangelical infrastructure. The argument made here is that scholars do not unravel "the care of souls" from the extraction of labor. They should remain analytically intertwined, not only because this is how the Jesuit administrator lived out his vocation on the hacienda. Patriarchal containment of the passions was justified in terms of the need to shape servants and slaves into good laborers and moral subjects while gesturing toward freedom deferred in the "colorless" afterlife. But documents like the *Instrucción* are part of a larger history of race and religion in Latin America that point to the critical importance of what Larissa Brewer-Garcia has called Catholicism's "gestures of inclusion."[99] The "care as containment" that is described here is in line with scholarship that demonstrates how racialization in colonial Latin America is relational, religious, intimate, and unstable.[100] Accordingly, these "gestures" were actualized by the Indians, slaves, and freedmen who took them up and, in the complex history of Latin American freedom-making, these historical actors worked and prayed in ways that brought about slavery's "slow and unremarkable death" in the central valley of Mexico.[101]

Notes

1. Francois Chevalier, ed. *Instrucción que han de guardar los hermanos administradores de haciendas del campo* (México: Centro de Investigaciones Superiores INAH, 1950), para. 77.
2. Ibid.
3. The manuscript was not published until the twentieth century, the result of Francois Chevalier's dissertation work on the Jesuit-run hacienda. Relying upon in-text citations, Chevalier dates the manuscript to the eighteenth century and suggests that it could not have been written prior to 1723. Ibid.,"Prólogo y notas," *Instrucción*, 11. In-text references include Esteyneffer's *Florilegio medicinal*, which was first published in 1712. In the Asian context, a Jesuit instruction manual pertaining to coconut production titled *Arte Palmorica* is discussed by Xavier and Županov. Angela Barreto Xavier and Ines Županov: 104–6. They give no indication that aspects of the Jesuit administrator's vocation were at stake.
4. For an overview of recent literature on religion and race in the colonial Americas, see Jessica L. Delgado and Kelsey C. Moss, "Religion and Race in the Early

Modern Iberian Atlantic," in *The Oxford Handbook of Religion and Race in American History*, ed. Paul Harvey and Kathryn Gin Lum (Oxford: Oxford University Press, 2018) and the introduction to Larissa Brewer-Garcia, *Beyond Babel: Translations of Blackness in Colonial Peru and New Granada* (Cambridge: Cambridge University Press, 2020).

5. Daniel Nemser, *Infrastructures of Race: Concentration and Biopolitics in Colonial Mexico* (Austin: University of Texas Press, 2017), 12.

6. On continence and conversion, see Christopher Wild, "Conversion and the Art of Spiritual Navigation" in *Konversion Als Medium Der Selbstbeschreibung in Spätantike, Mittelalter Und Früher Neuzei*, ed. Werner Röcke, Ruth von Bernuth, and Julia Weitbrech (Berlin: De Gruyter, 2016). "Virtue is continence that has matured with practice and habit, becoming more stable, effective, and self-aware." Geoffrey Scarre, "The Continence of Virtue," *Philosophical Investigations* 31, no. 1 (2013): 3.

7. Pablo Sierra Silva, *Urban Slavery in Colonial Mexico: Puebla De Los Ángeles, 1531–1706* (Cambridge: Cambridge University Press, 2018), 9.

8. Ursula Ewald, *Estudios Sobre La Hacienda Colonial En México: Las Propiedades Rurales Del Colegio Espíritu Santo En Puebla*, trans. Luis R Cerna (Wiesbaden: Franz Steiner Verlag GMBH, 1976), 31.

9. Herman L. Bennett, *Colonial Blackness: A History of Afro-Mexico* (Bloomington: Indiana University Press, 2010).

10. Silva's works are the latest in a growing body of literature that shows how slaves carved out emancipation. Bianca Premo, *The Enlightenment on Trial: Ordinary Litigants and Colonialism in the Spanish Empire* (Oxford: Oxford University Press, 2017) is an excellent recent example of how slaves made use of courts to litigate against slaveholders and secure emancipation. Bennett refers to these communities as "the New World's first culture of freedom." Bennett, *Colonial Blackness: A History of Afro-Mexico*, 16.

11. See Andrew Redden's cautionary stance in this volume.

12. Stephen Greenblatt, "A Mobility Studies Manifesto," in *Cultural Mobility: A Manifesto*, ed. Stephen Greenblatt (Cambridge: Cambridge University Press, 2010), 252.

13. Ewald, *Estudios sobre la hacienda colonial*, 24.

14. Chevalier, *Instrucción*, 101. This chapter is titled "De lo que han de guardar en la economía de las cosas del campo, y primero en lo tocante a sus aperos/That which they are to observe regarding the economy of the things pertaining to the country, first, those that pertain to implements/tools."

15. The first chapter is titled "De lo que han de guardar los hermanos administradores en la observancia regular, y en el porte de sus personas/That which brothers administrators are to guard in their regular observances and in the comportment of themselves."

16. J. Gabriel Martínez-Serna, "Procurators and the Making of the Jesuits' Atlantic World," in *Soundings in Atlantic History: Latent Structures and Intellectual Currents, 1500–1830*, ed. Bernard Bailyn and Patricia E. Denault (Cambridge: Cambridge University Press, 2009).

17. *Instrucción*, para. 13.

18. *Instrucción*, para. 1.

19. *Instrucción*, para. 1.

20. *Instrucción*, para. 2. In other parts of the *Instrucción* not discussed in this essay, the Jesuit college remains an "off-stage" presence, its rhythms working with and against the agricultural rhythms of planting and harvesting.

21. *Instrucción*, para. 4.

22. *Instrucción*, para. 2.

23. *Instrucción*, para. 5.

24. See John W. O'Malley, *The First Jesuits* (Cambridge, MA: Harvard University Press, 1993), 60–61, 79–80, 345–47.

25. *Instrucción*, para. 6.

26. *Instrucción*, para. 9.

27. *Instrucción*, para. 1, p. 2.

28. *Instrucción*, para. 14.

29. *Instrucción*, para. 15.

30. *Instrucción*, para. 16.

31. *Instrucción*, para. 17. A similar examination of the books is to be executed whenever the padre provincial visits the college. See *Instrucción*, para. 18.

32. For Jesuit modes of masculinity, see Ulrike Strasser, *Missionary Men in the Early Modern World: German Jesuits and Pacific Journeys* (Amsterdam: Amsterdam University Press, 2020). On the patriarchal values that underwrote legal norms and shaped colonial governance in the Americas, see Bianca Premo, *Children of the Father King: Youth, Authority, and Legal Minority in Colonial Lima* (Chapel Hill: University of North Carolina Press, 2005).

33. Ewald, *Estudios sobre la hacienda colonial*, 30–31.

34. But in Ewald's study of the haciendas affiliated with the *Colegio Espíritu Santo*, she finds that while higher status "servientes de razón" had initially referred to *españoles* and *criollos*, by the eighteenth century this category also included mestizos and sometimes Indians. On the mestizo as an indeterminate category, see Joan Rappaport, *The Disappearing Mestizo: Configuring Difference in the Colonial New Kingdom of Granada* (Raleigh, NC: Duke University Press, 2014).

35. *Instrucción*, para. 19 and 20.

36. Juan Martínez de la Parra, *Luz de verdades Católicas y explicación de la Doctrina Christiana que siguiendo la costumbre de la Casa Professa de la Compañía de México . . . se plática en su iglesia* (Mexico: En la imprenta de Diego Fernandez de Leon, 1691–1696).

37. Ibid., vol. 1, 198.

38. On references to the spiritual beauty of blackness in a Jesuit missionary context, see Brewer-Garcia, *Beyond Babel*, 164–206.

39. "Esso es lo que no quisieron dar a entender con este nombre nuestros mayores, que ni los senores se hagan odiosos con el entono de su dominio, ni a los esclavos se

les de siempre en cara con lo abatido de su fuerte." Parra, *Luz de verdades Católicas*, 198. On Seneca's qualified defense of the humanity of slaves, William Watts, "Seneca on Slavery," *The Downside Review* 90, no. 300 (1972): 189.

40. *Instrucción*, para. 21.

41. *"Porque al común no se le haga pesada esta devota distribución."* *Instrucción*, para. 7.

42. *Instrucción*, para. 23.

43. *Instrucción*, para. 24.

44. *Instrucción*, para. 22.

45. *Instrucción*, para. 25.

46. *Instrucción*, para. 26. He refers here to P. Bartolomé Castaño, S.J., *Catecismo breve de lo que precisamente ha de saber el cristiano* (1644).

47. *Instrucción*, para. 30.

48. *Instrucción*, para. 8.

49. *Instrucción*, para. 27.

50. *Instrucción*, para. 28.

51. *Instrucción*, para. 29.

52. Ignatius of Loyola advocated frequent communion, not only for the clergy, but "once per week" for the students at Jesuit colleges, with daily communion for the more spiritually advanced, advising his women followers that they would benefit from daily communion if they have done the work to assure that their consciences were clear.

53. William B. Taylor, *Magistrates of the Sacred: Priests and Parishioners in Eighteenth-Century Mexico* (Palo Alto, CA: Stanford University Press, 1996), 241–42.

54. Nemser has documented a similar occurrence, when parish priests demanded access to urban domestic Indian servants who lived in the homes of Spanish men and women, the latter locked the doors. Nemser, *Infrastructures of Race*, 109–10. Nemser calls these domestic spheres a "counter-sovereign," but Steve Stern's notion of a pluralized patriarchy may work better to set up the varying venues through which one might alternatively appeal for support or relief to a priest, judge, or patron. See Steve Stern, *The Secret History of Gender: Women, Men, and Power in Late Colonial Mexico* (Chapel Hill, NC: University of North Carolina Press, 1997).

55. *Instrucción*, para. 33.

56. *Instrucción*, para. 31.

57. *Instrucción*, para. 32. "And it will be most fruitful if one of the padres is 'lengua'— literally that he has the 'tongue' to speak to the Indians in their own language."

58. Me, Selwyn, Chatelier.

59. *Instrucción*, para. 34.

60. *Instrucción*, para. 34.

61. *Instrucción*, para. 35.

62. Ewald, *Estudios sobre la hacienda colonial*, 31, 33.

63. *Instrucción*, para. 56.

64. *Instrucción*, para. 57.

65. *Instrucción*, para. 58.

66.   Jessica L. Delgado, *Laywomen and the Making of Colonial Catholicism in New Spain, 1630–1790* (Cambridge: Cambridge University Press, 2018).

67.*Instrucción*, para. 59.

68. *Instrucción*, para. 47.

69. *Instrucción*, para. 47.

70. *Instrucción*, para. 48.

71. *Instrucción*, para. 49.

72. *Instrucción*, para. 46.

73. *Instrucción*, para. 36.

74. *Instrucción*, para. 38.

75. *Instrucción*, para. 37.

76.   Yasmin Haskell shows how Jesuit neo-Stoic poetry advocated "a manly virtue of the sage who withstands the storm of emotions, appeals to decorum and glory, and especially to 'constancy,' the title of Justus Lipsius' best known work." She also reminds us that self-control was linked to issues of physical health, as anger was linked with disease status in the early modern period. Yasmin Haskell, "Early Modern Anger Management: Seneca, Ovid, and Lieven De Meyere's *De Ira Libri Tres* (Antwerp, 1694)," *International Journal of the Classical Tradition* 18, no. 1 (2011): 39, 52.

77.   "No quieran llevarlo todo por el rigo, que no harán nada, y ellos virvirán descontentos y servirán forzados, y su servicio será violento y mal hecho," *Instrucción*, para. 39.

78. *Instrucción*, para. 39.

79.   *No sean amigos de que siempre resuene el estruendo de masas, y grillos, y cadenas y cepos*, *Instrucción*, para. 40.

80. *Instrucción*, para. 40.

81.   Raphaele Garrod and Yasmin Haskell, eds., *Performing Jesuit Emotions between Europe, Asia, and the Americas*, vol. 15 (Leiden: Brill Publishers, 2019).

82.   For an understanding of practices of virtue that saw habituation as a process of moral development that could cause anxiety about "authenticity," see Jennifer Herdt, *Putting on Virtue: The Legacy of the Splendid Vices* (Chicago and London: University of Chicago Press, 2008). To see Jesuits at the heart of debates about "dissimulation" in Europe and abroad, see Stefania Tutino, "Between Nicodemism and 'Honest' Dissimulation: The Society of Jesus in England," *Historical Research* 79, no. 206 (2006). Ines G. Županov and Pierre-Antoine Fabre, eds., *The Rites Controversies in the Early Modern World* (Leiden and Boston: Brill, 2018).

83. *Instrucción*, para. 42.

84.   "Porque si en tales casos se muestran inexorables, a mas de faltar en esto al respecto que deben a la persona humana que se interpone, sucederá que los esclavos, viendo que no vale ni humildad ni patrocinio, una vez huidos, no volverán mas a la hacienda, sino que darán en ladrones y se perderán."

85.   *Instrucción*, para. 43.

86. *Instrucción*, para. 44.

87. *Instrucción*, para. 45.

88. *Instrucción*, para. 61.

89. *Instrucción*, para. 54.

90. *Instrucción*, para. 50.

91. *Instrucción*, para. 51.

92. *Instrucción*, para. 64.

93. *Instrucción*, para. 65.

94. *Instrucción*, para. 66.

95. *Instrucción*, para. 63.

96. José Felix de Sebastián, *Memorias De Los Padres Y Hermanos De La Compañía De Jesus De La Provincia De Nueva España Difuntos Despues Del Arresto Acaecido En La Capital De Mexico El Día 25 De Junio Del Año 1767* (Bolonia: Archiginnasio, 1767–1796).

97. Pierre Bourdieu, *Outine of a Theory of Practice* (Cambridge: Cambridge University Press, 1977), 72.

98. The foundational comparative study is Frank Tannenbaum, *Slave and Citizen: The Negro in the Americas* (New York: Vintage Books, 1947). Tannenbaum's findings have been contested and nuanced over the years as scholars have turned from legal and economic structures to take a closer look at the lives of slaves who became citizens. For overviews of recent scholarship on race in the Americas that pulls together the disparate threads of law and religion, as well as notions of "lineage" and practices of freedom, see the introduction to Brewer-García, *Beyond Babel*.

99. *Beyond Babel*, 21.

100. For insistence that suppositions about "fixity" be rejected in favor of understanding historically differentiated modes of discrimination, see Kathryn Burns, "Unfixing Race," in *Histories of Race and Racism: The Andes and Mesoamerica from Colonial Times to the Present* (Durham: Duke University Press, 2011).

101. Silva, *Urban Slavery*, 8.

CHAPTER SIX

"The Most Barbarous and Fierce Peoples in the New World"

Decoding the Jesuit Missionary Project in Colonial North Mexico

SUSAN M. DEEDS

"MY LORD, I HAVE assembled in this history the accomplishments of the sons of the Company of Jesus—Your Majesty's most humble chaplains—which have been wrought through the preaching of the Gospel to the most barbarous and indomitable peoples in the New World."[1]

So begins the letter written by Jesuit Andrés Pérez de Ribas dedicating his *History of the Triumphs of Our Most Holy Faith Amongst the Most Barbarous and Fierce Peoples of the New World* to King Philip IV of Spain in 1645. The book chronicles the Jesuit missionary enterprise in late sixteenth- and early seventeenth-century northwest Mexico. Is the title, which may seem offensive (even racist) to the modern reader, an accurate representation of how Pérez de Ribas characterized Indigenous peoples of that region? To answer this question requires reading the account "against the grain" in an ethnographic sense to determine Jesuit attitudes regarding the peoples they proposed to convert to Christianity in an area that includes present-day Sinaloa, Durango, and southern Chihuahua. The scholarship focusing directly on this area does not explicitly address the question of whether the Jesuit project and the social transformations it wrought were forms or manifestations of racism.[2] Instead, the litreature has explored the social hierarchies that underpinned wide-ranging issues of cultural change and interethnic relations in colonial northern Mexico.[3] This chapter examines primary sources and secondary works to recreate and analyze shifting Jesuit perspectives that transitioned from Christianizing the "other" toward constructing markers of difference across ethnic groups or racializing difference in the northern missions.[4]

The idea of race in Spain evolved from an emphasis on purity of blood (*limpieza de sangre*) that distinguished Christians from Jews and Muslims. In *Genealogical Fictions: Limpieza de Sangre, Religion, and Gender in Colonial Mexico*, María Elena Martínez explores how lineage taxonomy based on religious and genealogical difference transitioned into the *sistema de castas*—a hierarchical system of social classification—in colonial Mexico. She describes the complex, gendered, and historically changing meanings of limpieza de sangre. According to Martínez, "in the second half of the colonial period, multiple, overlapping, and even competing discourses of blood purity operated in Mexico. Some stressed Christian bloodlines, some Spanish ancestry, and some skin color.... No racial discourse is ever entirely new; as social and historical conditions change, race builds on old beliefs, tropes, and stereotypes."[5] Her analysis shows that it is crucial to understand how terms employed to categorize people were used in specific historical contexts.

The factors that determined where an individual fell in the social structure of colonial Mexico were constantly evolving.[6] Accordingly, an arising question is how did the concept of race develop as an organizing principle for early modern Jesuits in conjunction with other understandings of social or cultural difference? For example, how did racial categories diverge the categories officially imposed by Spanish authorities on ethnic or social groups? How did Jesuits theorize racialized topics such as the "shortcomings" of Indigenous peoples?

The purpose of this chapter is to address these questions within an examination of Jesuit interactions with Indigenous peoples in northwest Mexico during the seventeenth and eighteenth centuries. It will contextualize Pérez de Ribas's views alongside the experiences of Jesuit missionaries on the ground. Why did Pérez de Ribas describe Indigenous peoples of northwest Mexico as the most barbarous and fierce peoples of the New World in a treatise that also heavily accentuated the values of martyrdom? At first glance, one sees that the tract was intended primarily to secure continued royal subsidies for missions. He wrote it at a time when the Jesuits faced harsh criticism from other religious orders and from the archbishop and then viceroy of New Spain, Juan de Palafox y Mendoza, regarding their allegedly mercenary motives.[7] This chapter demonstrates the fruitfulness of a deeper reading, or differently informed reading, to shed more light on Pérez de Ribas's constructions of difference.

Pérez de Ribas, a former missionary and then head of the Jesuit province in Mexico, appealed to the Spanish king by construing conversion of the Indians as a royal spiritual mandate, while not denying the potential economic benefits to the Spanish empire.[8] He characterized the evangelizing process as a battle between the Jesuits and the devil who controlled Native souls. As soldiers of God, the Jesuits were instruments of providentialism or divine will, subject to the supreme sacrifice of martyrdom in the same way as the apostles of the early church. Pérez de Ribas situated the semisedentary groups of the north as belonging to a category of wild savages or barbarians, childlike in their need of salvation. In this regard, he followed José de Acosta's 1588 classification of non-European peoples. In the first category, Acosta placed highly sophisticated cultures like the Chinese and Japanese, while the second included the Aztecas and Incas, "as rather sophisticated." His third grouping comprised "the barbarians, by nature a mixture of man and beast, whose customs render them human monsters. . . . They have to be given treatment that is partly human and kind, but also firm and violent if necessary."[9] In Pérez de Ribas's essentially optimistic characterization of this group, he did not doubt their capacity, although somewhat limited by their "barbarous" customs, to receive the faith if they could be released from the devil's snare.[10] In addition, he shared Acosta's belief that the way to accomplish this conversion was to learn their languages and customs in order to effectively combat Native shamans who served as messengers of the devil.[11]

In order to highlight the difficulty of the task, Pérez de Ribas emphasized not only the ferocity of the Indigenous peoples but also the magnitude of work and sacrifice, including Jesuit martyrdom, needed to bring such hostile societies and territories under Spanish control. Using a sophisticated discourse on martyrdom and the desire for it, he wielded a double-edged sword in which the unfavorable consequences (individual death) were outweighed by the image of Jesuit altruism/superiority in serving the crown. At the same time his propagation of symbols of martyrdom exalted the Jesuit calling as part of an agenda to attract recruits to the Order.[12]

Pérez de Ribas' reiteration of the savagery of Indigenous peoples was intended above all to emphasize the magnitude of the difficulty in bringing them into the fold for the purpose of embellishing the divine nature of the Jesuit mission. His descriptions of these Natives and their customs reflect cultural presuppositions of difference. They were barbarous or less than civilized because they had neither an urban mode of political organization nor Christianity. The emphasis was on converting them to living in towns as Christians—*vida política y cristiana*. Given this understanding of how Jesuits perceived Indians as different and deficient, we need to probe how and when the tendency to naturalize difference and link character or behavior to genealogy was deployed.[13] Ultimately discrimination based on religious or cultural difference came to function like racial "othering." What the Jesuits implemented in a hierarchical system designed to save souls had the potential to destroy cultures and lives—a process of marginalization that continues to this day.[14]

The "Civilizing Mission" in The Early Period

Such an outcome was not how Joan Font, a Jesuit missionary from Catalonia, perceived his mission when he wrote to Ildefonso de Castro, the head of the Jesuit order in Mexico, in 1608. Soon after his arrival in southern Chihuahua at the age of thirty-four, Font was filled with enthusiasm for his mission to evangelize Tarahumaras whom he characterized as having "reasonable capacity" for conversion. He added: "I am content and excited to see the door opened to a massive conversion, even greater because it is being undertaken without the expense of captains and soldiers. I have always endeavored to avoid extraordinary spending so that the ministers of the king will be more amenable to send priests to convey the doctrine. And there is no doubt that the natives are pleased to see us alone in their lands, absent the Spaniards whom they fear and distrust."[15]

Father Font's optimism about the civilizing mission in Chihuahua echoed Jesuit attitudes that had guided their early work among the Acaxees, Xiximes, and Tepehuanes in Sinaloa and Durango. Conversion would be accomplished by organizing previously more dispersed Indigenous peoples in mission villages where urbanity, separation from the natural environment, and social stratification would be employed to "civilize" them. Here, where they were exempted from ecclesiastical and royal taxes (tribute), they could be taught (ideally in their own languages) the Christian doctrine, urban sociopolitical organization, and agricultural practices to assure daily sustenance.[16] How did Jesuits articulate these goals and the practices to achieve them?

They were directed by the rules of their order to live in the world.[17] In the case of northwest Mexico, where they encountered nomadic and semisedentary peoples, the Native world had already been breached by Spaniards searching for silver and laborers to work in mines.[18] Labor was appropriated haphazardly and often violently through proscribed slavery and legally sanctioned coercive institutions like *encomienda* and *repartimiento*.[19] Initial fierce resistance from Indigenous groups was counteracted not only by Spanish military force but also by decimating epidemic diseases to which Natives had no immunities. Then Jesuit missionaries entered their territories, often bearing material gifts, to reorganize them into mission villages with Native political and religious officials. Located near sources of water, these new congregations were intended to convert Indians but also to enable production of agricultural goods that could be marketed to surrounding mines as well as to introduce Natives to Spanish norms of civilized life.[20] To facilitate these activities, the Jesuits recruited converted Tlaxcalans and Tarascans from central Mexico to serve as examples of Christian and sedentary living to the local Indigenous peoples.[21]

The process of religious conversion was not simply one of implanting new spiritual beliefs. It involved a major transformation in lifeways passed on from one generation to another related to land use, material culture, gender roles, and family practices. These ancestral patterns embraced a combination of physical, intellectual, and moral characteristics that came under attack from conditions imposed by the Jesuits and other colonizers. In the conflict that ensued, multigenerational differences in lifeways become racialized over time. How did this transpire?

The system imposed by Jesuits conflicted with local Indigenous social and spatial organization.[22] Their use of wilderness for hunting and gathering and its importance as a locus of myth and supernatural power was seen as unproductive by European missionaries. The emphasis on the accumulation of surpluses clashed with Indigenous custom, which, while not eschewing petty trade, embraced more immediate uses for material goods in consumption, gift-giving, and spiritual offerings. The introduction of a set of missionary-approved governing officials disrupted a less hierarchically differentiated social structure and introduced new parameters for social and economic divisions within Indigenous polities. Furthermore, the moral authority of Native elders was called into question by missionaries who chose assistants to aid them in religious matters and manipulated the selection of governing officials.[23] And missionary attempts to eliminate warfare among traditionally hostile groups stripped males of a source of power and prestige.[24]

Other impositions destabilized kinship bonds. Missionary emphasis on the sanctity of marriage and the nuclear family unit along with taboos regarding sexuality challenged existing male-female ties, reproductive patterns, kinship arrangements, and a social order based on reciprocal work arrangements. By singling out children as more malleable converts, missionaries introduced tensions that upset inter-generational relationships.[25] Christian concepts of sin and salvation required a greater emphasis on the individual than existed in societies whose religion and economy were based on the complementary roles of females and males and the cooperative efforts of extended families. Missionaries attempted to end ceremonial practices that reinforced social networks and traditional beliefs regarding well-being. In particular, they attacked ritual drinking parties that accompanied cooperative exchanges of manual labor as promoting sexual promiscuity and alcoholic brawling. For Pérez de Ribas, these were manifestations of the power of the devil, who taught them "superstitions, idolatries, and barbarous and savage customs."[26]

Despite all the potential for conflict, Indigenous peoples sometimes invited missionaries to enter their territories. One reason may have been the potential material and spiritual comfort offered by missionaries in the wake of devastating smallpox and measles epidemics that produced huge demographic losses.[27] According to this argument, the Jesuits filled a void and helped reconstitute Native adaptive strategies in a period of immense stress.[28] The thousands of baptisms performed by missionaries in the early contact period suggest that Indians may have incorporated this act into their ritual systems as a possible protection against disease.

Other reasons may explain early, more peaceful acceptances; for example, desire for material benefits that might accrue from farming, an expanded diet, and tools introduced by missionaries. Compared to the slave-hunting expeditions of early Spaniards, there was a relative absence of coercion by Jesuits, aided by Indigenous peoples from central Mexico and Spanish soldiers who could provide protection from traditional enemies.[29]

The Devil's Tricksters Foment Rebellion

Nonetheless, Indigenous peoples did not simply acquiesce. In the case of all four groups mentioned above, the imposed regimes that disrupted Native systems for maintaining well-being prompted armed resistance. All of these "first-generation" rebellions were defeated by Spanish militias, often aided by Indigenous allies.[30] Jesuits interpreted the rebellions as having been instigated by the devil through Native shamans or *hechiceros* and noted that elder Indians were the most recalcitrant converts because they had been possessed by the devil for much longer.[31] They also blamed Spaniards who illegally appropriated Native labor for mining in harsh conditions.[32] Pérez de Ribas wrote extensively about the rebellions and provided highly graphic biographies of Jesuits martyred in these revolts led by Indigenous shamans who were deemed demonic familiars.[33]

These accounts of combat and martyrdom all end with the triumph of God over the devil, told either through the death of sorcerers or the salvation of individuals freed from diabolic control through exorcisms or sudden divine intervention. "Even though he [the devil] is a wolf, he is able to dress in sheep's clothing, and although a demon, he can transform himself into an angel of light. . . . Once again, however, God, who knows the ways of the devil, did not allow him to succeed."[34] The holy faith would prevail even when martyrdom was the necessary sacrifice for furthering the evangelical enterprise. After recounting the death of the martyred Father Gonzalo de Tapia, Pérez de Ribas continues: "The devil certainly thought, and better to say incorrectly thought, that he had achieved a victory with the death and removal from earth of the founder of the Sinaloa mission—he who had laid the foundations for that extensive Christianity. But the devil's plans had the totally opposite effect, just as they did when he spilled the blood of the [ancient] martyrs. The latter's blood always fertilized the fields of the Church; each additional [sacrifice] multiplied the evangelical harvest. And so it was in Sinaloa . . . "[35]

Pérez de Ribas went on to describe Jesuit efforts to convert Tepehuan peoples, filling several chapters with the details of their rebellion, which began in 1616 and took the lives of the eight Jesuits. "There was only one cause of what happened here—it was a scheme invented by Satan and welcomed by these blind people. [The scheme] enraged their spirits to take up arms against the Faith of Christ and all things Christian."[36] Pérez de Ribas seems to suggest here that the Tepehuanes were not innately flawed by lineage; rather they had been blinded by the devil, who promised them that they would become lords of the land and finish off all the Spaniards and priests in their ancestral lands.

An Idealized Mission Compromised

Aided by Spanish soldiers who suppressed the revolts, the Jesuits renewed the mission project. They chose resettlement in places located farther away from Spanish towns and mines, to discourage interference and find spaces more suitable for farming.[37] In this process, they accepted Spanish force, including the execution by hanging of recalcitrant Indigenous leaders, combining it with gift-giving and less confrontational methods to deal with drunkenness and illicit unions.[38] Jesuits stepped up their efforts to bring lands around missions under cultivation. The Natives provided labor to plant and harvest on individual plots, as well as on communal lands, where they also raised cattle and mules. In reporting on corn and bean production and increases in livestock at his mission of San Pablo in 1662, Father Gerónimo de Figueroa emphasized that economic well-being in the missions was the essential foundation for promoting and assuring their spiritual vigor.[39]

There and in other areas Jesuits tended their flocks of neophytes. They described progress in the construction of churches, the teaching of the catechism, and the celebration of religious holidays.[40] Whatever hope they once had for martyrdom had been superseded by the importance of their work for God and the Spanish crown.[41] In one of the many optimistic letters, Father Rodrigo del Castillo reported on the conversion efforts in his mission of San Miguel de las Bocas. The children attended catechism classes in the church patio twice daily, and their parents could recite prayers. They were particularly receptive to the music (voice and instrumental) introduced by the Jesuits as an evangelizing tool.[42] The Jesuit highlighted their devotion to the fiestas of Our Lady of Angels and Corpus Christi, celebrated with altars adorned by flowers, the singing of *villancicos* (carols), and processions. He recounted in detail how his parishioners had participated enthusiastically in the dedication of a painting of the Virgin of Guadalupe, inspired by the story of her appearance to the Indian Juan Diego.[43] The descriptions of devout, industrious, and cooperative Indigenous peoples abound in many of the Jesuit reports, however tempered by paternalistic rhetoric and a tone of wariness regarding the Indians' capacity for change.

As time went on, the Jesuits increasingly related obstacles to the missionary project, especially setbacks in deaths from epidemics and periodic raids by unconverted Indians throughout the seventeenth century. Perhaps more alarming for the long term, they testified to the growing numbers of Spaniards and ethnically mixed peoples living near the missions. This challenged Jesuit authority, making the segregation of Indigenous peoples more difficult, particularly in economic terms as free-wage labor attracted Indians to work on Spanish haciendas and mines, adding to the coerced exodus of workers in repartimiento.[44] The mix of free and unfree labor persisted, resulting in the instability of mission populations.[45] Jesuit attempts to prohibit labor drafts were only partially successful, and some Natives left of their own accord, lured by economic incentives. As the numbers of Natives working in the missions dropped, production even for mission sustenance declined, prompting some Natives to leave missions to hunt and gather. As migratory strategies proliferated, interethnic contacts between missions, haciendas, mines, and Spanish towns intensified. Mission populations became less ethnically Indigenous.

The missionaries' hopeful outlook for change that had prevailed in the seventeenth century, even in the face of formidable Indigenous resistance and high death tolls from epidemics, had been on the wane. The raison d'être of the Jesuit mission program became increasingly undermined by movements in and out of the pueblos caused by factors outside of Jesuit control. Veteran missionary Tomás de Guadalajara reflected on the conditions in 1715: "In these mountains of the older Tepehuan and Tarahumara missions, we are experiencing extreme necessity. In part this is due to the relentless assaults on these frontiers, to the point that the villagers have barely enough to survive, but it is also because of the continuous labor drafts and the mustering of Indian fighters to take part in the campaigns against enemy Indians."[46] After visiting his diocese in the same year, the bishop of Durango, Pedro Tapis, wrote to the Spanish king arguing that excessive and unlawful demands on Indigenous labor undercut the advances taking place in the missions.[47]

The escalating battle for scarce labor resources was paralleled by Spanish efforts to acquire land. In the eighteenth century, demographic patterns—the slowing of Indigenous rates of decline and the growth of the non-Indian population—produced especially intense conflicts over land acquisition and ownership. Silver mining, which had fallen off in the late seventeenth century, revived with new discoveries near Chihuahua and attracted newcomers. Enterprising agricultural entrepreneurs sought land to supply a growing market. Competition for land with reliable water sources in the semiarid north became particularly acute and made mission lands more coveted.[48]

By 1716, Nueva Vizcaya Governor Manuel San Juan de Santa Cruz sought to bring order to the chaotic situation of land encroachments and labor drafts. He visited haciendas in areas between Parral and Chihuahua City to determine labor needs.[49] In attempting to reorganize the labor pool, he supported the founding of new Franciscan missions among less sedentary Indians and increased the number of labor drafts from Jesuit missions. Trying to reduce the growing numbers of non-Indians living in missions, in 1718 he issued a decree calling for stiff fines to be levied against "Spaniards, blacks, mestizos," and other outsiders who introduced gambling and alcoholic beverages into the villages and took advantage of Indians through trickery. Their destabilizing presence made labor drafts more difficult.[50] The Jesuits also decried the presence of Spanish and ethnically mixed, non-Indians in the missions who, "like the Indians, live by their own labor, their fields rarely yield more than [a little] corn, not even enough to meet costs . . . they also eat wild foods and occasionally butcher a cow, although it is difficult to raise cattle because they are easy prey for mountain lions and other wild beasts."[51] In many missions, residents were absent for months working in mines, on haciendas, and in transporting goods, leaving women and children to tend to meager crops of corn and beans, as well as a few animals.

The Waning of Apostolic Zeal

By the mid-eighteenth century, a number of Jesuits, including some who had served for years in missions, had become disheartened. The 1738–1739 epidemic of *matlazahuatl* (perhaps typhus) had resulted in high death rates among the region's laboring population, threatening economic enterprise in the north. As demand for scarce labor escalated even more, missions were hard put to provide subsistence for their inhabitants. Spanish officials argued that many of them were missions in name only;[52] the few Indians who remained were forced to seek provisions elsewhere, often defying missionary control.

Native disobedience and unrest increasingly moved Jesuits in the oldest missions to describe their behavior in essentializing, disparaging characterizations as lascivious, depraved, and perverted. Indians who engaged in foot-dragging and work slowdowns were "lazy and slothful." When they left the missions to hunt and gather, they were "vagrant and idle." False deference was interpreted as "insolence," just as other psychological defenses such as gossip and slander were "audacious and impudent." Pilfering to get their due was unmitigated "thievery." Assertive behavior was "stubbornness."[53] It was reported that "the Indians of the sierra are predominantly *ladinos* [acculturated]—lazy, impertinent, and badly influenced by Spaniards. . . . In sum, they are without shame, without fear, and without respect. We have learned from experience that the only way to live with them is to expect nothing."[54]

Frustrated by what they now saw as Native intransigence and incapacity to change, they read actions that have been described as "weapons of the weak" from a perspective far different than the one Pérez de Ribas had attributed to the devil's machinations.[55] They could call on God to deal with the devil, but they were less successful in preventing worldly intrusions and stresses introduced by the growing numbers of non-Indians, both inside the missions and in neighboring areas. And their will to try to stem abuses was compromised by shifting, more negative views of their "ungrateful" charges.[56] Changing population dynamics had contributed to a growing tendency to racialize difference by creating specific markers for ethnic groups.

The undermining of the missionary enterprise coincided with massive demographic changes and increasing pressure from the Spanish Bourbon monarchy to reduce the power of the church in temporal affairs and to secularize missions under the control of the diocesan clergy. The latter should become parishes in which Natives would pay not only ecclesiastical fees for services but also other taxes, thus saving the costs to the Spanish treasury that subsidized missions.[57] Royal officials had begun to investigate ways to strengthen the mining economy in Chihuahua and to offer proposals to resolve chronic shortages of labor and supplies in the province.[58]

Except in the northernmost Jesuit missions, the Indigenous population had shrunk drastically by 1740 while non-Indian settlements were on the rise. From approximately 80,000 Indians at the beginning of the seventeenth century, the missions claimed less than 20,000 in the middle of the eighteenth.[59] Faced with mounting criticism from secular authorities at a time when Jesuits hoped to expand the mission enterprise into upper California, the Order's father general in Rome directed the Mexican province to look into the possibility of turning over some of their missions to the bishop of Durango.[60] In accordance, Provincial Father Cristóbal Escobar y Llamas instructed Father Juan Antonio Balthasar to undertake a general visitation of missions in 1743.[61] The reports from his inspection over a two-year period confirmed the dire conditions of many of the missions. Neither self-sufficient nor closed to influences from outside, their ethnic composition was mixed with Indianness on the wane, at least biologically if not culturally.[62] Mindful of official complaints and lawsuits involving land and labor disputes in the missions, Balthasar worried about the waning enthusiasm within the Order itself: "If the truth be known, many of the [royal] complaints have a basis in fact ... there are very few missionaries who are highly motivated."[63]

Rendering unto Caesar and the Diocesan Church

On November 30, 1745, Father Escobar y Llamas sent a proposal to the king offering to cede to the bishopric of Durango twenty-two mission districts in Sinaloa, Durango, and southern Chihuahua, in order for the Jesuits to undertake expansion into California.[64] These missions had been chosen, he argued, because they were located near parishes, towns, and mining settlements closest to the seat of the bishopric. The king approved the offer nearly two years later after a new bishop was installed.[65] Even then the transfer was not completed until 1755. Bishop Pedro Anselmo Sánchez de Tagle was taken aback after receiving the reports he had requested from individual Jesuits on their populations and assets and realizing how difficult it would be to find priests to staff the new parishes.

Lengthy negotiations ensued regarding the disposition of their material possessions, which included land and livestock. Where Jesuits had purchased adjacent lands beyond the original legal allocation to the mission, questions arose as to their ownership. Did the properties belong to the church or the community? Ethnically mixed mission inhabitants and adjacent populations of mestizos, Afro-European, and poor Spaniards that had been ministered to spiritually by the Jesuits objected to the transfer, which meant they would now have to pay for sacramental services. The reduced numbers of Indians who remained would be subject to ecclesiastical tithes and royal tribute. The resolution of these issues and conflicts dragged on as the bishop's fears that the diocese was acquiring a liability grew.[66]

It is not difficult to imagine his reaction upon reading Father Marcelo de León's description of his mission of San Ignacio. Only three houses were made of adobe; the rest were mud and wattle constructions with thatched roofs.[67] His commentary on Native spirituality would have been even more unsettling to the bishop: "Even though they have been exposed to Christian beliefs for a long time, there is still a great deal to fear from them. Their faith seems to be stuck together with pins, and could unravel on a moment's notice." The turbulence that characterized the secularization process was worsened by an extended drought and an epidemic of measles in 1748. Nonetheless, despite the bishop's misgivings, the Jesuit surrender of the missions began in August of 1753 and was completed at the beginning of 1754.[68]

Assessing the Outcome

Was this finale the "triumph of the holy faith over barbarous peoples" so passionately articulated by Andrés Pérez de Ribas more than a hundred years earlier?

> Doubts might arise ... upon hearing that the Gospel is being preached in these missions to peoples who are as uncivilized, ignorant, and down-trodden as those described herein. It may seem that these missions do not possess the same degree of worth, or that one cannot expect the same fruits as those produced in missions to the world's noble, famous, and civilized nations. ... The object of my efforts here is to prove that the very same circumstances and characteristics that appear to tarnish, humiliate, and debase our missions actually exalt them and substantially increase their value in the eyes of God, who is never deceived.[69]

What had happened to this undertaking so valuable in the eyes of God? As the evangelizing project earlier envisioned by Pérez de Ribas had evolved through different stages, its goals and expectations for Indian "others" had changed. Looking back on it from the eighteenth century, the vision could not have resounded so convincingly with his successors who had experienced the steady erosion of the missions. Their very inception had sown the seeds of their destruction. The act of congregating previously dispersed peoples made them vulnerable to epidemic diseases and to appropriation of their labor, however unforeseen by Jesuit missionaries. From a Spanish Christian perspective, the laudable effort to save souls could not be frozen in time. The inexorable march of time and changing population dynamics registered phases of idealism, zeal, martyrdom, optimism, tenacity, and disillusionment that shaped Jesuit views of Indigenous peoples and their activities among them.

By the time of secularization, the few thousand Acaxees, Xiximes, Tepehuanes, and Tarahumaras living in missions were at different stages of material, cultural, and ethnic change. How they identified themselves varied considerably since the changing demographics of racial mixing produced biological difference but did not determine ethnic identification. Nonetheless, only a few of them maintained corporate bonds as Indigenous communities. From a modern perspective, the damage done to Indigenous cultures by the mission system as it evolved in conjunction with Spanish society cannot be denied.

Returning to the issue of race, how had the Jesuits' attributions of difference to Indigenous peoples influenced the outcomes I have described? If we conceive of race as a social construction that creates categories or markers of difference that are not necessarily biological but cultural or behavioral within societies, then the Jesuit assertion of religious and cultural superiority had profound consequences for cultural and ethnic persistence, as well as gendered roles. Over time, social and cultural differentiation occurred within the Indigenous groups considered here, and multiple associations were created across and outside of them. I have described these processes elsewhere as a labyrinth of *mestizaje* or ethnic mixing.[70] Today their mestizo descendants are imagined as predominantly white. At the same time, many people who still consider themselves to be fully Tarahumara live in the mountains of Chihuahua, where their struggles resemble those of the colonial period: conflicts over land and natural resources, recurrent battles with disease and malnutrition, and the effort to maintain cultural autonomy.

Notes

1. *Historia de los triunfos de nuestra santa fé entre gentes las más bárbaras y fieras del Nuevo Orbe* (Madrid: A. de Paredes, 1645). The title in English refers to the translation by Daniel T. Reff, Maureen Ahern, and Richard K. Danford (Tucson: University of Arizona Press, 1999). The introduction by Reff provides an excellent critical analysis of Pérez de Ribas' motivations and goals for writing the book.

2. Susan M. Deeds, *Defiance and Deference in Mexico's Colonial North: Indians under Spanish Rule in Nueva Vizcaya* (Austin: University of Texas Press, 2003), 29–38; Deeds, "Indigenous érez Rebellions on the Northern Mexican Mission Frontier: From First-Generation to Later Colonial Responses," in Donna J. Guy and Thomas E. Sheridan, eds., *Contested Ground: Comparative Frontiers on the Northern and Southern Edges of the Spanish Empire* (Tucson: University of Arizona Press, 1998), 32–51.

3. Deeds, "Labyrinths of Mestizaje: Understanding Cultural Persistence and

Transformation in Nueva Vizcaya," in Danna A. Levin Rojo and Cynthia Radding, eds., *The Oxford Handbook of Borderlands in the Iberian World* (New York: Oxford University Press, 2019), 660–708.

4. This chapter will focus only on the Indigenous peoples of the missions. The Jesuits did have slaves in their northern *colegios*, or colleges; they worked primarily on the haciendas that supported the missionary endeavor; Deeds, *Defiance and Deference*, 15–16, 122–3, 134, 141, 176–77. Although racial mixing between African Americans and Indigenous peoples occurred in missions from the early sixteenth century over time, Pérez de Ribas does not discuss the presence of blacks or Afro-Europeans in missions because such an acknowledgement would undermine the underlying rationale for congregating exclusively Indian neophytes in missions for the purpose of conversion.

5. María Elena Martínez, *Genealogical Fictions: Limpieza de Sangre, Religion, and Gender in Colonial Mexico* (Palo Alto, CA: Stanford University Press, 2011), 270. The book strives to address the critical question of "how a concept that had strong religious connotations came to construct or promote classifications that presumably were based on modern notions of race," (page 2).

6. See, for example, Norah L. A. Gharala, *Taxing Blackness: Free Afromexican Tribute in Bourbon New Spain* (Tuscaloosa, AL: University of Alabama Press, 2019), 9–10. She bases her study of the classification of social differences in the multifaceted concept of *calidad*, or status, arguing that a system of exclusively racial classification never existed in colonial New Spain, page 3.

7. Several studies have analyzed his motivations for writing this history. Guy Rozat Dupeyron, *América, imperio del demonio* (Mexico City: Universidad Iberoamericana, 1995); Daniel T. Reff, "Critical Introduction: The *Historia* and Jesuit Discourse," in *The History of the Triumphs* (Tucson: University of Arizona Press, 1999), 11–46; Maureen Ahern, "Martyrs and Idols: Performing Ritual Warfare on Early Missionary Frontiers in the Northwest," in Susan Schroeder and Stafford Poole, eds., *Religion in New Spain* (Albuquerque, NM: University of New Mexico Press, 2007), 279–97. See also Asunción Lavrin, "Dying for Christ: Martyrdom in New Spain," in Stephanie Kirk and Sarah Rivett, eds., *Religious Transformations in the Early Modern Americas* (Philadelphia: University of Pennsylvania Press, 2014), 131–57.

8. That Pérez de Ribas was well aware that he needed to convince the king that the Jesuits were furthering the economic interests of the crown is quite evident in the draft of a letter he wrote to an official of the Council of the Indies. In it he scores out references to pernicious Spaniards and substitutes a line emphasizing how crucial the Jesuit pacification of Indigenous peoples was to the production of silver in the north. Biblioteca Nacional, Madrid, ms. 3000, fols. 238–41.

9. José de Acosta, *De Procuranda Indorum Salute*, book V, ch. 11.

10. Pérez de Ribas, *History of the Triumphs*, part 1, book 7, ch. II.

11. Pérez de Ribas, *History of the Triumphs*, part 1, book 1, ch. VI. 6.

12. For more on the links between evangelization, martyrdom, and imperial expansion, see Alejandro Cañeque, "Mártires y discurso martirial en la formación de

las fronteras misionales jesuitas," *Relaciones: Estudios de historia y sociedad* 145 (Winter 2016): 35; Cañeque, "'Letting Yourself be Skinned Alive': Jerónimo Gracián and the Globalisation of Martyrdom," *Journal of Modern History* 24, no. 3 (2020); and Cañeque, *Un imperio de mártires: Religión y poder en las fronteras de la monarquía hispánica* (Madrid: Marcial Pons, 2020).

13.   In the preface to the English translation cited above, the editors offer this appraisal of Pérez de Ribas: "This guarded acceptance of native peoples as rational beings often empowered him as an ethnographer, predisposing him to cultural rather than abjectly racist or tautological explanations of native values, beliefs, and behaviors" (p. 4). See also Joshua Goode, *Impurity of Blood: Defining Race in Spain, 1870–1930* (Baton Rouge: Louisiana State University Press, 2009), 25.

14.   Relevant here is the last sentence in Daniel T. Reff's critical introduction to the English version cited at the beginning of this chapter: "In reading the *Historia* the key challenge is to avoid anachronistic judgments; that is, evaluating Pérez de Ribas' account of the Jesuit mission enterprise from a wholly modern perspective. A context-sensitive reading of the text provides a window on both the encounter and our own modern predicament," 46. His perspective allows us to see stages in a process that continues to marginalize peoples today.

15.   Durango, April 22, 1608, reprinted in Luis González Rodríguez, *Crónicas de la sierra tarahumara* (Chihuahua: Editorial Camino, 1992), 180.

16.   Deeds, *Defiance and Deference*, 18–19. These policies were clearly assimilationist and patronizing, but not designed to exterminate the "other."

17.   Charles W. Polzer, S.J., *Rules and Precepts of the Jesuit Missions of Northwestern New Spain* (Tucson: University of Arizona Press, 1976). The distinction between regular priests and secular priests should be noted. Jesuits and members of other Orders (e.g., Franciscans, Dominicans) were called regular clergy and took vows of obedience to the rules (*regulas*) of their order in an organization separate from secular clergy, or the diocesan church.

18.   Because the Jesuits arrived in Mexico well after mendicant friars, they were assigned to evangelize those Indigenous groups not yet firmly under Spanish control in the far north of New Spain.

19.   These were grants of Indigenous labor to Spaniards; the latter was more restricted in time and scope and included modest remuneration.

20.   Relación que el Hermano Juan de la Carrera hizo al padre Antonio de Mendoza, 1597, Archivo Romanum Societatis Jesu, Rome (copy in University of Saint Louis Vatican Film Library) [hereafter cited as ARSI], vol. 16, fols. 152–7; letter of padre Francisco de Arista, Topia, n.d. ca.1599, in Félix Zubillaga, S.J., and Ernest J. Burrus, S.J., eds., *Monumenta mexicana*, 8 vols. (Rome: Instituto Historicum Societatis Jesu, 1956–1981), appendix 5, 689. These processes are summarized in the next few paragraphs, but detailed descriptions can be found in Deeds, *Defiance and Deference*, ch. 1.

21.   Cuentas de la Real Caja de Durango, May 22, 1591, Archivo General de Indias, Seville (hereafter cited as AGI), Contaduría 929; carta ánua, 1615, ARSI, Provincia

Mexicana, vol. 15, reel 140. For more on Indigenous migrants from central Mexico in the north, see David B. Adams, *Las colonias tlaxcaltecas de Coahuila y Nuevo León en la Nueva España: un aspecto de la colonización del norte de México* (Saltillo: Archivo Municipal de Saltillo, 1991); Dana Velasco Murillo, *Urban Indians in a Silver City: Zacatecas, Mexico, 1546–1810* (Palo Alto, CA: Stanford University Press, 2016) and Laurent Corbeil, *The Motions Beneath: Indigenous Migrants on the Urban Frontier of New Spain* (Tucson, AZ: University of Arizona Press, 2018).

22. Deeds, *Defiance and Deference*, ch. 2 describes the environment and culture of the region.

23. Annual letters of Juan Font, 1611 and 1612, in González Rodríguez, *Crónicas*, 171–74; 186–93.

24. Precontact raiding aimed to acquire foodstuffs and women for sexual partnerships, both necessary for survival; report of Juan de la Carrera, Topia, ca. 1602, ARSI, Provincia Mexicana, vol. 14.

25. Carta ánua, 1606, ARSI, Mexicana, vol. 14, fols. 468–70; report of Joseph Tardá and Tomás de Guadalajara, August 15, 1676, ARSI, Provincia Mexicana, vol. 17, 355–72.

26. Pérez de Ribas, *History of the Triumphs*, part 2, book 10, ch. XXX, 623. The devil also intervened by causing Spaniards to sow discord among them. See, for example, Padre Joseph Tardá, Carta ánua de 1674, Archivo General de la Nación, Mexico City (hereafter cited as AGN), Jesuitas III-29, exp. 27; and Padre Diego de Alejos, Teguciapa, May 18, 1617, AGN, Archivo Provisional, Misiones, Caja 2.

27. The earliest annual letters from Jesuits in the late 1590s report massive numbers of deaths from smallpox and measles; Deeds, *Defiance and Deference*, ch. 1; for an example, see carta ánua, 1596, AGN, Historia, vol. 19, exp. 5.

28. Daniel T. Reff, *Disease, Depopulation, and Culture Change in Northwestern New Spain, 1518–1764* (Salt Lake City: University of Utah Press, 1991). Although Spanish medicine was mostly ineffective against epidemic diseases, Jesuit priests provided comfort with foodstuffs to ailing people; carta *ánua*, Sept. 3, 1599, in *Monumenta Mexicana*, vol. 6, 625.

29. Noticias de las misiones de Durango, n.d., ARSI, reel 577. Responding to the Ordenanzas del Padre Provincial Rodrigo de Cabredo (1610) that they must treat Indians with benevolence and care, the missionaries argue that they are preventing Spaniards from taking mission Indians to work for them while at the same time encouraging them to plant *"para evitar ociosidad y tener vida más política* (avoid idleness and live as a citizen in an organized urban polity)."

30. Details on the rebellions of Acaxees, Xiximes, Tepehuanes, and Tarahumaras can be found in Deeds, *Defiance and Deference*, 23–38, 91–103 and Deeds, "First-Generation Rebellions in Seventeenth-Century Nueva Vizcaya," in Susan Schroeder, ed., *Native Resistance and the Pax Colonial in New Spain* (Lincoln: University of Nebraska Press, 1998), 1–29.

31. Carta ánua, 1598, in *Monumenta mexicana*, vol. 6, 427; Carta ánua, 1616, AGN, Jesuitas, III-29, exp. 21. Pérez de Ribas' *Historia* is replete with anecdotal experiences

of daily Jesuit battles intended to upstage hechiceros. In seeking permission from the Jesuit order to publish it, he foregrounds his optimism regarding the missionaries' victories achieved among people who seemed indomitable, unconquerable, and almost without hope of salvation. These means were employed in order to drive the Prince of Darkness from the fortress that was his empire; *History of the Triumphs*, part 2, book 8, ch. 8.

32.   Their opinion was seconded by the bishop of Guadalajara, Alonso de la Mota y Escobar, in a letter to the viceroy, noting that abusive Spaniards had turned sheep into lions; May 20, 1602, Colección Pastells, Razón y Fe Library (copy in the Saint Louis Vatican Film Library), vol. 2, 597–604.

33.   *The History of the Triumphs*, see especially part 2, books 8 and 10.

34.   *The History of the Triumphs*, part 1, book 2, ch. XIII, 675.

35.   *The History of the Triumphs*, part 1, book 2, chs. VII-X; quote on 130.

36.   *The History of the Triumphs*, part 2, book 10, ch. VIII, 594.

37.   Report from Santiago Papasquiaro, Mar. 18, 1623, AGN, Jesuitas, III-16, exp. 7; carta ánua, P. Juan Florencio, May 16. 1624, AGN, Misiones, vol. 25, fols. 90–92.

38.   Carta ánua, 1626, AGN, Misiones, vol. 25, fols 164–65; carta ánua, P. Pedro Gravina, Santa María Utais, Mar. 11, 1629, AGN, Misiones, vol. 25, fols. 241–2; Traslado de los autos . . . hechos en la pacificación y asiento de los indios tepehuanes y tarahumaras, Oct.–Dec. 1635, Colección Pastells, vol. 6, 291–410.

39.   Puntos de ánua, San Pablo, June 8, 1662; AGN, Jesuitas III-15, exp. 26; see similar reports in AGN, Jesuitas I-16, exp. 17.

40.   Carta ánua, San Miguel de las Bocas, 1663; AGN, Misiones 26, fol. 180; puntos de ánua de la misión de Topia, 1663, AGN, Misiones 26, fols. 190–2; carta ánua, padre José Pascual, San Felipe, Jun. 24, 1651, AGN, Jesuitas III-15, exp. 7.

41.   Report of Juan María Ratkay, Carichic, Mar. 20, 1683, translated from the Bolton Collection in the Bancroft Library, Berkeley; copy in the University of Arizona Special Collections Library, ms. 226.

42.   Kristin D. Mann, *The Power of Song: Music and Dance in the Mission Communities of New Spain* (Palo Alto, CA: Stanford University Press, 2010).

43.   Carta ánua, padre Rodrigo de Castillo, Bocas, AGN, Misiones, vol. 26, fols. 180–1.

44.   Deeds, *Defiance and Deference*, 67–69. Respuesta del obispo Bartolomé de Escanuela, Nov. 15, 1681, Biblioteca Nacional, Mexico, Archivo Franciscano, caja 12, 200.

45.   Complaints presented to Gov. Joseph García de Salcedo, San Bartolomé, June and July 1674, Archivo de Hidalgo de Parral, Chihuahua, microfilm copy in the University of Arizona Library (hereafter cited as AHP) reel 1674d, frames 1970–99; hechos para que los indios vayan a trabajar a la hacienda de los Molinos, Topia, Jul.–Nov. 1707, AHP, reel. 1709, frames, 4–19, 81–98.

46.   Padre Tomás de Guadalajara to P. Procurador Juan de San Martín, Huejotitlán, Feb. 24, 1715, AGN, Jesuitas, IV-7, exp. b22.

47. Cusiguiriachic, Aug. 26, 1715, AGI, Guadalajara 206. Conversion or acculturation may not have been deemed advances by the Natives whose cultures were being devalued by the evangelical project.

48. Deeds, *Defiance and Deference*, 106–9.

49. Visit of Governor Don Manuel San Juan de Santa Cruz to the San Francisco de Cuellar jurisdiction, Nov.–Dec. 1716, AHP, reel 1716a, frames 283–307. See also Catherine Tracy Goode, "Corrupting the Governor: Manuel de San Juan y Santa Cruz and Power in Early Eighteenth-Century Chihuahua" (master's thesis, Northern Arizona University, 2000).

50. Que los españoles no se introduzcan a los pueblos de indios, Jan. 18, 1718, AHP, reel 1718a, frames 12–17.

51. Report of Padre Miguel Joseph González, Los Remedios, Jun. 22, 1749, Archivo de la Catedral de Durango (hereafter cited as ACD), Varios, Año 1749.

52. Silvestre Soto y Troncoso to viceroy, San Felipe el Real, Sept. 11744, DHM, 4–4, 39–47.

53. Deeds, *Defiance and Deference*, 151; Padre Ignacio Xavier de Estrada to Padre Provincial Juan Antonio de Oviedo, Temeichi, Nov. 23, 1730, AGN, Archivo Histórico de Hacienda, Temporalidades (hereafter cited as AHH, Temp.), leg. 278, exp. 7.

54. Report of Padre Andrés Javier García, Topia, ca. 1740, AGN, AHH, Temp., leg. 1126, exp. 4.

55. James C. Scott, *Weapons of the Weak: Everyday Forms of Peasant Resistance* (New Haven, CT: Yale University Press, 1985).

56. Padre Juan Antonio Balthasar to Padre Cristóbal Escobar y Llamas, Durango, Dec. 28, 1744 and Mar. 12. 1745, AGN, AHH, Temp., leg. 1126, exp. 3 and leg. 2009, exp. 20.

57. Auditor de Guerra Marqués de Altamira to viceroy, Oct. 2, 1747, AGN, AHH, Temp., leg. 278, exp. 40.

58. Exchanges on these issues between the Audiencia de Guadalajara and the king, 1739–1742, in Biblioteca Pública del Estado de Jalisco, Archivo Judicial de la Audiencia de Nueva Galicia, Civil, caja 166, exp. 3.

59. See the population chart in Deeds, *Defiance and Deference*, 127.

60. Padre General Francisco Retz to Padre Provincial, Rome, Jan. 8 and Apr. 2, 1740, Archivo Histórico de la Provincia de los Jesuitas en México, Mexico City, nos. 1307, 1308.

61. Visita documents, 1743–1745, AGN, AHH, Temp., leg. 2009, exps. 20, 47.

62. Deeds, *Defiance and Deference*, ch. 7

63. Padre Balthasar to padre Retz, Mexico City, Apr. 17, 1745, AGN, Misiones, vol. 22, fols. 382–91.

64. AGN, Misiones, vol. 22, fols. 212–39.

65. Real cédula, Dec. 4, l1747, AGN, Reales Cédulas, vol. 67, exp. 32.

66. The secularization process is described in detail in Deeds, *Defiance and Deference*, chs. 7 and 8.

67.   Padre Marcelo de León to bishop, San Ignacio, June. 30, 1749, ACD, Varios, Año 1749.

68.   Governor Mateo Antonio de Mendoza to King, Durango, May 16, 1754, AGI, Audiencia de Guadalajara, leg. 401. In the end, the Jesuits were not assigned the mission fields in California. Already experiencing hostility in Europe and Mexico from Bourbon administrators, they would be expelled from New Spain in a little more than a decade.

69.   Pérez de Ribas, *History of the Triumphs*, part 1, book 7, ch. I, 435.

70.   See note 3.

CHAPTER SEVEN

The Memory of Slavery at Saint Louis University

NATHANIEL MILLETT

AS YOU WALK ACROSS Saint Louis University's midtown campus, you are struck by a number of banners that proudly claim an impressive series of firsts. First university founded west of the Mississippi River in 1818, first medical degree granted west of the Mississippi River in 1839, and first university in a former slave state to establish an official policy admitting African American students in 1944 are three of the more notable banners. If the university wanted to, SLU could add banners that read: "first university west of the Mississippi River to own slaves, employ slaves, be built—at least in part—by slaves, and house students and their slaves," "first university west of the Mississippi River whose original campus was built on land owned in the name of a former slave woman," or "only university anywhere whose current campus is built on top of Dred Scott's first burial site."[1]

While there are many reasons why such a trio of banners will never fly above SLU's campus, this essay will examine the most important and complex of these reasons: the existence of slavery in SLU's past has been largely forgotten or misinterpreted to be so insignificant that it warrants virtually no attention by the university community, outside scholars, and the public. This act of forgetting or misremembering has been a complicated historical process that has spanned nearly a century and a half. This process has been contributed to equally by people of different political orientations and races for a host of motives and reasons, which will be explored in this essay. The current state of awareness about slavery in SLU's past contrasts starkly with developments at institutions such as Brown University, the University of Alabama, and the University of Virginia. Each of these universities has embarked on an often-painful process of coming to grips with the role of slavery or the slave trade in their respective pasts.[2]

At the outset, it should be noted clearly that SLU, unlike Brown, the University of Alabama, or UVA, was not a university that varyingly gained great wealth from the fruits of slavery or the slave trade, was built in large part by slaves, was situated squarely within a major slave society, and/or had a campus population in which slaves were a large percentage of the total population. Yet, at the same time, SLU is not Brown, the University of Alabama, or UVA in a number of other important ways. Namely, SLU is a Jesuit university that is located along the Mississippi River in a city situated squarely in a border state with a French and Spanish colonial past.[3] Furthermore, SLU's fortunes have been intimately intertwined with the broader city of St. Louis, a city that has had a complex and frequently difficult history with issues relating to race. Each of these distinctions makes the fact that slavery at SLU has been forgotten or misinterpreted both that much more remarkable and, by the same token, understandable. In an attempt to unravel this paradox, the essay will begin by briefly outlining the role of slavery at SLU before turning to an extended examination and analysis of the process by which this role has been forgotten or misinterpreted.[4] In turn, I will suggest throughout the essay that the existence of slavery at SLU has been forgotten or misinterpreted by different generations of scholars and observers due largely to given contemporary concerns about issues relating to race and SLU's public image.

The history of slavery at SLU began in 1823, when, at the invitation of Bishop William Dubourg of Louisiana, the Jesuits took control of Saint Louis College, a Latin school for boys that had been founded five years earlier. The Latin school was essentially a high school where local boys and boarders received an education that was primarily humanistic and religious in content. By 1828 the college had grown into Saint Louis University. The timing of SLU's founding occurred in the midst of an important period in the history of American slavery, the early republic, St. Louis, and western expansion.[5] This timing would shape the course of SLU's future, placing the university squarely at the center of America's torturous experience with race as the young republic careened toward the Civil War.

Officially founded by French fur traders in 1764, deep in the heart of a continent that was dominated by Native Americans, St. Louis was acquired by the United States in 1803 as part of the Louisiana Purchase.[6] Over the course of the nineteenth century, St. Louis would grow into one of the largest and most important cities in the United States. At the time of SLU's founding, the city was already a bustling center of trade that was inhabited by French- and English-speaking whites, Native Americans, slaves, and free people of color. The presence of slaves in St. Louis, and Missouri more broadly, was contentious and fateful in shaping antebellum America's debate over slavery and the expansion of the institution.[7] Most notably, the Missouri Compromise in 1819–1820 and the Dred Scott decision in 1857 intensified the national debate over slavery and sectionalism.[8]

The era of SLU's founding occurred at an equally important period in the history of the Society of Jesus. The order of priests had been founded by the Spaniard Ignatius of Loyola in the 1530s amid the tumult of the Catholic Counter-Reformation.[9] From the Order's inception, the Jesuits, with an emphasis on order, discipline, and rigorous training, excelled as teachers and scholars, at evangelization, and in apostolic ministry. Beginning not long after their founding and spanning the early modern period, Jesuits were active across Europe, the Ottoman Empire, Asia, French North America, and the Spanish Americas.[10] In the Western Hemisphere, the Jesuits worked to convert Native Americans to Catholicism while serving as vital agents of French, Spanish, and Portuguese imperial designs. This was most notable in the missions of French Canada and reductions of Brazil and Paraguay.[11] Other Jesuits, particularly in the Spanish and Portuguese empires, founded schools, colleges, and universities that were central to the intellectual life of colonial Latin America.[12] Over the course of the 1760s, the fortunes of the Jesuits changed drastically as the Order was barred from the kingdoms and empires of France, Portugal, and Spain before being formally suppressed by Clement XIV in 1773.[13] As the result of the suppression, the Jesuits were limited to the Kingdoms of Prussia and Russia with the largest concentrations to be found in Poland. In 1814, the orders of suppression were lifted, and the Jesuits once again became active in Western Europe and the Americas. This included the young United States, where the first postsuppression Jesuits soon appeared in Maryland and Louisiana.[14]

On the eve of SLU's founding, Bishop Dubourg understood well both the history and the reputation of the Jesuits and the current cultural, social, and economic status of St. Louis and the surrounding region. Based on this intertwined knowledge, Dubourg orchestrated the Jesuit move to St. Louis in the hopes that the city would become a staging ground for Jesuit missions to the Indians of the Midwest and far West. The Jesuits that were invited to St. Louis were members of the Maryland novitiate. Largely hailing from Belgium, the priests, among a variety of responsibilities, ran Georgetown College and a series of plantations, both of which utilized slave labor.[15] The Maryland Jesuits' ownership of slaves was one chapter in the long and complicated relationship of the Catholic Church and individual Catholics to slavery. This relationship is best understood in the relevant historical context. In the case of the Society of Jesus, the order—and most individual Jesuits— accepted slavery on moral, religious, legal, and economic grounds prior to, during, and after their suppression. This stance was in keeping with the position of the Catholic Church and that of the governments of most nations and empires on both sides of the revolutionary and nineteenth-century Atlantic. Thus, the Jesuit position on slavery should not be surprising. Slightly surprising, however, was the extent and frequency of Jesuit involvement with slavery in the Americas. Of particular note was Jesuit slaveholding in colonial Latin America.[16] Here, the Jesuit order owned many slaves who labored in difficult conditions on large and lucrative plantations. The wealth derived from these plantations was central to the Order's finances in presuppression Latin America. While nothing in the United States rivaled the Jesuit plantations of Latin America, most American Jesuits regarded slaves as a useful form of labor that could allow the priests more time to tend to spiritual matters. With a few exceptions for individuals, Jesuits continued to accept slavery until emancipation in the mid-nineteenth-century United States and late nineteenth-century Spanish Empire and Brazil. Thus, the slave-owning Jesuits from the Maryland novitiate who founded SLU fit squarely within both the Order's long- and short-term history with slavery.

Accordingly, the Maryland Jesuits brought half a dozen slaves with them to St. Louis in 1823.[17] Upon arriving in Missouri, the Jesuits and their slaves were sent to a farm in Florissant, Missouri, approximately fifteen miles northwest of the city. At the time, it was not unusual for schools or universities to own farmland. The land served as an investment, the produce could be sold or consumed, and the work was meant to be community- and character-building. As was the case with the farm in Florissant, faculty, students, and an array of free and unfree laborers worked the land and, sometimes, lived on the property. For the enslaved, farm life and work were less onerous than many types of labor, but they would, nonetheless, have remained acutely aware that they were human property who labored without rights for the benefit of others.

Over the next year, the farm and novitiate began to flourish, and the number of slaves grew by two with the birth of a child and the purchase of a man. In 1828 construction began on what would become the main campus of SLU in downtown St. Louis on a parcel of land known as the Connor Addition. While no direct evidence survives among the extant documents about SLU's construction, it is virtually certain that slaves—either those belonging to the Jesuits or to firms that were hired by the Jesuits—participated in the construction of the early campus and indeed any major building project prior to 1865, such was the importance of slave labor in antebellum St. Louis. What is beyond doubt is that the Connor Addition was located on land that had once been owned, at least legally, by a former slave woman named Esther who spent decades fighting various legal battles to claim properties across the region which she alleged had been unfairly taken from her.[18] By 1829 enough buildings had been constructed on the Conor Addition to start classes.

By the 1830s, the student body at SLU was expanding rapidly as was the city of St. Louis and the institution of slavery within the municipality. During this period in SLU's history, slaves continued to labor at the farm in Florissant while a number of slaves lived and worked on the downtown campus.[19] Most of the slaves on campus were housed in a single brick building and worked as servants, cooks, or laborers. Some of these slaves were periodically hired out by the Jesuits to raise cash. Likewise, slaves owned by private individuals and companies would have come and gone from campus at the direction of their owners, on personal business, or in social capacities. Conversely, SLU students, faculty, staff, and Jesuits would have been aware of the size, importance, and impact of the city's slave population while both on and off of the campus. Somewhat morbidly, the medical school relied largely on the bodies of dead slaves for dissections during this period.[20]

During the 1850s, St. Louis was thrust onto the center of the national stage of the growing sectional crisis with the Dred Scott case.[21] SLU faculty and students followed this crisis closely. For example, shortly after the 1857 Dred Scott decision, SLU's Philalethic Society debated the question: "Has Congress the right to abolish slavery in the territories?"[22] Such debates and the broader sectional tensions that they embodied were felt intensely by SLU's student body. This was because, beginning in the 1830s, SLU attracted students from both slave and free states who would have brought an array of opinions and feelings about slavery with them to St. Louis. Of particular note was the large percentage of SLU's student body that came from the Deep South and Louisiana in particular.[23] It is probable that some of these students would have been accompanied by their slaves, but, as was the case with the construction of SLU, there is no archival evidence remaining that proves this among the extant sources. Whether any of these Deep South students brought slaves with them, they came to St. Louis with pro-slavery convictions that would later lead many of them to fight and die for the Confederacy.

It was during the growing sectional crisis that the role of slavery at SLU first placed the university community in an uncomfortable position due to racialized ironies. This occurred when the Jesuits began to minister formally to the city's small free black Catholic population, which had been organized into St. Elizabeth's Parish. The parishioners of St. Elizabeth's were largely former slaves who would have been, on one hand, grateful for the Jesuits' spiritual and pastoral role in their lives. On the other hand, however, the parishioners would have been uneasy with the same priests' involvement with slavery. In many ways, the uncomfortable ironies confronted by these antebellum Jesuits as they sought to reconcile their desire to work with the city's black population with their involvement with slavery would continue to bedevil the SLU community for the next 150 years. Forgetting or reimagining slavery was the primary means by which the later SLU community sought to deal with this irony. This was a luxury that was unavailable to the antebellum Jesuits.

The Civil War impacted the city of St. Louis and SLU greatly.[24] Due in large part to the fact that Missouri was one of four border slave states that remained in the Union, tensions between unionists and secessionists and pro-slavery and anti-slavery factions ran high across the region and city. Hundreds of the city's sons—many of whom were German immigrants— joined the Union or Confederate armies while those left behind lived in a tense and emotional atmosphere. Interestingly, Civil War St. Louis's darkest episode occurred on ground that is located on SLU's modern-day campus when non-uniformed pro-Union German soldiers killed over two dozen civilian captives who were men, women, and children in what has been remembered as the Camp Jackson Affair.[25] SLU and the broader city have shown an admirable willingness to remember and commemorate the Camp Jackson Affair that contrasts starkly with the role of slavery in SLU's memory. The best explanation for the willingness to remember the Camp Jackson Affair while forgetting slavery is that the former can be recalled as an anomalous wartime incident that was perpetrated by individuals who had no connection with the university while the latter demonstrates a commitment to slavery by the university community, which has potential implications for SLU's modern-day image.

As the city and nation entered four long years of grueling war, SLU shut briefly before reopening with a greatly depleted student body. This was because nearly all of the former southern students remained at home, many fighting for the Confederacy. Remarkably, the horrors of war and increasingly powerful political winds did little to shake the SLU Jesuits' commitment to slavery and, as late as December 1862, the Order purchased a slave.[26] From moral and financial perspectives, this money was poorly spent as slavery was abolished in Missouri on 11 January 1865. Like the rest of the nation, St. Louis and SLU were now faced with the challenge of navigating a postslavery world in which race continued to matter as much as ever.

As I have outlined to this point, slavery played an important role in nearly the first forty years of SLU's existence. The slaves of SLU helped build the university on land once owned in the name of a slave woman and contributed significantly to the running of the university and its prosperity. And yet from 1865 onward, the memory of these slaves and the role that they played in SLU's early history has receded into virtual oblivion. This is, on the surface at least, remarkable for a number of reasons beyond the simple fact that slaves and slavery were important to SLU's early history. First, as a matter of Jesuit mission, SLU is committed to social justice and a belief in the humanity and dignity of every individual. Second, SLU is a major cultural, social, and economic institution within the city of St. Louis that greatly impacts the lives of tens of thousands of residents regardless of religious affiliation or race. Third, SLU's archives and records teem with evidence that any number of faculty, either Jesuit or lay, might have drawn attention to. Fourth, SLU has a strong sense of its own history and the role that the university has played in the city of St. Louis. At the same time, each of these reasons also made SLU's history with slavery particularly painful, frequently difficult to square with given current events, and a challenge to the university's image. The remainder of this essay will examine how slavery was forgotten at SLU and suggest that it was largely because of the above reasons, not in spite of them, that slavery has been forgotten or misremembered by the SLU community over the last century and a half.

The best place to start an examination of the memory and interpretation of slavery at SLU is by looking at a sampling of the many official and unofficial histories that have been written about the university since the 1870s. The authors of these histories were each in a particularly strong position to be aware of the existence of slavery at SLU and to address this history. Many of these authors have been faculty members and/or Jesuits who had access to SLU's extensive archives. In turn, the university archives and other local holdings contain many letters, diaries, and official university papers that detail the role of slavery at SLU.[27] Furthermore, these men knew the history of SLU, the city, region, and country well. Likewise, many of these men were leading scholars in the humanities and social sciences, some of whom were actively committed to the cause of racial equality. By the same token, these men's position and politics frequently made the existence of slavery at SLU a painful, embarrassing, and inconvenient topic.

The first book-length history of SLU appeared in the 1870s as part of an extended fiftieth anniversary celebration. The richly detailed *Historical Sketch of the St. Louis University*, which was written by Walter Hill, discusses the founding of SLU, Indian missions, and identifies the Civil War as an important event in SLU's history, but never once mentions slavery or slaves.[28] A generation later, SLU presented itself to the world with its very own display at the 1904 St. Louis World's Fair.²⁹ Visitors from as far away as Japan, Germany, Australia, Italy, and France could look at SLU's curriculum, reading lists, syllabi, and, of course, a carefully prepared history of the university. In keeping with the general tone of the world's fair, this history was triumphant and inspiring, filled with noble and earnest priests, pious students, and an array of laudable firsts. Race was readily evident in this history—as it was across the fair—but it was in the form of "Indians," "savages," and "redskins" being converted by the Jesuits who contributed greatly to the westward march of civilization. This history ignored the role of slavery at SLU, changing slaves into "servants." While striking at first, these omissions and alterations make sense for multiple reasons upon closer examination. First, during the era in which these initial histories of SLU were written, scholars and the public had relatively little interest in the lives of slaves and the impact of the institution on a place like St. Louis. Even if aware of the existence of slavery at SLU, such authors would have had scant interest in drawing attention to this fact at a point in time when the nation and city were attempting to heal from the trauma of the Civil War or, during the era of the World's Fair, celebrate America's triumphant ascent to the status of international power. Regardless of authorial motivations, the earliest postemancipation histories of SLU established a narrative in which slavery had never existed at the university. This narrative would shape greatly future scholarly and public perception of SLU's relationship to slavery. Furthermore, this narrative would prove to be particularly powerful and alluring to future chroniclers and observers who sought to portray SLU as enjoying a relatively consistent history of pursuing racial justice. The allure and power of this narrative increased both with time and during periods in which SLU's campus and the city of St. Louis were enveloped by particularly racially charged atmospheres.

At first glance, the 1938 publication of Gilbert Garraghan, S.J.'s, massive three-volume *The Jesuits of the Middle United States* appeared to represent a shift in the treatment of slavery in SLU's past. Garraghan's history mentions, even if just in passing, that in 1829 SLU owned two slaves who were transferred from the farm in Florissant to the downtown campus.³⁰ For decades, however, this would be the sole scholarly mention of slavery at SLU for a number of reasons. Garraghan was a good historian who based his work on exhaustive archival research. More importantly, he was not from St. Louis, nor was he employed by SLU. Instead, Garraghan taught at Loyola University in Chicago. Thus, it was easier for the detached Jesuit to present his findings in a dispassionate and scholarly manner without having to worry about the implications of such a revelation in a way that was impossible for members of the SLU and St. Louis community. At the same time, however, Garraghan's publication makes it clear that future scholars interested in the history of SLU would have been aware of the existence of slavery at the university such was the impact of *The Jesuits of the Middle United States*. Thus, Garraghan's work strengthens the argument that the role of slavery at SLU was willfully marginalized or overlooked by many future scholars and observers.

Published just two years after Garraghan's history, *The Truth About St. Louis University* by Claude Heithaus demonstrates clearly a desire to avoid the topic of slavery at SLU.[31] Despite the titillating title, Heithaus's history— while providing an extended account of the university archives and a number of specific collections and their content, which would have included many references to slaves—makes no mention of slavery. This omission is particularly remarkable and informative given Heithaus's views on race and his personal role in SLU's history, not to mention the recent publication of Garraghan's work. Four years later, Heithaus delivered a radical homily at the college church in which he attacked the institution of segregation broadly and SLU's refusal to admit black students more specifically in deeply impassioned language.[32] The sermon began with the bold proclamation that "it is a surprising and rather bewildering fact, that in what concerns justice for the Negro, the Mohammedans and the atheists are more Christ-like than many Christians." Heithaus went on to proclaim that "the Blessed Trinity is pleased, and angels in heaven rejoice, when a Negro is united with Our Lord in Holy Communion" and that "Jesus denounced injustice in the highest places, and He threatened the oppressors of the downtrodden with hell-fire; but some people say that the Society of Jesus should connive at a wrong that cries out to heaven for vengeance." In the sermon the priest invoked "Cromwell and his self-righteous bullies, who proved their superiority over the defenseless white Catholics of Ireland by selling them into slavery with the Negroes of the West Indies," chided "Catholics, who do not know the history of this country," argued that "scholars know no color," and reminded the congregation that "for 125 years this University has been operated for the greater glory of God, and for that sole reason the bounty of God has kept it in existence. . . . And now I ask you Catholic students . . . will you not do something positive right now to make reparation for the suffering which this prejudice has inflicted upon millions of your fellow Christians?"

Heithaus's speech was a bombshell at SLU and in St. Louis more broadly. The sermon was instrumental in the integration of the university and sparked a vigorous conversation on race on the campus and across the city. Despite the fact that Heithaus's sermon discussed history, memory, slavery, racial justice, and the role of SLU, the priest chose not to broach the subject of SLU and slavery here or in any of his other writings. Heithaus clearly felt that mentioning SLU's relationship with slavery would complicate his task and steal much of his moral and rhetorical thunder. Indeed, few if any other combinations of topics without mentioning slavery at SLU could have better illustrated Heithaus's intentional decision to avoid the subject for fear of presenting SLU and the Catholic Church as having anything less than an unbroken history of pursuing racial justice. Nonetheless, Heithaus's sermon and its perceived consequences would factor greatly into the memory of the SLU community and much of the broader population of St. Louis for decades to come, something which the chapter will return to later.

Heithaus's sermon and the move toward integration did little to stimulate interest in the role of slavery in SLU's past. Indeed, if anything, postintegration SLU seemed committed to the willful forgetting or marginalization of slavery as the university and city walked a tightrope of racial tension, massive white flight, and declining economic fortunes. Strong evidence of this was published just a few years after Heithaus's speech in the *Diamond Jubilee History of Saint Elizabeth's Parish*.[33] As was discussed earlier, Saint Elizabeth's Parish was founded in the 1850s for St. Louis's black Catholics. It was located close to the university and ministered to by the Jesuits from SLU. Saint Elizabeth's first parishioners included former slaves, some of whom would have been owned by or labored at SLU. By the 1920s and 1930s, the Jesuits associated with the parish were radicals in questions of race and had founded the *St. Elizabeth's Chronicle*—a local and, later, national quarterly devoted to issues of race and Catholic social justice. The most notable of these SLU Jesuits associated with Saint Elizabeth's was William Markoe. Markoe was

deeply committed to racial equality and wrote numerous articles in the
St. Elizabeth's Chronicle with titles such as "The Negroe's Viewpoint," "The
Negroe's Progress," "Race and Religious Prejudice," and "The Catholic
Church and Slavery."[34] Markoe's writings attacked bigotry, racism, and Jim
Crow segregation. In the process, the priest called for religious, educational,
and legal equality for blacks in fiery language that would have shocked many
in Depression-era America. Markoe, who literally stood face-to-face with the
legacy of slavery at SLU when he met a former SLU bondsman in 1930 and
listened closely to his tales of life as a slave at SLU, began "The Catholic
Church and Slavery" with the sentence, "Slavery is a dead issue. Its wound
however, still rankles in the breasts of intellectual colored folks." Nowhere in
the article, which ranges from ancient Rome to Latin America to the
American Civil War, does Markoe hint that SLU once owned slaves or that
the Catholic Church had anything but an admirable history of struggling
against slavery that fit neatly with his present work for racial equality. SLU's
history of slavery, on the other hand, would have been embarrassing and
uncomfortable for Markoe, whose current parishioners included some
descendants of these slaves. Likewise, admitting that SLU once owned slaves
would also have undermined the effectiveness of one of Markoe's favorite
claims: that American blacks and Catholics had a common history of
oppression at the hands of white protestants. Accordingly, the *Diamond
Jubilee History of St. Elizabeth's Parish* made no mention of slavery.

SLU's firsthand experience with the Civil Rights Movement and 1960s
protests did little to increase awareness of the university's history with
slavery. If anything, this deeply racially charged era presented new obstacles
to the accurate remembering of slavery at SLU because this history was
potentially more uncomfortable than ever for the university community.
This era was a challenging time for the city of St. Louis, which had seen its
economy and population decline rapidly beginning in the 1950s.[35] Racial
tensions were intense in a city that was numerically dominated by African
Americans who frequently contended with poverty and a lack of adequate
social services. SLU's midtown campus, with its largely white and middle-
class student body, contrasted starkly with the surrounding neighborhoods.
In the late 1960s and early 1970s racial tensions boiled over at SLU as a small
black student body began a series of protests. The most dramatic events

occurred in the spring of 1969, when civil rights protestors occupied Ritter Hall. In a formal letter to the Board of Trustees, a coalition of black students proclaimed: "We, the black students of Saint Louis University are aware and have unassailable proof that racism on campus is rampant and that the administration is aware and does not act against it."[36] Later, the Association of Black Collegians made ten demands of SLU, which included a "program for incorporating Black culture into the various activities of Busch Center," "that there be more courses related to Black culture in these academic departments; English, History, Psychology, Sociology, Philosophy, Political Science, Religion, Economics, History [history was actually included twice on the list]," and "that the Urban Affairs Department involve more black people in policy making positions. That the Urban Affairs Department become more relevant to the Black Community."[37] Later demands reiterated the need to expand SLU's black history offerings and that these classes be taught by an African American because "the accomplishments of the black man in our country have been ignored and downgraded, and we feel that a black instructor would more earnestly and diligently present these achievements."[38] As a result of this demand and general climate on campus, the history department launched "Topics in US History: Black America" in the fall of 1969 and began a search for a black professor. [39]

And yet, even with discussions about SLU and race being so publicly and passionately debated, few if anybody thought it worth mentioning that the university had a history with slavery. Three facts illustrate clearly this disconnect between past and present. First was the demand by the student protestors that more black cultural events occur in the Busch Student Center with no apparent awareness that this building stood on top of Dred Scott's first grave.[40] Second, Walter Ong's public discussion of "Some Semantics of Racism," which was a centerpiece in the administration's efforts to reach out to black students, was a tremendously sophisticated analysis of racially loaded language and its negative impact on daily life at SLU, but made no mention of the role of African Americans in SLU's past.[41] This was particularly notable because Ong was one of twentieth-century America's most original and sophisticated thinkers whose theories challenged how scholars understand culture, communication, and history.[42] Finally, History 149-H, A Course in the Negro in American History, which was taught by an

African American and sought to serve as an "exploration of the background of the American Negro as found in the culture of Africa, Spain, France, Ancient Greece, Ancient Rome, Russia, Germany, and Japan," made no mention of the existence of slavery at SLU.[43]

Despite the fact that race, history, justice, memory, and identity were at the core of SLU's experience with the Civil Rights Movement—topics that made the university's history with slavery particularly relevant—over 100 years had now passed since the last of SLU's slaves were freed. In the intervening century, conventional wisdom had come to accept that SLU had no meaningful history with slavery. St. Louis's racial climate and SLU's emotional experience with the Civil Rights Movement made the weight of this history even greater as many of the people who were in the best position to uncover and address this history would be reluctant to exacerbate tensions and undermine SLU's image by drawing attention to the university's experience with slavery. This argument is supported further by the fact that post-civil-rights-era official histories of SLU, the Missouri Province, and Jesuits in the Midwest continued to ignore the role of slavery in the university's past. For example, 1968's *Better the Dream: Saint Louis: University and Community, 1818–1968* noted that on the eve of the Civil War, "Missouri was a peninsula of slavery stretching into a sea of free states" before discussing the impact of the war on SLU and the role that SLU alumni played in the conflict.[44] Despite the fact that the meticulously detailed and well-researched book, which ran to 445 pages, was authored by the longtime SLU history professor William Faherty, S.J., it made no other mention of slavery nor did it even hint that the university had been involved with the institution.

Faherty's later writings are informative and demonstrate the difficultly that even the most knowledgeable and progressive members of the SLU community had in acknowledging the existence, extent, and nature of slavery in the university's past. Indeed, as will be discussed below, in the 1990s, various media outlets interviewed Faherty about SLU's integration because he had come to be identified as the expert on the history of race at the university. In 1977 Faherty published *The Religious Roots of Black Catholics in St. Louis* with no mention of slavery at SLU.[45] *Jesuit Roots in Mid-America*, published in 1980, is notable because it made passing reference to slavery at SLU, but did so with a considerable license.[46] Faherty starts encouragingly by admitting that the Maryland Jesuits had arrived in St. Louis with "three young Negro married couples, Tom and Polly, Moses and Nancy, and Isaac and Suzzy," who had been donated by a cousin of Charles Carroll.[47] He then proceeds to describe life at the farm in Florissant as something akin to an interracial commune where priests and slaves worked the fields together with little regard for race or status. Faherty even describes how the head of the Jesuits at the farm, "Van Quickenborne liked to work with the slaves on the rich acres in front of the Seminary buildings. . . . On such occasions, the slaves would come into his room to wake him and find their morning chores."[48] Elsewhere Faherty asserts that "another divergence of viewpoint arose out of the reliance on slave labor to carry on the religious venture . . . the Florissant Jesuits did not traffic in human beings, nor separate families. They referred to the blacks as 'servants' never as 'slaves.' The younger Jesuits did not approve of the slave system." Faherty then argues that prior to emancipation in Missouri, "finding a situation of true freedom for blacks in rural Missouri presented growing difficulties as the slave question grew more embattled." The author suggested that freed Missouri slaves faced the strong possibility of being kidnapped and sold back into slavery in the Deep South before noting that the SLU Jesuits were also concerned with the slaves' spiritual welfare. According to Faherty, contemporary Jesuit beliefs held that "those freeing slaves made sure that the blacks had an environment where they could readily practice their Catholic faith, recognizing implicitly that blacks, even when enslaved, had full spiritual equality with whites."[49] These statements were the last on the subject of slavery in *Jesuit Roots*, which made no mention of the institution after 1824.

Faherty's treatment of the nature of slavery at SLU demonstrates the extent to which the institution, when remembered at all, had been reimagined into a more serviceable narrative that might be prepared to admit grudgingly that the institution had existed at the farm in Florrisant for half a decade, but was benevolent to the point of being virtually unrecognizable as slavery. The reality was that, regardless of terminology, the Jesuits supported slavery, bought and sold slaves, and utilized slave labor until the day the state of Missouri forced the university to emancipate its slaves. Furthermore, there is no evidence to support Faherty's dual argument that the SLU Jesuits did not emancipate their slaves because they were worried about their safety and salvation. Nonetheless, these claims were reprinted in 1988 in *Jesuit Roots and Pioneer Heroes of the Middle West*, which was published by the St. Stanislaus Jesuit Historical Museum in Florissant, and co-written by Faherty and five other authors.[50] Twenty years later, Faherty's *Saint Louis University, a Concise History (1818–2008)*—the most recent extended treatment of SLU's history—had returned to not mentioning the existence of slavery at SLU.[51] Ultimately, Faherty's writings, which spanned nearly half a century, failed to describe accurately the role of slavery at SLU due to a pair of intertwined and mutually reinforcing reasons. First, by the time Faherty began to write, there existed a strong and appealing narrative about slavery and SLU that dominated the secondary works and institutional memory on which the Jesuit based his scholarship. Second, Faherty's desire for SLU to be seen as a progressive beacon of racial justice and inclusion in the frequently choppy seas of twentieth-century St. Louis race relations made the priest less likely to rigorously pursue archival evidence of slavery at SLU that he would have come across in the course of his work. Combined, these reasons led Faherty away from more accurately describing the nature of slavery at SLU.

Faherty was not the only chronicler of SLU and the Jesuits to shy away from discussing the role of slavery and the university during and after the Civil Rights Movement. In the 1970s, John Francis Bannon, S.J., published *The Missouri Province S. J. A Mini-History*, which identified the same three black couples accompanying the Jesuits to Missouri but made no mention of them being slaves.[52] Later, under the suggestive bold-faced heading "**The Jesuits and the Blacks**," Bannon noted that "from the very early days the Jesuits of Missouri were acutely aware of the pitiable condition of the blacks, especially of the Free Negroes in the Midwestern cities. For some years, however, they simply did not have the manpower to meet this apostolic challenge in formal fashion" before the 1858 founding of St. Elizabeth's Parish.[53] There was no mention of slavery here or anywhere else in the volume, however. Bannon, a historian of the Spanish Borderlands who also had a keen interest in local history and knew the content of SLU's archives well, was aware that people of color played a major role in North American history and that of SLU. Indeed, large portions of *The Missouri Province* were devoted to Native American history. Furthermore, Bannon's interest in the university's past was so intense that he published a chronicle of the history department entitled *The Department of History, Saint Louis University, 1925–1973: An Historical Sketch.*[54] Likewise his knowledge of the university archives was so deep that Bannon compiled *Notes for an Academic History of Saint Louis University: Suggested by the Record of Degrees Awarded during its 163 Years of Service* based on exhaustive work in SLU's special collections.[55]

A 1970 speech by Bannon further complicates efforts to understand why he did not address the history of slavery at SLU more directly. The speech was titled "A New All-University Award Proposed."[56] In the speech, Bannon claimed to have recently become aware that the Board of Trustees was planning to create the "Neville Chamberlain Award." According to Bannon, "the prime qualification for consideration will be a supreme disregard, by choice or ignorance, of the lessons of history" as well as a lack of courage, common sense, and decency. The speech foresaw the biggest problem with the award being the overwhelming number of qualified recipients and the sheer expense of providing the winners with their prizes. Tellingly, Bannon suggested that the prizes could be paid for by cutting "proper salary increments for dedicated leaders guiding and abetting the despotism and tyranny of militant minorities against the rights and preferences of the majority." On one hand, the sheer irreverence of the speech makes it clear that Bannon had little regard for upsetting the SLU administration or casting a negative light on the school more generally. In this light, Bannon seems like a man who would not think twice about presenting the university with unpleasant truths from its past. On the other hand, Bannon makes very clear his displeasure with the recent civil rights protests that had rocked the SLU campus, forcing the university to address questions of race. This is not to suggest that Bannon was a racist; however, his feelings toward the movement may well have discouraged him from more fully exploring and publicizing the role of slavery at SLU.

Documentary film must be added as another medium that overlooked the history of slavery at SLU. In celebration of SLU's 1968 sesquicentennial, a documentary history of the university titled *Knowledge and the Future of Man* was produced by the university. The primary purpose of the well-produced film was to serve as a recruiting tool for the university. Accordingly, its content was little different from that of the printed official histories of the university, and it made no mention of slavery at SLU. Interestingly, SLU's student paper printed an impassioned review of the film that praised its technical proficiency, but criticized it for offering "no challenge," never going "beyond the conventional," and presenting an image of SLU where "everything is neat, ordered, and in its place. The problem being that on college campuses in general, and even at St. Louis University, things are not quite that tidy."[57] At least in the mind of one earnest young journalist, the official story of SLU's history seemed whitewashed and unsatisfying.

Over the years, SLU's curriculum has come tantalizingly close to or maddeningly far from addressing the role of slavery in the university's past. Beginning in the 1960s when course materials survive, SLU's departments of history, theology, and American studies offered an array of classes that might have dealt more extensively with this past including a history special topics course entitled The Jesuits.[58] The course was team-taught by professors from the history, theology, philosophy, and English departments and addressed slavery on days devoted to Jesuits in Latin America and the Paraguay Reductions, but not, apparently, during the discussion of Jesuits in the Midwest. The 1982 course Social History of the United States focused on race and local history.[59] Students had to write two papers for this class: first, a family history, and second, a social history of St. Louis between 1865 and 1912. Unfortunately, these dates would have led students away from the topic of SLU and slavery. A couple of years later, The History of St. Louis was offered.[60] The course broke the history of St. Louis into eighteen topics and a series of subtopics. Not until week 16 (St. Louis Blacks: Emancipation and After) and 17 (St. Louis Blacks: 1915–1970) was the history of African Americans in St. Louis addressed in the course. The dates of the coverage obviously meant that the topic of slavery at SLU was not addressed in the class, however. A pair of interesting urban/architectural history courses titled The Architectural Heritage of St. Louis and Henry Shaw and St. Louis Parks: A Study of Urban Development, Environmentalism, and Social History of the 19th Century both provided students with detailed views into the physical and built environment of nineteenth-century St. Louis, but appear to have skipped the role that slaves played in these spaces.[61] The syllabus for Special Topics: Jesuit Education at Saint Louis University stated that the course's first goal was to "address the history of Jesuit education at Saint Louis University in the context of Jesuit higher education from its inception."[62] Yet the class used two textbooks that largely ignored the history of slavery at SLU. A pair of 1983 graduate classes were ideally suited to finally unlock the history of slavery at SLU. First, St Louis in the Westward Movement: Myths and Realities required students to write a primary source-based research paper that addressed a little-known topic in St. Louis history using the "more than adequate" local resources, which included "the University Library, Washington University, the Missouri Historical Society, the Jefferson National Expansion Memorial Archives, the Archives of the Saint Louis Archdiocese, the Mercantile Library and many others."[63] Second, Introduction to Archival Administration used SLU's archives to familiarize students with cutting-edge archival technology.[64] The very detailed syllabus made it clear that students in this course would gain both a deep familiarity with archival theory and practices and the content of SLU's archives. Unfortunately, there is no existing evidence that either course addressed the history of slavery at SLU. In the case of curriculum and the classroom, I think the omission of slavery at SLU was largely the role of a century of historical gravity. That is, by the 1960s, when the historical profession became more attuned to such topics, a strong alternate narrative had been constructed and accepted in which slavery had not existed at SLU or was so unimportant as to not warrant attention. At the same time, this was a convenient narrative that suited the SLU community and easily became conventional wisdom. This narrative dominated histories of the university, making scholarly inquiries into the role of slavery at SLU seem in equal measure pointless and potentially incendiary depending on the given racial climate on campus and in the city.

Tellingly, SLU was not always so reluctant to embrace its past struggles with issues relating to race. Most notably, in the mid-1990s the administration, students, alumni, and local media devoted much energy to celebrating the fiftieth anniversary of integration at SLU. Father Heithaus's radical homily received particular praise. In the 1994 narrative—which is largely unchanged today—Heithaus's speech was remembered as the spark that lit the fuse of a fairly seamless integration in which a handful of old bigots were overwhelmed by the forces of change and justice. According to a 1994 article in the St. Louis Review, which extensively quoted Faherty in his role as historian of SLU, "the process toward integration at SLU caught fire with Heithaus' [sic] words."[65]

A few months later, the *St. Louis Post Dispatch* ran an article with the headline "SLU Celebrates Its Pioneering of Intergration."[66] The piece focused on the experience of Walter Douglas, an African American who graduated from SLU in 1948 before detailing the array of events that the university had planned to commemorate integration. Less than a year later, SLU's official magazine, *Universitas: The Magazine of Saint Louis University*, ran an extended piece entitled "History Lessons."[67] The piece, which also quoted Faherty extensively, provides a standard treatment of the impact of Heithaus's speech before profiling some of the first black students to be admitted to SLU. The profiles echoed those contained in a special inlay included in the 11 February 1994 *University News* with a title that read "Fifty Years Ago" over a picture of Fredda Witherspoon, an African American woman who graduated from SLU shortly after integration.[68] Witherspoon, like Douglas, recounted a few mild cases of resentment from white classmates and faculty, but claimed that the overwhelming majority of SLU faculty and students were welcoming. Witherspoon and Douglas both proceeded to wax glowingly about the opportunities afforded by their SLU degrees. "Fifty Years Ago," once again, quoted Faherty.

The events surrounding integration were much more complex and frequently uglier than any of these pieces suggest. The reality of 1944 included Heithaus's banishment to Nebraska, the vitriolic condemnation of the bishop of St. Louis, and a difficult process of integrating black students that was so incomplete twenty-five years later that civil rights protestors argued that SLU's black students were subjected to intense racism. However, the narrative of Jesuits fighting nobly against Jim Crow a decade before *Brown v. Board of Education* is an appealing and useful one both for the university and for much of the city. In very clear terms, this narrative places SLU on the moral, just, and right side of history. Conversely the idea of SLU having a history with slavery—or indeed a less-than-easy process of integration or struggles over civil rights, for example—is the opposite and forces SLU to cede some of the moral high ground. Maintaining this moral high ground—especially when race is involved—is particularly important to SLU when one bears in mind the university's frequently uneasy relationship with the city of St. Louis. Since the 1950s, SLU has found itself in an often-difficult position of trying to balance an admirable commitment to social and racial justice while often butting heads with the local African American community over issues such as campus expansion, minority underrepresentation, and claims of racism. The backdrop to this delicate balancing act has been massive white flight, urban decay, and intense de facto segregation. The net result has been a deeply charged racial climate, which scholars, students, and Jesuits have been reluctant to exacerbate by drawing attention to the darker ingredients in SLU's history with race.

Recent events serve to underscore vividly these points and emphasize the extent to which these issues are as alive today as ever before. During the fall of 2014 hundreds of protestors marched on the SLU campus. Many of the protestors turned the march into an occupation, living in tents on the campus for weeks. The protests were sparked by the killings of Vonderrit Myers and Michael Brown and were based on the larger belief that St. Louis's African American community suffered at the hands of widespread police brutality and institutional racism, which had resulted in a lack of opportunity and dire standard of living for much of the city's black population. SLU was targeted by protestors because, as has been detailed throughout this essay, the university is a major cultural, educational, economic, and social force in the city of St. Louis, but one that is overwhelmingly white and middle-class in an area that is populated largely by lower-income African Americans. The protests, which remained peaceful, led to a tense atmosphere on campus as parents, students, the local population, and the protestors frequently disagreed on an array of topics. Throughout these events, SLU's president and administration built on decades of tradition when they reminded the protestors and larger community about SLU's historical commitment to racial justice, placing great emphasis on the integration of SLU and Heithaus's sermon. An equally telling example of history repeating itself came when the protestors submitted a series of demands that bore a striking resemblance to those made in the late 1960s by civil rights activists during SLU's last period of extended unrest. As a result of negotiations between the protestors and SLU's president, the so-called Clock Tower Accords were signed in late 2014. Whether or not the administration's promises to expand African American studies course offerings, increase SLU's black student body, and tackle racial injustice will increase awareness about the university's involvement with slavery remains to be seen.

These recent events grow directly out of a century and a half history that explains why SLU's memory of its own involvement in slavery is so hazy when the campus archives and libraries abound with evidence of this role, when the university has employed excellent scholars who have greatly advanced humanistic and social scientific knowledge, and when the Jesuit order more broadly has been fairly honest and forthright in discussing their past with slavery. This is not to suggest that SLU has consciously sought to cover up the role of slavery in its past. Rather, bringing the topic up in the midst of the Jim Crow era, during the Civil Rights Movement, or in the present day as SLU finds itself front and center in events related to national civil rights protests, is difficult especially when a useful alternative narrative had developed by the early twentieth century. Given the renewed vigor of discussions about race on campus, perhaps it is now time for slavery to factor more prominently in SLU's memory to an extent that reflects historical reality.

Notes

1.   Walker Gollar, "Saint Louis University Slaves," *Missouri Historical Review* 105 (2011): 125–39 is the sole extended treatment of the history of slavery at Saint Louis University. For the case of Ester, a former slave woman who claimed to have owned the land on which SLU was built, see Julie Winch, *The Clamorgans: One Family's History of Race in America* (New York: Hill and Wang, 2011), ch. 2. On the death, memory, and legacy of Dred Scott in St. Louis, see Adam Arenson, "Dred Scott versus the Dred Scott Case. The History and Memory of a Signal Moment in American Slavery, 1857–2007," in David Thomas Konig, Paul Finkelman, and Christopher Alan Bracey, eds., *The Dred Scott Case: Historical and Contemporary Perspectives on Race and Law* (Athens: Ohio University Press, 2010), 25–46. Other Jesuit universities such as Georgetown University, Spring Hill College, and Loyola University in Baltimore would have been involved with slavery, as were various Catholic universities, seminaries, and schools that were located in slave states. An examination of slavery and its memory at any or all of these institutions would, of course, be important and valuable. This essay, however, is a case study of SLU that allows for a systematic analysis and detailed historical contextualization that might be less effective if examining the role of slavery at multiple or all Catholic educational institutions in former slave states. Likewise, as will be detailed throughout this article, given the importance of the city of St. Louis to the history of nineteenth- and twentieth-century America and, in turn, the role of SLU within the city, a case study of the university leaves readers with much to consider.

2.   In the past decade or so there has been a steady increase in interest about the

role of slavery in American universities. This interest has manifested itself in various forms, including scholarly monographs, essays, conferences, websites, inquiries by journalists, official reports, and student projects. Craig Wilder, *Ebony and Ivory: Race, Slavery, and the Troubled History of America's University* (New York: Bloomsbury Press, 2013) is the best extended treatment of the topic. In February of 2011, Emory University hosted a conference entitled Slavery and the University: Histories and Legacies. In 2003, Brown University commissioned a Steering Committee on Slavery and Justice, followed a decade later by the University of Virginia's Commission on Slavery and the University, and in February 2014, the University of Alabama's library presented the exhibit Unchaining Alabama: An Exhibition of Student Research on Slavery at the University.

3.   For colonial and nineteenth-century St. Louis, see: Adam Arenson, The *Great Heart of the Republic: St. Louis and the Cultural Civil War* (Cambridge, MA: Harvard University Press, 2011); Patricia Cleary, *The World, the Flesh, and the Devil: A History of Colonial St. Louis* (Columbia, MO: University of Missouri Press, 2011); and James Primm, *Lion of the Valley: St. Louis, Missouri, 1764–1980*, 3rd ed. (St. Louis: Missouri Historical Society Press, 1998). The collected essays in George Traub, ed., *Jesuit Education Reader* (Chicago: Loyola Press, 2008) are the best introduction to Jesuit education.

4.   It is important to note at the outset that the primary purpose of this essay is to present a discussion of the memory of slavery at Saint Louis University, not to serve as an exhaustive history of the institution of slavery at Saint Louis University. Likewise, the essay does not seek to provide an exhaustive or comparative history of the Jesuit order and its relationship to slavery across the Americas. The essay is a case study of historical memory.

5.   Daniel Walker Howe, *What Hath God Wrought: The Transformation of America, 1815–1848* (New York: Oxford University Press, 2009) is a magisterial treatment of American history during this era.

6.   For the history of St. Louis and the surrounding region prior to 1803, see: Cleary, *The World, the Flesh, and the Devil*; Kathleen Duval, *Native Ground: Indians and Colonists in the Heart of the Continent* (Philadelphia: University of Pennsylvania Press, 2007); M. J. Morgan, *Land of Big Rivers: French and Indian Illinois, 1699–1778* (Edwardsville, IL: Southern Illinois University Press, 2010); and Primm, *Lion of the Valley*. Peter Kastor, *Nation's Crucible: The Louisiana Purchase and the Creation of America* (New Haven, CT: Yale University Press, 2004) is the best single volume on the Louisiana Purchase.

7.   A tiny sampling of the best works on Antebellum American slavery includes: Ira Berlin, *Generations of Captivity: A History of African-American Slaves* (Cambridge, MA: Belknap Press, 2004); David Brion Davis, *Problem of Slavery in the Age of Emancipation* (New York: Knopf, 2014); Walter Johnson, *River of Dark Dreams: Slavery and Empire in the Cotton Kingdom* (Cambridge, MA: Belknap Press, 2013); Matthew Mason, *Slavery and Politics in the Early American Republic* (Chapel Hill, NC: University of North Carolina Press, 2006); and Adam Rothman, *Slave Country: American*

Expansion and the Origins of the Deep South (Cambridge, MA: Harvard University Press, 2007).

8. The Missouri Compromise occurred when Missouri applied to join the United States as a slaveholding state. To maintain a balance in Congress between slave and free states, Maine was admitted to the union as a free state at the same time. Likewise, a line along the boundary of the territory acquired in the Louisiana Purchase was extended west to divide future free (to the north) and slave (to the south) territories and states. The debate surrounding the admission of Missouri was contentious and represented one of the first and most serious sectional rifts in the young United States. See Mason, *Slavery and Politics*, ch. 8 for the Missouri Comprise. In the Dred Scott decision, the Supreme Court held that African Americans were property with no rights associated with citizenship. According to the court, the federal government thus had no right to regulate the institution in the western territories. The decision was deeply divisive and factored into increasingly acrimonious sectional tensions, which would soon lead to the Civil War. For Dred Scott, see: Don Fehrenbacher, *Dred Scott Case: Its Significance in American Law and Politics* (New York: Oxford University Press, 2001); David Thomas Konig, Paul Finkelman, and Christopher Alan Bracey, eds., *Dred Scott Case* (Athens: Ohio University Press, 2010); and Earl M. Maltz, *Dred Scott and the Politics of Slavery* (Lawrence: University Press of Kansas, 2007).

9. John O'Malley, *The First Jesuits* (Cambridge, MA: Harvard University Press, 1995) is an excellent history of the early Jesuits. Thomas Worcester, ed., *Cambridge Companion to the Jesuits* (Cambridge: Cambridge University Press, 2008) is a strong overview of the Order's broader history.

10. See, for example, Liam Brockey, *Journey to the East: The Jesuit Mission to China, 1579–1724* (Cambridge, MA: Belknap, 2009); Luke Clossey, *Salvation and Globalization in the Early Jesuit Missions* (Cambridge: Cambridge University Press, 2011); Allan Greer, *Mohawk Saint: Catherine Tekawitha and the Jesuits* (Oxford: Oxford University Press, 2006); Tracy Leavelle, *Catholic Calumet: Colonial Conversions in French and Indian North America* (Philadelphia: University of Pennsylvania Press, 2011).

11. See Takao Abe, *Jesuit Mission to New France: A New Interpretation in the Light of the Earlier Jesuit Experience in France* (Leiden: Brill, 2011); Carole Blackburn, *Harvest of Souls: Jesuit Missions and Colonialism in North America, 1632–1650* (Montreal: McGill-Queen's University Press, 2000); Thomas Cohen, "Racial and Ethnic Minorities in the Society of Jesus" in Thomas Worcester, ed., *The Cambridge Companion to the Jesuits* (Cambridge: Cambridge University Press, 2008); Barbara Ganson, *Guarani Under Spanish Rule in the Rio de la Plata* (Palo Alto, CA: Stanford University Press, 2003); Allan Greer, *The Jesuit Relations: Natives and Missionaries in Seventeenth-Century North America* (New York: Bedford/St. Martin's, 2000); C. J. McNaspy and J. M. Blanch, *Lost Cities of Paraguay: Art and Architecture of the Jesuit Reductions, 1607–1767* (Chicago: Loyola Press, 1982).

12. See Christopher Chapple, ed., *The Jesuit Tradition in Education and Missions: A 450-Year Perspective* (Scranton, PA: University of Scranton Press, 1993); Joseph

Gagliamo and Charles Ronan, eds., *Jesuit Encounters in the New World: Jesuit Chroniclers, Geographers, Educators, and Missionaries in the Americas, 1549–1767* (Rome: Instititutum Historicum, 1997); O'Malley, *The First Jesuits*, ch. 6; and Traub, S.J., ed., *A Jesuit Education Reader*.

13. Wright, "The Suppression and Restoration" in *The Cambridge Companion to the Jesuits* is a good overview of the Suppression era.

14. The best single volume history of the Jesuits in the United States is Raymond Schroth, *The American Jesuits: A History* (New York: New York University Press, 2007).

15. Thomas Murphy, *Jesuit Slaveholding in Maryland, 1717–1838* (New York: Routledge, 2001) examines Jesuit slaveholding in the Maryland Novitiate prior to and after the suppression. In recent years, the faculty and students at Georgetown University have explored the role of slavery in their university's past. The Jesuit Plantation Project can be found at: http://units.georgetown.edu/americanstudies/jpp/.

16. See Dauril Alden, *The Making of an Enterprise: The Society of Jesus in Portugal, Its Empire, and Beyond, 1540–1750* (Palo Alto, CA: Stanford University Press, 1996); Nicholas Cushner, *Jesuit Ranches and the Agrarian Development of Colonial Argentina, 1650–1767* (Albany, NY: SUNY Press, 1983), ch. 5; and Cushner, *Lords of the Land: Sugar, Wine, and Jesuit Estates of Coastal Peru* (Albany: SUNY Press, 1980), 87–101.

17. Gollar, "Saint Louis University Slaves," 126.

18. Winch, *Clamorgans*, ch. 2.

19. Gollar, "Saint Louis University Slaves," 134.

20. Frazier, *Slavery and Crime in Missouri, 1773–1865*, 45.

21. See note 7 for the importance of the Dred Scott case.

22. Quoted in Arenson, *Great Heart of the Republic*, 95–96.

23. William Faherty, *Better the Dream* (St. Louis, MO: Saint Louis University Press, 1968), 44–45.

24. See Arenson, *Great Heart of the Republic* and Gerteis, *Civil War St. Louis*.

25. James Covington, "The Camp Jackson Affair, 1861" (master's thesis, Saint Louis University, 1943) is still the most extended treatment of the Camp Jackson Affair. In May 2011, the SLU history department led a ceremony at the site of the massacre to commemorate the 150th anniversary of the Camp Jackson Affair.

26. Gollar, "Saint Louis University Slaves," 137.

27. More information about SLU's archives can be found at: http://libraries.slu.edu/special_collections/archives_manuscripts. Other relevant local archives include the Midwest Jesuit Archives, http://libraries.slu.edu/special_collections/archives_manuscripts; the Saint Louis Mercantile Library, http://www.umsl.edu/mercantile/; and the State Historical Society of Missouri Saint Louis Research Center, http://shs.umsystem.edu/about/stlouis.shtml.

28. Walter Hill, *Historical Sketch of the St. Louis University: The Celebration of its Fiftieth Anniversary or Golden Jubilee on June 24, 1879* (St. Louis, MO: Patrick Fox, 1879).

29. Saint Louis University Historical Records [Doc Rec 1] Series 14: Louisiana Purchase Exposition (World's Fair).

30. Gilbert Garraghan, *Jesuits of the Middle United States. Volume I* (Chicago: Loyola Press, 1983 original 1938), 291.

31. Claude Heithaus, *Truth about St. Louis University* (St. Louis, MO: Saint Louis University Press, 1940).

32. One of the many places that the text of the sermon can be found is in the 11 February 1944 issue of *The University News*.

33. *Diamond Jubilee St. Elizabeth's Parish.*

34. "The Negro's Viewpoint," *St. Elizabeth's Chronicle* April 1928, 3–4, 16, 22, and 32; "The Negro's Progress," *St. Elizabeth's Chronicle* June 1928, 3–4, and 14; "Race and Religious Prejudice," *St. Elizabeth's Chronicle* May 1928, 3–4, and 18; and "The Catholic Church and Slavery," *St. Elizabeth's Chronicle* August 1928, 3–5, and 9.

35. See Colin Gordon, *Mapping Decline. St. Louis and the Fate of the American City* (Philadelphia: University of Pennsylvania Press, 2008).

36. "The Black Students of Saint Louis University" to the Trustees, May 1970. History Department Records, 1928–1984. Series 6/Sub-Series 5: Black History, 1969–1971, SLUSC

37. *The University News*, May 2, 1969.

38. Geoffrey Carter to Robert Henle, S.J., February 4, 1969. History Department Records, 1928–1984. Series 6/Sub-Series 5: Black History, 1969–1971, SLUSC.

39. John Francis Bannon, S.J., to Trafford Maher, S.J., May 28, 1969. History Department Records, 1928–1984. Series 6/Sub-Series 5: Black History, 1969–1971, SLUSC.

40. See note 1.

41. *The University News*, May 15, 1970.

42. Thomas Farrell and Paul Soukup, eds., *An Ong Reader: Challenges for Further Inquiry* (Cresskill, NJ: Hampton Press, 2002) is a good introduction to the work of Ong. Ong's most famous work is *Orality and Literacy*.

43. "A Syllabus for a Course in the Negro in American History," Herman Dreer, instructor. History Department Records, 1928–1984. Series 6/Sub-Series 5: Black History, 1969–1971, SLUSC.

44. Faherty, *Better the Dream*, 133–46.

45. William Faherty, *The Religious Roots of Black Catholics in St. Louis* (St. Louis, MO: Saint Louis University Press, 1977).

46. William Faherty, *Jesuit Roots in Mid-America* (Florissant, MO: St. Stanislaus Jesuit Historical Museum, 1980).

47. Faherty, *Jesuit Roots in Mid-America*, 10–11.

48. Faherty, *Jesuit Roots in Mid-America*, 13.

49. Faherty, *Jesuit Roots in Mid-America*, 17.

50. John Killoren, NiNi Harris, Nancy Merz, David Suwalsky, Thomas Nickolai, and William Faherty, *Jesuit Roots and Pioneer Heroes of the Middle West* (Florissant, MO: St. Stanislaus Jesuit Historical Museum, 1988).

51. William Faherty, *Saint Louis University, a Concise History (1818–2008)* (St. Louis, MO: Saint Louis University Press, 2008).

52.   John Bannon, *The Missouri Province S.J.: Mini-history* (St. Louis: Missouri Province, 1977), 8.

53.   Bannon, *The Missouri Province*, 23.

54.   John Bannon, *The Department of History, Saint Louis University, 1925–1973: An Historical Sketch* (St. Louis, MO: Saint Louis University Press, 1980).

55.   John Bannon, *Notes for an Academic History of Saint Louis University* (St. Louis, MO: Office of the Registrar, 1982).

56.   John Bannon, "A New All-University Award Proposed." John F. Bannon Manuscript Collection. Series 5: Manuscripts, c. 1947–1982/sub-series 27, SLUSC.

57.   *The University News*, December 13, 1968.

58.   Syllabus for "The Jesuits." Coordinator: R. J. Henle, S.J., 1978 or 1979? History Department Records, 1928–1984. Series 6: Departmental Curriculum, 1940–1984/sub-series 14: course syllabi, 1940–1984.

59.   Syllabus for "Social History of the United States." Instructor Sr. Elizabeth Kolmer, 1982. History Department Records, 1928–1984. Series 6: Departmental Curriculum, 1940–1984/sub-series 14: course syllabi, 1940–1984.

60.   Syllabus for "History of St. Louis." Instructor William Faherty, S.J., 1984. History Department Records, 1928–1984. Series 6: Departmental Curriculum, 1940–1984/sub-series 14: course syllabi, 1940–1984.

61.   Syllabus for "The Architectural Heritage of St. Louis." Instructor not listed, 1983. Syllabus for "Henry Shaw and St. Louis Parks: A Study of Urban Development, Environmentalism, and Social History in the 19th Century." Instructor not listed, 1982. Both in History Department Records, 1928–1984. Series 6: Departmental Curriculum, 1940–1984/sub-series 14: course syllabi, 1940–1984.

62.   Syllabus for "Special Topics: Jesuit Education at Saint Louis University." Instructors Walter Ong, S.J., and Anthony Daly, S.J., 1984. History Department Records, 1928–1984. Series 6: Departmental Curriculum, 1940–1984/sub-series 14: course syllabi, 1940–1984.

63.   Syllabus for "Seminar in United States History—St. Louis in the Westward Movement: Myths and Realities." Instructor Martin Towey, 1983. History Department Records, 1928–1984. Series 6: Departmental Curriculum, 1940–1984/sub-series 14: course syllabi, 1940–1984.

64.   Syllabus for "Introduction to Archival Administration." Instructor not listed, 1983. History Department Records, 1928–1984. Series 6: Departmental Curriculum, 1940–1984/sub-series 14: course syllabi, 1940–1984. History Department Records, 1928–1984. Series 6: Departmental Curriculum, 1940–1984/sub-series 14: course syllabi, 1940–1984.

65.   *St. Louis Review*, February 11, 1994.

66.   *St. Louis Post Dispatch*, January 31, 1995.

67.   *Universitas: The Magazine of Saint Louis University*, Spring 1995.

68.   *The University News*, February 11, 1994.

CHAPTER EIGHT

A Challenge to Our Sincerity

American Jesuits Discover "The Negro"

JAMES M. O'TOOLE

THOUGH HE HAD PERSONALLY visited the United States only twice, Pedro Arrupe, the superior general of the Society of Jesus, knew in 1967 that it was a nation in turmoil. Opposition to involvement in the war in Vietnam was growing more insistent as body counts from the battlefield rose steadily. Nonviolent, morally unambiguous civil rights demonstrations had given way to bitter summer seasons of rioting in cities across the country. An incipient new wave of feminism and a controversial youth culture were challenging behavioral norms across the board. Of these, Arrupe thought, the "urgent and complicated" problem of race was the most serious, requiring sustained reflection and action, and in a circular letter addressed to all American Jesuits in November of that year he called them to this work. "The racial crisis," he said, "involves, before all else, a direct challenge to our sincerity in professing a Christian concept of man." Whenever a Jesuit used the word "our," he meant to denote a very specific group of people, and so it was here. Enduring questions of race in the United States were not someone else's concern; they demanded with special insistence a response from Jesuits themselves, individually and collectively.[1]

After reviewing the history of slavery and discrimination in America, including a brief, "chastening" acknowledgement of Jesuit slaveholding before the Civil War, Arrupe's letter laid out the political and religious case against any form of racism. The Declaration of Independence; decisions of the United States Supreme Court; documents from the recently concluded Second Vatican Council; statements from Pope Paul VI and from the American bishops; and an earlier letter from Jean-Baptiste Janssens, his own predecessor as general, all supported the view that "racism in all its ugly manifestations, . . . whether in public life or private life, is objectively a moral and religious evil." While it was true that a handful of contemporary American Jesuits worked in self-described interracial apostolates, Arrupe had to conclude that "our record of service to the American Negro has fallen short of what it should have been," relying too much on "individual initiative and very little upon a corporate effort of the Society." It was especially "embarrassing" to note that "some of our institutions have effected . . . little more than token integration of the Negro" into their ministries.[2]

In assessing the work of American Jesuits on behalf of "the Negro," the general was right. As they had built their extensive institutional network of schools, colleges, parishes, and other programs, the Jesuits of the United States had overwhelmingly served the white ethnic Catholics who had been crowding into the nation's cities since the 1840s. Apart from the activity of a few solitary crusaders, any promotion of understanding and reconciliation across racial lines had been piecemeal affairs; taken together, these were not inaccurately characterized as "token." Arrupe's letter marked the beginnings of change. In the years that followed, new forms of "corporate effort," expressing a commitment to serving the African American community, would emerge and spread. The years that had preceded these beginnings of change, however, demonstrated how much work there was to be done, how much the concerns of the black community in America had been thus far left off the Jesuit agenda. Even as the nation as a whole began to rethink its racial arrangements in the years immediately following the Second World War, so American Jesuits of the time had to assess what they had and had not done, a first step toward discovering and exploring new possibilities. That process was a slow one, and still often uncoordinated. Only gradually did they discern what new actions were required of them on behalf of "the Negro."

Jesuits had been in what Europeans called the New World almost from the time of the Order's founding in the sixteenth century, but it was the arrival in 1634 of three of them with settlers of the colony of Maryland that marked the start of a continuous tradition in the territory that would become the United States. Three centuries later, they had grown to impressive numbers. By the end of the Second World War, their personnel and their organizational infrastructure touched every corner of the nation. The American "Assistancy" (as they called it) was divided into eight geographic provinces, supervising the work of almost 3,500 priests. When the ranks of lay brothers and scholastics in training were included, the total Jesuit population came to nearly 6,500. Moreover, young men were joining them as never before: 169 new priests were ordained in 1946 alone. Enrollments in the schools and colleges where many of these Jesuits worked were healthy and getting healthier. Thanks partly to benefits provided by the G.I. Bill, nearly 82,000 students attended one or another of the twenty-six colleges and universities run by the Order in that year—one of these had just opened, two more would join them in the next decade—with another 23,000 students in their thirty-eight high schools. The future promised even further growth as a nationwide "boom" of babies was underway: there were about 4,600 seniors in those high schools, but already 6,800 freshmen.[3] The prospects for continued expansion seemed almost endless.

These schools, both secondary and higher, were resolutely local institutions, drawing their students mostly from the communities in which they were situated. Especially in the Catholic heartland of northeastern and midwestern cities, it was the sons (only rarely, for now, the daughters) and grandsons of European immigrants who filled their halls and classrooms. Student populations mirrored their surroundings with Irish, German, Italian, and other surnames predominating as local demographics dictated. High school buildings identified with and anchored their neighborhoods, and, with few exceptions, it was much the same with the colleges, which were populated mostly by "day hops"—students who lived at home and commuted to campus every day for class. Some (most notably Georgetown in the nation's capital) had dormitories for students from "away," but any college wanting to open a dorm was warned not to cast its net too broadly, lest it poach from Jesuit institutions elsewhere. One college president, seeking his provincial's permission in the 1950s to construct a new residence hall, got the approval he wanted, but he was told to "take care of the necessities of the students of the city in which the College is situated" and "not seek students from other areas." In the North no less than in the South, this meant that very few

African American students ever came within the orbit of these schools. Persistent patterns of residential segregation were redoubled by the fact that so few black Americans were Catholics. Only about four hundred thousand of the nation's fifteen million African Americans were members of the church, and they were a double minority, comprising less than one percent of the country's forty-two million Catholics. The rare black face that looked out from the pages of a Jesuit school's yearbook was an exception, graphically proving a rule that otherwise seemed ironclad.[4]

That rule made almost any African American presence in a Jesuit institution newsworthy, sufficiently unusual for the locals to call it to the attention of their Jesuit fellows in publications that were meant to be read only by members of the Order. Two high schools in the Chicago province (Saint Ignatius in Chicago and the University of Detroit High School) "this year opened their doors to Negro students," the *Jesuit Educational Quarterly* reported proudly in 1945, though it did not specify how many had actually walked through those doors. Ten years later, when two black students enrolled in Dallas Jesuit High School, the *Quarterly* ran its two-sentence notice of the event under the headline "History Made." The boast was true enough, since this was "the first time Negroes have been admitted to an all-white high school in Dallas." Whenever there was any contact between Jesuits and members of the black community, someone was quick to make note of it. In 1949, an exhibit of the sculpture of Richmond Barthe, "one of our foremost negro [sic] artists," had opened in the library of Saint Peter's College in Jersey City, for example, and also that year "three Negro doctors" were teaching at the Saint Louis University medical school.[5] Each of these developments meant something in its own particular setting, but together they did little to counter—and much to support—Arrupe's later assertion that they were merely "token."

Even so, they represented the dawning of a realization that structural racial problems might require something more than small, local solutions, a recognition that was beginning to spread generally throughout America. The war and its aftermath had challenged the accepted political, legal, and social systems pertaining to race. The struggle against an overtly racist enemy in Nazism had prompted at least some Americans to reflect on their nation's own failings. African Americans had fought in the war (although in segregated units), and that service gave their returning veterans a claim on better treatment at home; when President Harry S. Truman ordered the desegregation of the armed forces in 1948, a significant barrier to equal opportunity was breached. A Swedish economist, Gunnar Myrdal, commissioned by the Carnegie Corporation, had published his landmark work, *An American Dilemma*, in 1944, exploring (in the words of its subtitle) "the Negro problem and modern democracy." The book, which sold out more than two dozen printings, highlighted the vast distance between the lofty national rhetoric of equality and the actual lived experience of African Americans, suggesting the need for a collective reexamination of conscience. A decade later, the historian C. Vann Woodward would demonstrate that the rules of Jim Crow segregation, thought to be eternal and immutable, were in fact of much more recent vintage and thus susceptible to amendment or repeal. The ruling of the Supreme Court in 1954 that "separate but equal" schools were inherently unequal and therefore unconstitutional—Myrdal's study was footnoted in the court's unanimous decision—began the dismantling of much of the legal foundation for segregation.[6] To be sure, the 1950s also witnessed the rise of southern white "massive resistance" to desegregation, but the arc of American racial consciousness was beginning to bend. In that context, Jesuits' pride in the rare occasions when they had crossed paths with African Americans was a tepid response to social change.

Any progress toward making Jesuit schools and colleges more readily accessible to African American students and their families could not begin, however, until there was a better understanding of exactly how things stood. Assembling some basic facts about policies, enrollments, and programs was a necessary first step. That step had been taken not by a Jesuit, but by Richard Roche, a priest of the Oblate order, who prepared a dissertation in sociology at the Catholic University of America, published in 1947 under the title, *Catholic Colleges and the Negro Student*. Just as the war was ending, Roche had surveyed Catholic colleges of all kinds—men, women, coed—conducted by any religious order (male or female) or by diocesan authority. He received usable responses from 154 of them, a return rate of more than 90 percent of those contacted. He followed this up with selective interviews and more in-depth studies of particular schools, none of which he identified by name. His most fundamental findings drew a baseline against which any future developments could be measured. Seventy-six of the colleges reported that they had at least one African American student, either currently or at some point in the past; seventy-seven had never had a black student; and one answer was unclear. Perhaps more telling, twenty-four of the colleges reported that they either currently had or had once had an explicit policy that excluded blacks. Most of these were in the South or in Border States, but colleges elsewhere might fall into this category too: there were two in the Northeast, two in the West, and three in the Midwest that systematically barred African Americans.[7]

The reasons Catholic college leaders gave for this segregation in their institutions, whether outright or de facto, were many, especially in the states of the former Confederacy. "No school in the South will admit Negroes to mix and mingle with whites," one administrator told Roche; "to do so would be to invite boycott and disaster." Some even believed (incorrectly) that state laws mandating the segregation of public schools applied no less to private schools. But fear that the admission of blacks would drive away white students, leading to precipitous declines in enrollment and then bankruptcy, was widespread, transcending region. This had never actually happened— "in no discoverable case," Roche concluded, had white student flight been "a problem to any institution which has admitted Negro students"—but that did not seem to matter; the excuse persisted anyway. An air of easy indifference was common. Most colleges did not have a policy on admitting blacks because they thought they did not need one. "We do not have the applications," a registrar explained. That might suggest an openness to black admissions in future, but at least in this case exactly the opposite was true. "I personally believe," this administrator continued coolly, "a policy of restriction would be a practical necessity if we had a large number of applications [from African Americans], and I do not doubt that such a policy would be officially or unofficially put into effect." Roche pointedly observed that attitudes of this kind represented a distinctly unedifying "clash" between "religious beliefs" about the equality of all humankind and a school's "practical policies." In most cases, however, he concluded with a note of sadness, "American race relations patterns have had much greater influence on the educators than the requirements of their Catholic faith."[8]

Roche's study of Catholic colleges in general prompted Jesuit officials to examine the place of African Americans in the institutions they ran, and a succession of surveys of black enrollment in Jesuit high schools and colleges followed. The vehicle for this was the Society's newly-formed Institute for Social Order (ISO). By the 1940s, a generation of papal statements had been promoting the application of Christian ideals to the concerns of this world. Pope Leo XIII's *Rerum Novarum* (1891) had defended private property and condemned socialism, but it also supported the right of workers to organize unions and to demand decent working conditions and a fair wage. In 1931, Pope Pius XI's *Quadragesimo Anno* reiterated those principles and adapted them to the changed circumstances of economic depression and impending war. These documents, which had said nothing specifically about race, were familiar texts in Jesuit theology and philosophy classes, but many felt the need for greater emphasis in all the Order's ministries. Accordingly, one hundred and forty Jesuits from around the country, four provincials among them, had convened in the late summer of 1943 at the theologate in West Baden, Indiana. Never before in the Society's entire history, one participant quipped, had that many Jesuits eaten meals together in the same place at the same time. More seriously, they had come together to plan for better correlation of local efforts, a coordination that might enable all Jesuit institutions and programs "to lay more stress on the social problems of our chaotic age." Put under the directorship of the indefatigable Daniel Lord, a popular pamphleteer and national supervisor (based in Saint Louis) of the student sodalities on all Jesuit campuses, the ISO added a committee on interracial relations to its larger program of social and economic reform.[9]

With this expansive mandate, the ISO took it upon itself to extend and refine the data that Roche had begun to collect, and it enlisted the labor of scholastics at the Woodstock seminary in Maryland to contact individual Jesuit schools and colleges and to analyze the results. The first report appeared just after Roche's book, and it counted only twenty African American students (out of a total enrollment of 23,000 for the 1946–1947 school year) in twenty-six responding Jesuit high schools, a dozen of which said that they did not admit blacks as a matter of policy. Where a black student had been enrolled, he was most likely alone. Saint Ignatius in Chicago and Gonzaga High School in Spokane, Washington, were outliers, reporting six and five black students respectively, but Bellarmine in San Jose, California,

Boston College High School, and Saint Peter's Prep in Jersey City were more typical, with one black student each. Most had none, and Creighton High School in Omaha reported that three blacks had started the year, but they all left partway through for unspecified reasons. It was much the same with the colleges: 436 African Americans amid a total enrollment of about 82,000. These were obviously statistically insignificant percentages, but Francis Drulet, author of this first report, nonetheless found the numbers "heartening." Protesting a bit too much, he reassured fellow members of the Order that "Jesuits do educate Negro students." Four more surveys followed, compiling data through the 1952–1953 school year and producing numbers that showed only slight improvement. By then, there were eighty-four blacks in Jesuit high schools and about one thousand in the colleges and universities, representing black/white ratios of 1:639 and 1:74, respectively.[10]

Drulet and his successors analyzed these data in terms that had already become familiar on many individual campuses. In an era when a non-Catholic student in a Jesuit school (especially a high school) was even rarer than an African American, the small percentage of blacks who were Catholics seemed most significant in holding the numbers down. Financial considerations were also important. "How many Negro families in the average community can afford the tuition rates prevailing in most of our schools?" the author of the 1950–1951 study asked. Even segregated public high schools could seem preferable, though some families were apparently inclined to save up in order to pay for college tuition, hoping for a better return on their investment through the upward mobility that an undergraduate degree might bring. Psychological factors could enter in as well: A single black high schooler in an otherwise all-white school would undoubtedly find it hard to fit in, though things might be better in higher education. "Being maturer in age and experience than high school students, Negroes in college find it easier to fuse with their fellow students," Drulet thought. The most serious impediment, however, was the demanding nature of Jesuit education, again, especially obvious at the high school level. "Our schools are classical and moderately scientific in their curriculum; consequently their appeal is limited," Drulet said proudly. "It can be safe to say that our Jesuit education is not yet the food of the majority of that race [i.e., blacks]. . . . They will seek to be educated for the most part along mechanical and technical lines." The stereotypes built into that argument seem obvious today, but Jesuit readers at the time would probably have been reassured that their schools had indeed made "a good beginning"—or perhaps a good *enough* beginning—at providing the "special care and comfort which the Negro needs in the field of education."[11]

Smug self-congratulation could be undercut by racial attitudes common among Jesuits themselves. Roche had already noted that even people who had taken religious vows sometimes let the customs and norms of contemporary society trump the acknowledged demands of Christian charity, and American Jesuits were no more immune to this than anyone else. The president of Loyola University in New Orleans took note of "a few remarks on the part of two or three of Ours" after several black Sisters of the Holy Family were allowed to take special Saturday courses there in the fall of 1950 and one black lay man enrolled in an evening program. A new provincial, taking charge of the New Orleans province at the same time, told the General in Rome that his men were divided into three "race camps." There were "men of action" who wanted immediate change, others who "violently opposed" any challenge to Jim Crow, and a "middle-of-the-road" group (by the far the largest) who thought that "segregation is an explosive issue that can best be broken by indirect means." Open hostility among these factions was often so intense that the provincial even had to mandate strict enforcement of traditional Jesuit rules governing seating at meals—on entering the dining room, each man was expected to take the nearest open place, regardless of his immediate tablemates—so that those with whom one disagreed could not be avoided and like-minded cliques could not cluster. But physical proximity over lunch and dinner did not necessarily bring community concord. One older Jesuit in the segregationist camp complained to the provincial that the "men of action"—too many of them young and not originally southerners, he thought—had "had racial equality pumped into them" in a way that was not "helpful."[12]

Even those who were most involved in interracial apostolates might still see "the Negro" as someone fundamentally other than themselves. The executive committee of the ISO, for instance, had gathered in Chicago in April 1945 to discuss, among other issues, "an interracial problem." The "problem" was so obvious that it could be hard to see: the complete absence of any American Jesuits who were themselves black. Desegregating Jesuit schools was one thing, but what about accepting black candidates for entry into the Society itself? Someone had suggested that the ISO make a bold statement, going "on record" as favoring the idea, and the proposal prompted a frank discussion, summarized in the privately circulated minutes of the meeting. A participant from the Maryland province said that this was a step that should have been taken long ago, while another Marylander countered that their province simply could not think of such a thing, citing the familiar fear that accepting blacks would scare whites away. Another participant, though sympathetic to the idea, argued against making any statement, as doing so would only call attention to the fact that they had not done it already. An older Jesuit from New York candidly confessed that, at one time, having African Americans in the community with him "might have been a test of his vocation. He now says it no longer would be." Even John LaFarge, widely known for his sometimes-single-handed promotion of the Catholic Interracial Council movement and other efforts, warned against doing anything that might embarrass members of the New Orleans province in particular or other Jesuits generally, whether northern or southern. Later that year, LaFarge would publish a denunciation of "false prudence, a sham excuse" in racial matters, but the impulse toward prudence could be powerful. Racial diversity within the Jesuit order was a long-delayed goal never really achieved.[13]

In these discussions, the story of the one black American who had been a Jesuit in the nineteenth century was overlooked, whether unknowingly or deliberately. Patrick Healy was the mixed-race son of an Irish immigrant to Georgia and his black slave and common-law wife, but he had a light enough complexion to "pass" as white throughout his life. It had to be so: his superiors would probably never have chosen him to be the president of Georgetown in 1873, less than a decade after the end of the Civil War, had his racial origins been generally known. In 1942, a young Jesuit pursuing graduate studies had hoped to write a doctoral dissertation on Healy and his family, emphasizing their ambiguous racial identity, but he was warned off the topic by a senior scholar. "You must know as well as I the effect of any disclosure of this nature," the established historian told the younger man; "in a case like this, silence is golden." Albert Foley, a Jesuit sociologist at Spring Hill College in

Alabama, had also begun to study the family and, though he did publish a biography of Patrick Healy's brother James (who had been the bishop of Portland, Maine), his work had limited effect. Foley had also drafted a book-length biography of Patrick, but it remained unpublished until he himself had it printed privately in 1976.[14] Much of the Jesuits' own history was still too problematic to be applied expressly to the discussion of current racial issues; golden silence was preferable. Better to take comfort in the more encouraging view expressed at the end of Drulet's survey, that a "good beginning" had been made by the Society in working with the African American community.

Sunny assessments of that kind had an enduring life of their own. "Ministry among the Negroes," another Jesuit had written at the time, was "zealously promoted by Ours from the very dawn of American Catholicity in colonial Maryland," a view that conveniently overlooked the fact that those "Negroes" had been the property of the people ministering to them. But changing times were beginning to demand a better response, and the Society needed to commit itself to cracking the patterns of enforced segregation in its schools. Any such effort would be particularly difficult in the South and in Border States, making those regions the likeliest, but nevertheless problematic, places to start. Saint Louis University, known familiarly on and off campus as SLU, provides the most dramatic case. Saint Louis was a strictly segregated city, and schools there, both public and parochial, adhered to the expected norm. The longtime archbishop, John Glennon (made a cardinal shortly before his death in 1946), was a confirmed segregationist, refusing to consider any challenge to the established order. Other local institutions were little better. Cross-town Washington University allowed blacks only in its graduate programs, and the University of Missouri, several hours away in the middle of the state, restricted African Americans to those programs and degrees that were not available at the historically black Lincoln University in Jefferson City.[15]

Despite this unanimity of practice, a core group of Jesuits at SLU pushed the effort to desegregate their school. In the lead were two brothers, John and William Markoe, originally from Minnesota. William had entered the Society in 1913 and was ordained in 1926. John graduated from West Point (where he had played on the football team with Dwight Eisenhower), commanded a regiment of black troops on the Mexican border during the First World War and, after a dishonorable discharge for his many hard-drinking exploits, reformed himself and joined the Jesuits at the war's end. The brothers pledged themselves to work on behalf of the black community, repeating daily a personal vow "to give and dedicate our whole lives and all our energies . . . for the work of the salvation of the Negroes in the United States." William served as the pastor of Saint Elizabeth's, a black church in the city; John's challenges to the local Jim Crow system, implying as they did a criticism of Archbishop Glennon, soon got him transferred to Creighton in Omaha, where he organized an interracial "DePorres Club," named for the seventeenth-century saint who had ministered to slaves in Peru. Joining these two was George Dunne, a Californian by birth who, after missionary work in China, had completed a PhD in international relations at the University of Chicago. A broadcast radio sermon of his on the subject of integration was deemed insufficiently deferential to the archbishop and to local customs, and he was warned to be careful when speaking in public. Last but in the end most decisive was Claude Heithaus, a local lad who joined the Jesuits after graduating from SLU, later earning a doctorate in archaeology from University College, London, and then returning home to teach.[16] Together, these Jesuits constituted a critical mass for change.

They pressed the newly installed president of the university, Patrick Holloran, to form a committee to explore the possibility of integration. The group agreed on the principle, expressed cautiously in a passive voice, that "steps should be taken," but no specific plan was outlined. Concerned about the effect any such move might have on students, parents, faculty, and alumni, Holloran decided to conduct an informal poll. At the end of January 1944, he sent out a letter to about one hundred "friends of the University," hoping to gauge reaction before going ahead. Accordingly, he enclosed a small postcard that respondents could return after checking off the answers to two yes-or-no questions: Would you "look favorably" on admitting blacks, and would you be "less inclined to send a son or daughter" to the university if blacks were admitted? His concerns were the now-conventional ones: that whites would withdraw if blacks were allowed in and that blacks were unprepared for the rigors of a Jesuit education, thus undermining standards. He tried to reassure his friends that the monumental change would really be no change at all. "There will never be any lowering of academic standards in the admission of colored students," he said; "they will satisfy all requirements or will not be considered." Moreover, he expected that the number of African American students "will never be great. . . . I do not think the number will reach twenty in the next twenty years."[17]

Holloran intended his inquiry to remain private, but the letter was immediately leaked to the local press, perhaps by one of the Markoe brothers. No formal tabulation of the responses was made, at least none that has survived, but apparently there was less opposition to integration than the president had anticipated. Lest he waver, however, Heithaus now stepped forward to keep up the pressure. At a regular weekday Mass in the university's church on February 11, he preached a carefully crafted sermon (which he himself then sent to the newspapers). Relying on the doctrine of the Mystical Body of Christ—this was less than a year after Pope Pius XII had issued an encyclical letter, establishing this image as a central metaphor for the church, in which all members, regardless of their differences, had an important role to play—Heithaus decried segregation as sinful, and he asked the congregation to recite a prayer with him: "Lord Jesus, we are sorry and ashamed for all the wrongs that white men have done to Your Colored children. We are firmly resolved never again to have any part in them, and to do everything in our power to prevent them. Amen."[18]

The sermon had the desired effect of steeling the president's nerve, but first, Holloran and Heithaus were summoned to a meeting with Archbishop Glennon. He was angry at all this having gone public, though not angry enough to derail the movement, contenting himself with an order that Heithaus would not speak openly about race again. Heithaus did not obey. In March he preached another sermon, this one comparing preists who tolerated segregation in deference to local custom with missionaries who overlooked cannibalism because it was a "local custom." This got him officially reprimanded and reassigned, first as an army chaplain in Kansas and then to the faculty at Marquette in Milwaukee. Nevertheless, at the end of April, Holloran announced that qualified African Americans would henceforth be admitted to the university, and five were accepted for the summer session of 1944: two undergraduate males in arts and sciences, together with two men and one woman (all of them public school teachers) taking graduate-level education courses. Thereafter, Holloran's projection of low numbers was almost immediately proved wrong. By the 1950–1951 school year, there were about 350 black students in all programs at SLU—undergraduate, graduate, and professional—out of a total enrollment of nearly 7,500. There were also four black faculty: three in the medical school and one in arts and sciences, teaching speech.[19]

This was undeniably a historic step, but the Jim Crow regime persisted in other ways. In an address at the beginning of the new school year in September 1944, Holloran assured the campus that desegregation would bring with it no movement toward "social identity." The phrase, together with its frequent cognate "social equality," was a redolent one. Segregationists deployed it as a scare tactic. Integration, they said, meant accepting the notion that blacks and whites actually were equal; if associations between them in business and social life became normal, society would be on a very slippery slope down to the scariest prospect of all—intermarriage. Even those who thought of themselves as liberal on race matters felt compelled to deny that anything of the sort was their goal, asserting instead that, even if the two races were to "mix and mingle" (as the anonymous college administrator had put it to Roche), white people could still think of blacks as inherently inferior to them and could keep their distance. At SLU, black students were therefore reminded that admission brought with it certain opportunities but not others. Social activities remained segregated, though black students could now have access to university facilities for their own events. This rule was tested when an African American couple showed up at a university-sponsored dance in April 1945. The dean of men "politely and without incident" barred their entrance, the university's public relations officer explained afterward, and "the colored boy and his date politely left." The emphasis on politeness was obviously deliberate, confirmed by an assessment that, in general, "Negro students have conducted themselves in [a] gentlemanly and exemplary fashion." Change would come, if slowly and mostly from the bottom up. White students—the PR man had been heartened by the "magnificent acceptance of [desegregation] by our own students," a phrase suggesting that black students were somehow not the university's "own"—apparently began to pressure restaurants and other businesses in the neighborhood to serve their black friends.[20] Meanwhile, the first movement toward integration had been a cautious one.

Other Jesuit schools proceeded with similar care, insisting along with SLU that no standards would be lowered in the process. "Same requirements for all students," the University of Santa Clara board of trustees noted tersely in authorizing admission of its first black student, who arrived in 1949. Newly admitted blacks remained few in number on most campuses, as the ISO surveys documented. At Boston College, there was usually one black in each of the graduating classes in the years immediately after the end of the war—in two years, there were as many as three—but, thanks to the cohort of returning veterans, the size of those senior classes had grown from just over 200 in 1947 to about 1,200 in 1950, leaving any black students all the more in the minority. (In two cases, the graduating black student was not an American, having come to Boston from Saint George's, the high school in Jamaica that was staffed by Jesuits from the New England province.) Sometimes it took successive attempts by African Americans before a university admitted any. In 1934, a black senior at Xavier, one of the two high-powered secondary schools run by the Jesuits in Manhattan, had gone uptown to Fordham to register for the fall. Normally, this was a pro forma transaction, with graduates of Xavier and its companion school, Regis, admitted automatically, a practice that helped keep bright students within the Jesuit fold. This lad's white friends were let in, but he was rejected. Not until 1943 did a black student enter Fordham, at first in an accelerated wartime program; he then left for service in the navy, returned in 1946, and received a degree the following year. Elsewhere, too, African Americans might have to find their way into a school via a summer course or other special circumstance. Spring Hill College in Mobile, Alabama, allowed some black nuns to take summer classes in 1949, and in 1954 it admitted its first full-time black undergraduate as part of what the school's Jesuit consultors called a "great experiment." That was doubly the case: the applicant was a woman, and the college had just recently decided to become fully coeducational.[21] The abandonment of previous patterns of exclusion was, as always, uncoordinated from campus to campus, but there was nonetheless a growing realization among American Jesuits that they should be more active in opening their schools and other ministries to African Americans.

The emergence of the modern Civil Rights Movement in the 1950s and

1960s worked a profound change in the larger societal context surrounding race, and it also prompted Jesuits to more concerted efforts. Personal prejudices no doubt persisted among some members of the Order, but overt expressions of racism were becoming unacceptable behavior, replaced by other attitudes. Equating segregation and cannibalism might be deliberately provocative, as it had been for Claude Heithaus, but others too were now wondering whether one of those practices was more tolerable than the other. Shouldn't Jesuits be doing something? Participation by members of the Society in civil rights demonstrations around the country quickly became commonplace. Forty-one people (six priests and thirty-five scholastics) from Woodstock participated in the massive March on Washington in August 1963, unfurling a banner that identified them as "Woodstock Catholic Seminary for Equal Rights." They were joined by delegations from Gonzaga High School and Georgetown Prep in Washington, from Loyola High School in Baltimore, and from Fordham and LeMoyne in New York; the LeMoyne delegation was led by Daniel Berrigan, then embarked on the early years of his political activism. One hundred students from Georgetown University had assembled in their chapel for Mass that morning and then marched in a body to the Lincoln Memorial to participate in the event. "The demonstration seems to have been a turning point for the Negro," one Jesuit wrote. Jesuits and other Catholics also participated in demonstrations elsewhere. Photographs of priests and nuns joining ranks and marching on behalf of voting rights in 1965 in Selma, Alabama became iconic images of increasing involvement. For leaders of the movement, theirs was an unexpected but welcome presence. "The only ones they hate more than Negroes down here," joked Ralph Abernathy, right-hand man to Martin Luther King, Jr., "are Roman Catholics."[22]

Beyond taking their places in national public demonstrations, some Jesuits began to develop programs in their own localities that sought to help African Americans. In 1963, the provincial in New York had asked those in his jurisdiction to "contribute as much as possible to the advancement of minority groups."[23] In response, one priest and five scholastics organized a summer tutoring collaborative for black and Puerto Rican students called the "Higher Achievement Program." Forty-five grade schoolers and thirty high school students "who had the academic potential . . . but who felt they needed help to develop this potential and to succeed in their further education"[24] were enrolled in the six-week curriculum. Classes were held daily at Regis, Brooklyn Prep, and Saint Peter's Prep in Jersey City, and sometimes the tutors visited students' homes for consultation with parents. The effort apparently paid off. "The reading and comprehension of most of the students showed a marked improvement," one participant said.[25] Two years later, a broader attempt at involvement in the black community began. Working from a community center in Harlem, a dozen young Jesuits fanned out into the neighborhood "to discover medical needs, food and income problems."[26] Sometimes they delivered groceries or clothes acquired from the local Salvation Army store. Similar programs popped up in other cities where the Jesuits had long been active. In Baltimore, three scholastics moved into an inner-city row house and "tried to live as good neighbors, . . . making our home and ourselves available to serve in whatever way seems best."[27] They spent three months conducting adult education classes and trying "to help in many day to day crises," one participant said, though in the end he had mixed feelings about the impact they had had.[28] It was "hard for me to say that I have made a difference in their lives," he concluded, but there was also a growing personal appreciation for "the systematic changes which must be effected—in education, job training, housing, welfare, etc."[29] All such programs were limited, in both scope and duration, but they were nonetheless giving members of the Society firsthand experience with individuals whom it had once been easy to lump together into the single, remote category labeled "the Negro."

Into this emerging pattern of direct Jesuit work in and on behalf of the African American community, Pedro Arrupe's letter of 1967 arrived. It was an open secret that the letter had been drafted for him by two Americans: William Kenealy, the former dean of the Boston College law school who later directed a national office for the Jesuit social apostolate; and Louis Twomey, an alumnus of the ISO who had gone on to direct an institute for human relations at Loyola, New Orleans, and who had assisted Archbishop Joseph Rummel in planning the desegregation of the parochial school system there in 1962. After assembling the catalog of the sins of racism and the inadequate Jesuit response, Arrupe outlined a number of specific directives, "lest my letter appear to be a mere enunciation of general principles." Provincials were ordered to assess all their current ministries "to discover how their potential can be focused most effectively upon the grave problems of race." Every province should form a planning committee to make specific recommendations, and those plans should be discussed at a joint meeting of all provincials in the United States within a year. Blacks should be welcomed in Jesuit parishes and retreat houses, and student sodalities should be used "to break down the un-Christian barriers of racial prejudice and discrimination." In the management of Jesuit institutions—"the signing of contracts for goods and services," for instance—superiors should "patronize only those business firms and construction companies which have adopted, and actually observe, the canons of fair employment practices." It was good that some members of the Society were participating in public protests, and Jesuits should continue "to cooperate with the many efforts being made by sincere, intelligent and courageous people, Catholic and non-Catholic, believer and non-believer, who are making substantial contributions to the cause of interracial justice." Finally, among Jesuits as individuals, any "uncritical acceptance of certain stereotypes regarding the Negro, acquired in youth," had to be identified and stamped out, and younger Jesuits still in formation should be particularly prepared to recognize and counter such prejudices.[30]

It was a long agenda, and it opened the door to a number of efforts, some of them experimental. Joseph Torrens, a California Jesuit with a PhD in English from the University of Michigan, used it as a warrant to accept a position on the faculty of the Tuskegee Institute in Alabama, leaving behind an appointment at Santa Clara. Founded in 1881 by Booker T. Washington, Tuskegee emphasized industrial training, but it also played a significant role in preparing black schoolteachers for service in segregated schools across the South. Torrens arrived for the start of the fall semester in 1968, one of the few white members of the faculty, and he had to address some unexpected questions. Should he wear clerical clothes, for example? He went back and forth on this. Fearful of standing out too much, he decided at first not to "wave a papal flag in addition to a white one," but that led the local chancery office to deny him permission to say Mass publicly. He relented for a while and got approval to celebrate the liturgy in the local church; then he went back to "civvies." He enjoyed his classes and relished any progress on the part of his students, though there were also tense moments. He participated in animated discussions within the English Department, for example, on the use of African American slang over "standard English." He stayed through the fall of 1970, uncertain in the end of how much good he had done. The impact on himself as he returned to California was clearer: "After Tuskegee, I could not possibly see a lot of things about our country and our Jesuit schools in the same light as before."[31]

Arrupe's letter had a more direct and immediate impact on those schools, especially the colleges, and deliberate efforts to recruit African American students were put into place on most campuses. The shrugging excuse of "we do not have the applicants" was no longer tenable. Special scholarship funds were designated to assist in this effort, an idea that the general had explicitly endorsed. Similarly, tutorial programs were designed to help those from poorer, inner-city high schools after they arrived at college. At Boston College, for instance, a Negro Talent Program—the name was quickly amended to "Black Talent," in line with the changing common usage—was begun in 1968, and about fifty African American freshmen (out of a total class of 1,300) enrolled that fall. One hundred thousand dollars had been set aside (from a total financial aid budget of about $1.5 million; tuition was $1,600 per year) to support them. The comparable effort at nearby Holy Cross was even more sustained and received support from the highest level. In the spring of 1968, John Brooks, a theology professor, personally drove to Philadelphia and other cities with a young admissions officer, visiting high schools and talking with students and guidance counselors to identify potential black applicants. Nineteen were enrolled that fall, still a small percentage of the 2,200 undergraduates, but when Brooks became president of the college two years later, he continued to devote his personal attention to the program and to the students it had brought to campus.[32] There were no dramatic increases in black enrollment at these or at the other Jesuit schools, but all of them made a commitment to increasing the racial diversity of their student bodies steadily over the coming years. Even if success was slow, the goal remained clear.

Less than a year after the distribution of Arrupe's manifesto to Jesuit houses in the United States, the *Woodstock Letters*, a quarterly journal published since

1872 and expressly identified on its title page as being "For Jesuit Use" only, devoted most of its summer 1968 issue to a candid discussion of the document and what would come next. One of the contributors, a university economics professor, spoke hopefully of its potential to "galvanize action in several directions. . . . I believe we will now act with a greater sense of urgency." There was much lost ground to make up, however, and easy optimism about what might be accomplished was dangerous. "We are jumping on a bandwagon that is pretty well past us," he said soberly, and it might take years to catch up.[33] But in the quarter century since the end of the war, American Jesuits had at least come to realize the scope of the work to be done and the pressing urgency of the task. Theirs had been, to no small degree, an extended process of "discovering" the African American community that was all around them, the injustices to which that community had been subjected, and the difficulties that would attend any attempt at improvement. The efforts of Jesuits in their schools, colleges, and other institutions to address those larger social problems would be varied, and not all of them would be effective or lasting; they continue, with both success and failure, to the present day. But a corner had been turned, and there was no going back.

Notes

1. Pedro Arrupe, "The Interracial Apostolate," *Woodstock Letters* [hereafter *WL*] 97 (Summer 1968): 291–302; the quotations are from paragraphs 1 and 2. The *Woodstock Letters*, together with the *Jesuit Educational Quarterly* (see note 5, below) and *Studies in the Spirituality of Jesuits* (note 13) are all available online at jesuitlibrary.com.

2. Arrupe, *WL* 19, 14, and 21.

3. For contemporary statistics of membership, see Arrupe, "Varia: American Assistancy," *WL* 75 (March 1946): 74–85; Arrupe, "Chronicle of the American Assistancy for 1946," *WL* 76 (March 1947): 64–71; and Arrupe, "Catalogue: Growth of the Provinces of the American Assistancy," *WL* 76 (December 1947): 310–15.

4. Population statistics are summarized in Michael Glazier and Thomas J. Shelley, eds., *The Encyclopedia of American Catholic History* (Collegeville, MN: Liturgical Press, 1997), 11. For the interplay of ethnicity, race, and neighborhood, see John T. McGreevy, *Parish Boundaries: The Catholic Encounter with Race in the Twentieth-Century Urban North* (Chicago: University of Chicago Press, 1996); for the experience of the African American "minority within a minority," see Cyprian Davis, *The History of Black Catholics in the United States* (New York: Crossroad, 1995). The warning about college residence halls is in William Fitzgerald to Joseph Maxwell, March 17, 1955, Provincial's

Records (Fitzgerald), Box 12, Folder 1, New England Province Archives, Jesuit Central Archives, Saint Louis, Missouri. For examples of black students in a Jesuit college, see the photos in the *Sub Turri*, the yearbook of Boston College, available at University Archives: Digital Library (libguides.bc.edu). In the volume for 1937, there was one African American (Caspar Ferguson) among 280 graduating seniors; in 1941 there were three (Louis Montgomery, Bernard Robinson, and Cornelius Vincent) among 273 seniors. On the origins of the Jesuit high school and college network, see Philip Gleason, "The First Century of Jesuit Higher Education in America," *U. S. Catholic Historian* 25, no. 2 (Spring 2007): 37–52 and Gerald McKevitt, "Jesuit Schools in the USA, 1814-c. 1970," *The Cambridge Companion to the Jesuits*, ed. Thomas Worcester (New York: Cambridge University Press, 2008), 278–97.

5.   "News from the Field," *Jesuit Educational Quarterly* [hereafter *JEQ*] 7 (January 1945): 188; "News from the Field," *JEQ* 18 (January 1956): 191; "News from the Field," *JEQ* 11 (March 1949): 256; "News from the Field," *JEQ* 12 (October 1949): 125.

6.   Gunnar Myrdal, *An American Dilemma: The Negro Problem and Modern Democracy* (New York: Harper, 1944); C. Vann Woodward, *The Strange Career of Jim Crow* (New York: Oxford University Press, 1955). For the integration of the military, see Richard M. Dalfiume, *Desegregation of the U. S. Armed Forces: Fighting on Two Fronts* (Columbia: University of Missouri Press, 1969).

7.   Richard J. Roche, *Catholic Colleges and the Negro Student* (Washington, DC: Catholic University of America Press, 1948); see ch. 2 for a description of Roche's survey method. On the impact of this study, see Philip Gleason, "The Erosion of Racism in Catholic Colleges in the 40s," *America* 173 (November 1995): 12–15.

8.   Roche, *Catholic Colleges and the Negro Student*, 61, 224, 73, and 223. For the mistaken belief that public school segregation required private school segregation, see "A Correction," *WL* 78 (May 1946): 106.

9.   On the origins of the institute, see Robert C. Hartnett, "The West Baden Conference: A Teacher's Workshop," *JEQ* 6 (October 1943): 88–94 and Hartnett, "The J. E. A. and the I.S.O.," *JEQ* 10 (June 1947): 23–30. Hartnett's report of the discussions at this meeting was accompanied by an explicit reminder from the *JEQ*'s editors that none of the details of the meeting were to be shared with non-Jesuits. See also Peter McDonough, *Men Astutely Trained: A History of the Jesuits in the American Century* (New York: Free Press, 1992), ch. 6. On Lord, see Raymond A. Schroth, *The American Jesuits: A History* (New York: New York University Press, 2007), 124–26.

10.   Francis K. Drulet, "Negro Students in Jesuit High Schools and Colleges, 1946–1947: A Statistical Interpretation," *WL* 76 (December 1947): 299–309; Martin J. Neylon, "Negro Students in Jesuit Schools and Colleges, 1948–1949," *Social Order* 2 (January 1949): 20–22; James F. Muldowney, "Negro Students in Jesuit Schools and Colleges, 1949–1950," *Social Order* 3 (January 1950): 23–26; Donald Campion, "Negro Students in Jesuit Schools, 1950–1951," *JEQ* 13 (March 1951): 223–28; Bartholomew Lahiff, "Negro Students in Jesuit Schools, 1952–1953," *JEQ* 16 (October 1953): 123–26. No statistics were published for the 1947–1948 and 1951–1952 school years.

11.   Drulet, "Negro Students in Jesuit High Schools and Colleges," 303–9.

12.   Quotations at R. Bentley Anderson, *Black, White, and Catholic: New Orleans Interracialism, 1947–1956* (Nashville, TN: Vanderbilt University Press, 2005), 80, 81–82, and 84. The dining room seating arrangements are described ibid., 123.

13.   "Minutes of the Executive Committee Meeting, Chicago, January 20–21, 1945," *ISO Bulletin* 3, no. 4 (April 1945): 4; John LaFarge, "Some Suggestions on Interracial Policy in the United States," *ISO Bulletin* 3, no. 7 (September 1945): 4–5. See also R. Bentley Anderson, "Numa J. Rousseau: Creole, Catholic, and Jesuit," *Studies in the Spirituality of Jesuits* [hereafter *Studies*] 42, no. 4 (December 2010): 1–35 and Gregory Chisholm, "On Being Black and Jesuit," *Studies* 33, no. 5 (November 2001): 9–14. For LaFarge, see David W. Southern, *John LaFarge and the Limits of Catholic Interracialism, 1911–1963* (Baton Rouge: Louisiana State University Press, 1996). For another discussion of desegregation in Jesuit ministries, see R. Bentley Anderson, "Black, White, and Catholic: Southern Jesuits Confront the Race Question," *Catholic Historical Review* 91 (July 2005): 484–505.

14.   See Albert S. Foley, *Dream of an Outcaste: Patrick F. Healy* (Tuscaloosa, AL: Portals Press, 1976; reissued 1989), and Foley, *Bishop Healy: Beloved Outcaste* (New York: Farrar, Straus and Young, 1954). Foley's "Adventures in Black Catholic History: Research and Writing," *U. S. Catholic Historian* 5, no.1 (1986): 103–18 contains some of his recollections about the difficulty of writing about the Healy family. The most recent treatment of Patrick Healy is James M. O'Toole, *Passing for White: Race, Religion, and the Healy Family* (Amherst and Boston: University of Massachusetts Press, 2002), esp. ch. 8. For the discouragement of the young Jesuit, see Peter Guilday to Thomas O'Donnell, June 20, 1943, Foley Papers, Box 7, Josephite Archives, Baltimore. O'Donnell did manage finally to publish something on the family: "For Bread and Wine," *WL* 82 (May 1951): 99–142.

15.   The practice of these other schools is outlined in John J. McCarthy, "Facing the Race Problem at St. Louis University," *JEQ* 14 (October 1951): 69–70. For reassurances by Jesuits that they were doing something for blacks, see Edward Reiser, "Parochial and Allied Ministries in the American Assistancy," *WL* 72 (December 1943): 308 and Edward D. Reynolds, *Jesuits for the Negro* (New York: America Press, 1949). For an analysis of the desegregation of Jesuit and other Catholic colleges elsewhere in the South, see Anderson, *Black, White, and Catholic*. See also Alexandria Griffin, "The Life and Afterlives of Patrick Francis Healy, S.J." (PhD diss., Arizona State University, 2020), Proquest Dissertations 27955677.

16.   On the Markoe brothers, see Davis, *History of Black Catholics*, 221–25; Matt Holland, *Ahead of Their Time: The Story of the Omaha DePorres Club* (Charleston, SC: CreateSpace Publishing, 2014), and Robert T. Reilly, "He Saved Us from Scandal: John Markoe, S.J.," *WL* 97 (July 1968): 361–66; the text of their vow is at 363. For Dunne, see Schroth, *American Jesuits*, 126–29. For Heithaus, see Daniel Van Slyke, "Claude Heithaus and the Integration of St. Louis University: The Mystical Body of Christ and Jesuit Politics," *Theology and Lived Christianity*, ed. Daniel M. Hammond (Mystic, CT:

Twenty-Third Publications, 2000), 139–73 and Paul Shore, "The Message and the Messenger: The Untold Story of Father Claude Heithaus and the Integration of Saint Louis University," *Trying Times: Essays on Catholic Higher Education in the 20th Century*, ed. William M. Shea (Atlanta, GA: Scholars Press, 1999), 135–52 .

17.   Van Slyke, "Heithaus and the Integration of St. Louis University," 144–45.

18.   Van Slyke, "Heithaus and the Integration of St. Louis University," 150–54; the prayer is at 150.

19.   For enrollments, see McCarthy, "Facing the Race Problem," 71 and 80.

20.   McCarthy, "Facing the Race Problem," 72–73. On the enduring power of the social equality phrase, see Nell Irwin Painter, "'Social Equality,' Miscegenation, Labor, and Power," in *The Evolution of Southern Culture*, ed. Norman V. Bartley (Athens: University of Georgia Press, 1988), 47–67.

21.   Gerald McKevitt, *The University of Santa Clara: A History, 1851–1977* (Palo Alto, CA: Stanford University Press, 1979), 300, 371; Boston College *Sub Turri*, 1945–1952, University Archives: Digital Library (libguides.bc.edu); Raymond A. Schroth, *Fordham: A History and Memoir* (Chicago: Loyola University Press, 2002), 173, 178; Charles S. Podgett, "'Without Hysteria or Unnecessary Disturbance': Desegregation of Spring Hill College, Mobile, Alabama, 1958–1854," *History of Education Quarterly* 41 (Summer 2001): 167–88.

22.   Daniel Degnan, "The Washington March: August 28, 1963," *WL* 92 (November 1963): 367–74. Abernathy is quoted in McGreevy, *Parish Boundaries*, 156.

23.   *WL* 93 (November 1964), 425.

24.   *WL* 93 (November 1964), 426.

25.   *WL* 93 (November 1964), 427.

26.   *WL* 94 (November 1965), 429.

27.   *WL* 97 (Summer 1968), 345.

28.   *WL* 97 (Summer 1968), 345.

29.   *WL* 97 (Summer 1968), 345, 353.

30.   Arrupe, "The Interracial Apostolate," no. 27 and 28. Identification of Kenealy and Twomey as authors of the letter is in James S. Torrens, "Tuskegee Years: What Father Arrupe Got Me Into," *Studies* 37, no. 3 (September 2005): 12.

31.   Torrens, "Tuskegee Years," 1–37.

32.   On Brooks and the students he recruited, both during their school years and after, see Diane Brady, *Fraternity* (New York: Spiegel and Grau, 2012); see also Anthony J. Kuzniewski, *Thy Honored Name: A History of the College of the Holy Cross, 1843–1994* (Washington, DC: Catholic University of America Press, 1999), 407–10. For the program at Boston College, see "$100,000 Scholarship Fund Established for Negroes," *The Heights*, March 5, 1967, and "Roxbury Area Responds to Increased Negro Aid," *The Heights*, March 26, 1967. *The Heights* is the Boston College student newspaper, available at University Archives: Digital Library (libguides.bc.edu).

33.   Robert E. McEwen, "Return to Mobility," *WL* 97 (Summer 1968): 332–35. McEwen also acknowledges Kenealy and Twomey as Arrupe's ghostwriters.

CHAPTER NINE

Trial by Fire

*Father George Dunne and
Race Relations in Cold War
Los Angeles*[1]

SEAN DEMPSEY, S.J.

THE POLICE CALLED IT an accident. Not long before Christmas in 1945, O'Day Short, along with his wife and two young children, burned to death in a fire in their suburban Fontana, California home outside of Los Angeles. The Short family was African American, and O'Day Short had been active in the local chapter of the NAACP, working courageously to desegregate Los Angeles area neighborhoods that still practiced racial exclusion through the use of restrictive covenants. When the Shorts had moved to their new Fontana home in the fall of 1945, they had been warned by local whites, who would later be characterized as vigilantes, to move out of the area immediately, lest they suffer the consequences of crossing the city's color line. Suffer they did. Although investigators from San Bernardino County would claim that there was no evidence of foul play, an independent investigation commissioned by the Los Angeles NAACP found that the Shorts' house had been doused with highly flammable oil sometime before the explosion that quickly consumed the house and claimed the lives of the entire Short family. No charges were ever filed, and after a brief moment of notoriety, especially among leftist political circles in Los Angeles, the Short case quickly faded from view, a footnote in the long and painful history of racial terror in the pre-civil rights era.

These are the contours of the Short case as they are recounted in Mike Davis's classic work of historical "excavation," *City of Quartz*, but they do not represent the entire story.[2] What Davis fails to mention is that the Shorts were black Catholics, and that shortly after the fire, Mrs. Short's sister called on Father George Dunne, a young Jesuit priest teaching political science at Loyola University of Los Angeles, as well as the attorney Dan Marshall, Dunne's friend and founder of the Catholic Interracial Council of Los Angeles, to relate the details of what she considered a case of racially inspired murder. Dunne responded by bringing the case to the attention of a national Catholic audience by writing two scathing articles indicting the San Bernardino district attorney for negligence in the liberal Catholic periodical *Commonweal* in 1946, and later writing a stage play called "Trial by Fire," based on the Short case that played to audiences throughout the country beginning that same year. While the tragic story of the Short family might never have received the attention it was due from either the mainstream media or the justice system, Dunne, Marshall, and other progressive Catholics in Los Angeles worked assiduously to make the story known to the wider public.

Dunne's involvement with the Short case was only one aspect of his wider political engagement with progressive causes, Catholic and otherwise, in the early years of the Cold War. In addition to writing about the tragedy in Fontana, Dunne was also involved in efforts to establish a permanent Fair Employment Practices Commission (FEPC) in California, supported Dan Marshall in the landmark California Supreme Court case *Perez v. Sharp*, which overturned the ban on interracial marriage in 1948, and played a pivotal role in assisting the insurgent Conference of Studio Unions (CSU) in their long and sometimes bloody battle with the Hollywood studios after the war. Moreover, Dunne provided an unambiguous theological and intellectual foundation for Catholic interracialism by becoming the first Catholic cleric to declare segregation a sin against charity in an article published in 1945, and even called for Catholics to work constructively with democratic socialists for the common good in another article that same year.

Dunne's activism also revealed fissures in the Catholic Church's struggle with race in the post-World War II period, as his arguments against segregation and racial violence brought him into conflict with his own religious superiors and conservative bishops that conflated racial justice with secularism and socialism, at a time when many American Catholics were energetically engaged in opposing both as the Cold War unfolded. Dunne's career in many ways foretold a post-Vatican II Catholic Church in which his fellow Jesuits would often be advocates for civil rights, racial equality, and universal human dignity. However, this future was hardly inevitable in the early Cold War years, as predominantly white American Catholics (and white Jesuits) slowly and even reluctantly turned their attention to issues of racial injustice in the United States.

Dunne's political and religious commitments in the immediate postwar years brought him into the same orbit as a host of activists that comprised the left/liberal/labor coalition in Los Angeles, especially on issues at the intersection of race and labor, that included figures such as Los Angeles CIO head Philip "Slim" Connelly, a practicing Catholic and Communist Party member who was among the many leftists purged from the labor movement in the late 1940s, as well as African American politicians such as Augustus Hawkins, who at that time was a member of the California state legislature and one of the leading figures in the FEPC campaign.

At the same time, Dunne was part of a larger institutional and transnational Catholic world as a Jesuit priest with significant previous experience as a missionary in China, where much of his reform-minded sensibilities were forged in the early 1930s. In addition, Dunne was closely linked with his fellow Jesuit, Father John LaFarge, the editor of the Catholic periodical *America* and founder of the national network of Catholic Interracial Councils who favored a more gradual approach to racial integration, as well as with fellow California Jesuits who worked alongside him on labor issues. Indeed, Dunne's status as a Jesuit priest and political activist in the early Cold War years would often lead him into conflict with a Church hierarchy that grew more militantly anticommunist during the period under the influence of bishops such as New York's Cardinal Francis Spellman and his protégé, Cardinal James Francis McIntyre of Los Angeles.

Yet, contests over Catholic anticommunism, its commitment to democracy, and Cold War politics more generally, were not limited to intra-ecclesial skirmishes. Shortly after Paul Blanshard published his best-selling anti-Catholic tract, *American Freedom and Catholic Power*, in 1949, Harvard Law School invited him and Father Dunne to square off in a public forum to debate the issues.[3] Blanshard's work had in many ways revived nineteenth-century nativist arguments that Catholics were incapable of voting their conscience, and instead would defer to the authority of priests, bishops, and the Pope. But Blanshard was not a conservative Know-Nothing, but rather a progressive that feared what he perceived as Catholicism's reactionary tendencies. The transcript of their discussion from 1950 provides a fascinating window into the intellectual, moral, and religious dimensions of still-developing Cold War politics. That Dunne, rather than a more "orthodox" spokesperson for the Catholic position, would be chosen to defend the Church's embrace of American values, speaks not only to the shifting ground of Cold War politics, but also to the political diversity within institutional American Catholicism in this period, which belies its reputation as monolithically anticommunist and increasingly conservative.

This chapter focuses primarily on Father George Dunne's political, religious, and intellectual activism in the brief, but remarkably eventful, period just after World War II, in which he engaged with a range of critical issues from racial violence and the strike wave of 1946 to national debates over the role of Catholicism in American public life and the struggles within the Church to define its Cold War politics. This chapter is also a modest attempt to bring Catholic history into dialogue with broader currents in American historiography. Dunne's activism does not fit neatly into conventional narratives of either the history of the postwar left or of the Catholic Cold War. Rather, it reveals the volatile boundaries between the political and the religious, the Church and the world, in a time of great struggle, from the streets of Fontana to the realm of international politics, over the direction of the nation and the Catholic Church, especially regarding race, labor, and broader questions of human dignity. As such, the title of Dunne's play about racial violence and the Short case was well chosen, for the immediate postwar years were indeed a trial by fire.

From China to St. Louis

When Dunne was a young Jesuit scholastic (as seminarians in the Society of Jesus are known) in the late-1920s, he volunteered for the China mission.[4] China had been missionary territory for the Jesuits and other Catholic religious orders since the sixteenth century, but the number of Christian missionaries in China, both Protestant and Catholic, was at an all-time high when Dunne arrived. The over 20,000 missionaries in Republican China constituted the largest foreign presence in the country, and they occupied important positions in schools and churches in major cities such as Shanghai and Beijing, as well as in the impoverished countryside.[5] European Jesuits, especially the French, had built up a robust network of Catholic institutions in a number of locations, but were increasingly in need of assistance as the number of Chinese Catholics steadily grew.

The California Province of the Jesuits, which had itself only ceased to be a missionary territory in 1909, agreed to send men to contribute to the China mission beginning in the late-1920s, and Dunne was one of the first to offer his services. He arrived in the French Concession of Shanghai in 1931 and set about learning Mandarin, teaching in the local Jesuit high school, and studying theology in preparation for his priestly ordination. However, Dunne's experience in China did more than enkindle his missionary zeal to save souls and convert the vast Chinese population to Catholicism. It also convinced him of the need for systematic social reform to prevent a Communist takeover of China.

Dunne witnessed firsthand the corruption of the Kuomintang government and the growing restiveness of the urban population that surrounded him in 1930s Shanghai. Although Mao's troops were at the time cordoned off in the south of China, Dunne interpreted the social unrest and poverty around him as ominous signs of the impending success of the Communist revolution. He wrote to his Jesuit superiors that unless China's Republican government instituted a host of critical reforms, China would fall into Communist hands by the 1960s at the latest. The dislocations of the Japanese invasion of China in 1937 significantly accelerated Dunne's timetable, and China was indeed in Communist hands by 1949.

Dunne's missionary experience in China was informed by a Catholic anticommunism that had been developing since the nineteenth century. Indeed, the pronounced anticlericalism of left-wing revolutionary movements in Europe since the French Revolution had placed the Catholic Church in a defensive, even reactionary, posture for well over a century by the time Dunne arrived in Shanghai. Yet the Catholic struggle against socialism and communism in Europe had a very different character than what Dunne had come to know in an Asian context. In Europe, the battle raged over the hearts and minds of the Catholic working class, whom the Church feared were rapidly exchanging their allegiance to priests and bishops for the radical possibilities of revolution. Much of the social teaching of the Catholic Church, which it began to promulgate in a serious way with Pope Leo XIII's encyclical, *Rerum Novarum*, in 1893, was an attempt to address the issue of labor from a pointedly anticommunist perspective, even as it acknowledged the dignity of labor and the rights of workers to organize into unions.[6]

Dunne's sojourn in China coincided with the next major development in Catholic social teaching, Pope Pius XI's 1931 encyclical, *Quadragesimo Anno*, written on the fortieth anniversary of Leo XIII's work. *Quadragesimo Anno* went much further than *Rerum Novarum* in providing a Catholic vision for government and the social contract, arguing essentially for a corporatist state, based on principles of subsidiarity, which would integrate the needs of labor, as well as management, into the body politic. In Europe, *Quadragesimo Anno* had an unforeseen influence on fascist political movements, adherants of which regarded the encyclical as a comprehensive and potentially powerful antidote to the threat of communism.

However, the impact of Catholic social teaching was far different in the United States, where it lent renewed legitimacy to social reform efforts such as the 1919 Bishops' Program of Social Reconstruction, written by Msgr. John Ryan, one of the leading figures of progressive Catholicism from the Progressive era through the New Deal. Ryan's signature contribution to American Catholic social thought was his insistence that the government provide a "living wage" to all workers, sufficient for a male breadwinner to support a family. Despite the deeply gendered character of such reforms, Ryan and the Bishops' Plan represented a remarkably progressive vision for American society that was less overtly concerned with the specter of communism than its European counterparts.[7]

Dunne carried this distinctively American version of Catholic social reform with him to China, where he realized the international dimensions of the problems of labor and capital. Understandably, however, his primary concern was safeguarding the integrity of the Jesuit missionary project in China, which had stretched back several centuries to the time of famed European missionaries such as Matteo Ricci and Ferdinand Verbiest during the Ming and Qing dynasties.[8] Dunne knew that a victory by Mao's People's Army would potentially have a devastating effect on the network of schools and churches that the Jesuits had constructed in hopes of converting China's massive population to Catholicism. Moreover, it would mean an end to the Catholic social vision in that country that was gaining at least some traction in Europe and the United States as the devastation of the Great Depression took hold.

When Dunne was forced to leave China because of health concerns shortly before his ordination to the priesthood, he did so with great regret. An academic center that he was helping to establish that would have brought Jesuit scholars from around the world to study and live in China was having difficulty getting off the ground, and Dunne despaired of its ultimate success. Nevertheless, Dunne's confrontation with the transnational dimensions of the need for social reform and a robust Catholic response to social inequality stayed with him through the remainder of his Jesuit formation, and it would color his future engagement with the issues of race and labor in Los Angeles and beyond after the war.

Dunne's time in China also reveals an overlooked dimension of progressive Catholic thought and practice in the United States—its inherent transnationalism. Much has been written about "home-grown" twentieth-century progressive Catholics such as Dorothy Day and Thomas Merton, both of whom were contemporaries of Dunne. Historian James Fisher has written of these Catholics as part of a distinctly American Catholic counterculture that defined itself partly in opposition to both mainstream American culture and the conservative hierarchy of the Church (although Day in particular was generally a supporter of the hierarchy).[9] Day's Catholic Worker movement, for example, is most often interpreted as an outgrowth of an American radical tradition to which Day added a personalist philosophy and Catholic doctrine to forge an incisive, activist critique of capitalism and dominant American values such as consumerism. Even as Day launched her assault on American materialism and excess, however, she embodied deeper American currents of utopianism, communitarianism, and a bohemian subculture.

While undoubtedly true, these portrayals leave out important American Catholic actors, particularly members of international religious orders, who had direct experience of nations and contexts beyond American borders and who occupied critical leadership positions within the US Catholic Church. For Dunne, this experience would not only shape his intellectual outlook, but also deeply informed his engagement with American politics, especially as the Cold War began to unfold.

After his return to the United States, Dunne continued to keep international politics in focus as he began doctoral studies at the University of Chicago in political science, specializing in Sovietology. Dunne was part of a growing cadre of Catholic clergy that were beginning to be educated in secular universities by the mid-twentieth century, breaking free of the constraints of Catholic seminary education, even if they were slated to return to Catholic universities to teach, as Dunne was. Dunne's first assignment after receiving his doctorate in the mid-1940s was to teach political science at St. Louis University, but his progressive politics soon brought him into conflict with other Jesuits in the university administration as well as the archbishop of St. Louis, John Glennon. The issue, however, was not over his interest in the Soviet Union, but over his stand on race.[10]

While in St. Louis, Dunne joined a group of progressive Jesuits and like-minded lay persons to push for the integration of the city's Catholic schools, much to the displeasure of the segregationist Glennon. Although St. Louis University itself had quietly begun admitting black students just before the end of the war, the archbishop's racial views made for an exceedingly delicate political situation for the Jesuit administrators. Dunne, who apparently could never be accused of subtlety, began broadcasting radio homilies in which he attacked segregation as inimical to the Gospel, and the archdiocese's continued policy of school segregation as inherently unjust. After several more incidents in which Dunne forcefully argued for the immediate desegregation of Catholic institutions in St. Louis, he was dismissed from the university by its president, Father Patrick Holloran. His fractious time in St. Louis over racial issues subsequently inspired Dunne to forge an intellectual and moral foundation for interracial politics that set him apart even from racial liberals such as the Jesuit Father John LaFarge, founder of the Catholic Interracial Council of New York and patron of its nationwide network.

The Sin of Segregation

After leaving St. Louis, Dunne's Jesuit superiors reassigned him to Loyola University of Los Angeles, a move that would bring him into the center of political conflicts over race and labor in the early postwar years. While he was transitioning to his new post, Dunne wrote two influential articles for the liberal Catholic periodical *Commonweal*, in which he staked out a position well to the left of most Catholics on racial integration and the prospects of Catholic cooperation with socialists. Taken together, these articles reveal not only Dunne's progressive credentials, but also the variety of Catholic political discourse available in 1945, before the hardening of lines during the McCarthy era and a more strident brand of Catholic anticommunism came to the fore.

In "The Sin of Segregation," Dunne, with the bitter aftertaste of his time in St. Louis still very much in evidence, wrote that "the racist mind has contrived an almost limitless number of evasive analogies to justify the unjustifiable," perhaps obliquely referring to Archbishop Glennon and other segregationist Catholics.[11] He went on to dismantle spurious claims about the ill effects of miscegenation, which he claimed owed more to the fascist thought of the Nazis than to believing Christians. Dunne's rationale was, admittedly, more philosophical than political. It was based on a vision of justice and natural rights that were normative in Catholic thought, even if Dunne was applying these ancient principles in new and controversial ways. Moreover, his starting place, as was true of most racial liberals of the time, was the individual's conscience and the ways in which racism conflicted with an individual's right to choose their own acquaintances and friends. However, Dunne quickly moved beyond this liberal focus on individualism to pose a more socially grounded set of objections to segregation.

Dunne continued his assault on racial exclusion by calling for an end to restrictive covenants and noting that white concerns over property values based on the alleged moral inferiority of racial minorities was an instance of utter hypocrisy, as many of these same people already invited blacks into their homes as domestic servants. Dunne also added another call for the immediate desegregation of all Catholic institutions, extending a line of argument that he had used in his controversial radio homilies in St. Louis.

Yet Dunne saved his most devastating critique of segregation, at least for any faithful Catholic, for the end of his long article in *Commonweal*. Dunne concluded that segregation was not only an illogical and unjust practice, but that it was a sin against charity itself. Although this might seem like a commonplace and uncontroversial statement in our post-civil rights era, it was far from that in the Catholic world of 1945. As historians such as John McGreevy have argued, the encounter with race was one on the most fractious issues to confront the US Church throughout the twentieth century. Most American Catholics, particularly those in urban neighborhoods in the Northeast and Midwest, lived in an almost entirely Catholic world, with a dense network of social institutions, schools, hospitals, and charitable organizations that structured Catholic life.[12] The most important institution in this Catholic world was the geographical parish, which not only organized social and spiritual life, but also sacralized Catholic neighborhoods, making them particularly defensive about encroachments by racial outsiders, especially non-Catholic African Americans. It would only be in the 1960s that the Church began to use its institutional weight to fully desegregate Catholic institutions, but even then, these efforts were often met by massive resistance on the part of the working-class Catholics in the pews.

Nevertheless, Dunne was not completely alone in his calls for greater racial inclusion in the Catholic community. John LaFarge worked for greater racial tolerance among Catholics through his many Catholic interracial councils, as well as through his editorship of the national Jesuit magazine, *America*. However, as historians have noted, there were clear limits to LaFarge's interracial politics, as he generally favored a gradual approach that would not alienate traditional Catholics and other conservatives among the faithful.[13] He was especially cautious on issues of interracial marriage, fearing that the offspring of such marriages would inevitably be subject to harassment and discrimination in the racist American culture.

Dunne, along with his friend Dan Marshall, the Los Angeles-based lawyer who had founded the short-lived Catholic Interracial Council of Los Angeles, were far more aggressive in their calls for racial equality and the immediate integration of Catholic institutions that set them apart from their East Coast counterparts. Marshall was especially concerned with LaFarge's gradualism with respect to interracial marriage, seeing in it a potentially dangerous justification for continuing racial intolerance.

In fact, Marshall, along with Dunne's support, petitioned the California Supreme Court in a landmark 1948 case *Perez v. Sharp* to overturn statewide restrictions on interracial marriage.[14] Andrea Perez was a Mexican American woman who wished to be married to Sylvester Davis, an African American man, which was prohibited under California state law because Mexicans at the time were considered to be white. Both Perez and Davis were Catholics and parishioners at Marshall's multiracial church, St. Patrick's in South Central Los Angeles. Marshall's argument before the court was not based solely on his legal convictions regarding the injustice of racial discrimination. Rather, he made *Perez v. Sharp* into a First Amendment case, arguing that the couple's religious freedom was being violated by the state by not allowing them to participate in the sacrament of marriage.

Marshall won the case in a 5:4 decision but was disturbed by the dissenting opinion of one of the judges that cited Lafarge's writings in the 1944 book, *The Race Question and the Negro*, as a rationale for the continued ban on interracial marriage. Marshall quickly fired off a letter to Lafarge, warning him about the ways that his moderate stance on racial issues was being appropriated by segregationists to uphold unjust legislation, and only thinly veiling his anger over LaFarge's go-slow approach to integration.[15]

Dunne, on the other hand, was no gradualist on racial issues and shared Marshall's concerns over LaFarge's policies. But Dunne also had an even larger, more global political project in mind in the immediate postwar years as the world reconfigured itself in the aftermath of the Allied victory. In another article published within a few months of "The Sin of Segregation," Dunne outlined the possibilities for Catholics and democratic socialists to work together to secure a more just social order—the one that he had first recognized the need for in his China days.

In "Socialism and socialism," which appeared in the pages of *Commonweal* in November of 1945, Dunne surveyed the postwar political landscape in Europe and was deeply disturbed by the ways in which the forces of unbridled capitalism were already working to assert control.[16] He wrote, "It is difficult to understand how anyone could have imagined that with the day of liberation there would come pouring out ... an army of capitalists bent upon restoring the old order of things that had preceded conquest." Dunne lamented that the solidarities forged in the dark days of the war were already disaggregating in the few short months since the defeat of Nazism, and that financiers and industrialists, who had done little to earn the victory, were moving swiftly to dictate the terms of the peace.

Dunne's proposed solution to the problems confronting postwar Europe involved the cooperation of Christian Democrats and Socialists to work together to create a more just and equitable social, economic, and political order. Doing so, he argued, required that Catholics learn to distinguish between the materialist philosophy of Socialism, which it must reject, and its program for economic restructuring and redistribution of goods, which it ought to embrace wholeheartedly as representative of Gospel values. In a similar manner, Dunne maintained that Socialists should give up their historical opposition to the Catholic Church as a bastion of reactionary social and political thought.

Dunne's call for cooperation between leftwing political groups and Christian Democratic parties was undoubtedly rooted in the distinctive brand of anticommunism that he had begun to develop as a China missionary in the 1930s. However, Dunne's anticommunism had significant room in it for endorsing an economic plan with strongly socialist components, even to the point of significantly redistributing wealth and curtailing the influence of capitalists. This political vision during the earliest years of the Cold War put him at odds with other American Catholics, who greeted the postwar years with increasing trepidation over the expansion of Soviet influence.

One of these prominent Catholics was Dunne's fellow Jesuit, Father Edmund Walsh, founder of the Georgetown School of Foreign Service and a militant anticommunist from the very first days of the Soviet Union.[17] Clerics like Walsh would have a major influence on a much more conservative strand of Catholic anticommunism, typified by bishops such as Cardinals Spellman and McIntyre, as well as postwar politicians such as the devoutly Catholic Joseph McCarthy, with whom Walsh had a close relationship. This more strident anticommunism steadily grew more prominent, and even normative, in Catholic circles as the Cold War developed in the 1950s, drawing into its orbit a cadre of conservative intellectuals such as William F. Buckley, and eventually providing a basis for cooperation between Catholics and conservative Protestants on issues of foreign policy. However, Dunne's article from 1945 suggests that Catholic anticommunism was far more fluid than sometimes imagined, especially in the volatile years immediately after the war, and that the advent of McCarthyism, fueled in part by the Catholic faithful, was far from inevitable.

Taken together, Dunne's two remarkable articles from 1945 represent his attempt to forge an intellectual and moral argument not only about race, but about the postwar future of the United States and the world based on principles of equity, social justice, and increasing cooperation between the left and the Catholic Church. For Dunne, this vision was deeply rooted in philosophical and theological concerns. In his memoir, Dunne admits that his knowledge of the history of racial discrimination in the United States and the Catholic Church was limited until much later in life.[18] What animated Dunne's activism was instead a pronounced sense of universalism in both the secular and religious meanings of that term. In Dunne's view, because the Gospel directed Christians toward a recognition of human dignity, this universal call should logically be extended to the granting of equal civil and political rights to all people, regardless of race. In a memorable confrontation with an unsympathetic Jesuit superior, Dunne argued that "Negroes had equal rights in the Church [and] by equal I mean equal, and cannot conceive of unequal equalities."[19] Despite their abstract philosophical origins, Dunne's ruminations on the pages of *Commonweal* would come vividly, and tragically, to life as he confronted the cauldron of race, labor, and politics in Los Angeles.

The Short Case and the Strike Wave

The Cold War was not only waged on the plane of geopolitics and national political concerns—it was also fought locally, often in battles over the color line, labor, and, in this case, religion. Viewing Cold War politics "from the bottom up" reveals the often-violent set of contests that played out in American cities and other locations over the meanings and directions of life in the postwar period.[20]

Los Angeles was one of the key places where these battles were fought in the mid- to late 1940s. The city's multiracial demographic, which made its color line far more protean than it was in Northeastern or Midwestern cities, also made it a primary place where the struggle against racial exclusion, restrictive covenants, and workplace discrimination took on the most urgency.[21] For Dunne, two crucial events critically shaped his understanding and engagement with local Cold War politics—the aforementioned Short case and the Hollywood strikes that began in 1945. Together, these incidents brought Dunne closer to the positions of a remarkable group of progressive activists, including members of the NAACP and the Los Angeles CIO, that historian Shana Bernstein has called "bridges of reform."[22] Perhaps inevitably, they also brought Dunne into conflict within both the Catholic Archdiocese of Los Angeles and the increasingly conservative political world of postwar Southern California.

As historian Josh Sides has argued, in many ways Los Angeles was a city of real opportunity for African Americans in the twentieth century.[23] Like many industrial cities, Los Angeles had attracted many blacks during both phases of the Great Migration, and the burgeoning metropolis provided ample job opportunities, even if they tended to be, as in most cities, at the bottom rung of the economic ladder. African Americans had slowly broken out from the Central Avenue corridor near downtown into several surrounding neighborhoods of South Central Los Angeles, a vast area that would become synonymous with the black Angelinos in the ensuing decades. Yet, many Los Angeles neighborhoods and suburbs remained closed to blacks, either through the use of restrictive covenants or more subtle forms of housing discrimination. In some cases, however, as in Fontana in December of 1945, racial exclusion took a violent turn.

After learning of the tragic events in Fontana, Dunne hastily wrote an article that appeared in March of 1946 in *Commonweal*. Entitled simply "The Short Case," Dunne recounted the visit by Mrs. Short's sister to a meeting of the Catholic Interracial Council of Los Angeles in which it was resolved to press the San Bernardino District Attorney's office to reopen its investigation of the fatal fire that claimed the lives of the Short family.[24] As historian Fay Botham has written, the Los Angeles chapter of the Catholic Interracial Council was a "short-lived, but influential organization" that brought together progressive white Catholics from around the city with Mexican Americans and African Americans around issues of racial justice. Much of the activity of the council was centered on St. Patrick's parish in South Los Angeles and home to many of the city's black Catholics, including the physician, Thomas Peyton, with whom Dunne's friend Dan Marshall often collaborated.[25]

In the article, Dunne fused biblical language with calls for social justice and restitution, writing that "there are no restrictive covenants in Jerusalem the holy city," and went on to attack the arbiters of "bourgeois morality" for turning a blind eye to racial injustice and even murder. Dunne was also clearly frustrated by the fact that any attempts to address issues of race in Los Angeles were invariably met with suspicions of communist influence. With the bitterest irony he also wrote that what Paradise needed, according to some, was "a Hearst newspaper and an American Legion." For Dunne, the Short family was not only a victim of racist vigilantes, but of the hypocrisy and facile politics of Los Angeles' conservative middle class, who made a mockery of both religious and political calls for justice.

After writing a follow-up article on the Short case for *Commonweal*, Dunne set about writing a stage play based on transcripts of the coroner's inquest that he and Dan Marshall had obtained, after much resistance, from the San Bernardino Sherriff's Department.[26] He had been encouraged to write a play by his friend, Sister Marie de Lourdes, mother superior at nearby Mount St. Mary's College and a teacher of theater arts. She was convinced that not only would the story of the Short tragedy make great theater, it would also be a way of publicizing the Short case beyond the limited readership of *Commonweal*.[27] Dunne agreed, rapidly writing what would be his first and only play, *Trial by Fire*, which premiered at the Wilshire Ebell Theater in Los Angeles in late-1946. In the next several years, it played before audiences in cities from New York to Chicago, receiving positive notices and even the occasional rave review (from no less an august figure than Langston Hughes) for its gutsy and emotional portrayal of racial violence and the nobility of the Short family's stand against restrictive covenants.[28]

During *Trial by Fire*'s initial run in 1946, Dunne and the actors used the play as a means of political mobilization in support of Proposition 11, which appeared on California's ballots in 1946. Prop 11 would have permanently established a Fair Employment Practices Commission (FEPC) in California, institutionalizing the expiring national FEPC put in place during the war by

President Roosevelt. The campaign for the passage of Prop 11 was itself a microcosm of the collision of Cold War politics and religion, as the Catholic Archbishop Cantwell came out strongly in favor, while Rev. James Fifield, the conservative head of the First Congregational Church of Los Angeles, and a leading figure in anti-New Deal political activism, opposed the measure with equal fervor. Prop 11 was defeated in 1946, caught in the middle of a widening political and religious chasm in the early Cold War.

In June of 1947, *Ebony* magazine ran a feature article on both Dunne and *Trial by Fire*, marking perhaps the only time a white Catholic priest has been so honored.[29] The article noted the "smear campaign" that Dunne and his play had been subjected to by some Catholics, who called him "a tool of the Communists subverting the American way of life." Moreover, the article noted the unusual intellectual position Dunne occupied regarding Catholic anticommunism, arguing that "[Dunne's] insistence that Catholics should devote their lung-power to being outspoken on American sore spots instead of upbraiding outspoken Communists, plus his alienation of reactionaries in general, are working against him."

As Dunne's play worked its way across the country, it was often produced under the auspices of civil rights organizations such as Chicago's Civil Rights Congress, which included many members of the Communist Party USA It was apparently at this time that the FBI began compiling a file on Dunne, deeming his activities potentially un-American and far too close to Communists for their liking. As the Cold War grew colder in the late-1940s, it became increasingly difficult for Dunne to speak out openly on issues of racial justice without coming into conflict with authorities, just as *Ebony* magazine predicted.[30]

However, *Trial by Fire* was not the sole cause of Dunne's travails during the early years of the Cold War. He also became deeply embroiled in the Hollywood strikes that began in 1945 and continued through 1946 and 1947, when the upstart Conference of Studio Unions began a strike against both the studios and the rival International Alliance of Theatrical and Stage Employees (IATSE), which by that time had strong ties to organized crime. It would be a long and bloody strike, devolving several times into violent episodes, and constituting a crucial part of the 1946 strike wave, the largest in American history.[31]

Dunne became a kind of unofficial chaplain to the CSU strikers, appearing at rallies to assure them that justice was on their side and to continue fighting against the studios and IATSE, and providing them, along with Dan Marshall, with strategic and legal advice. Accusations of Dunne's sympathies with communists once again circulated widely, provoking the ire of the then Archbishop of Los Angeles, John Cantwell, who was committed to seeking a peaceful and quick resolution to the strike and undermining communist influence in Hollywood. However, Dunne's critics were not limited to the Catholic hierarchy. When Dunne suggested that the Screen Actors Guild (SAG) join in a sympathy strike on behalf of the CSU, he was vehemently rebuffed in a face-to-face meeting by the union's president, Ronald Reagan, who was convinced that the Hollywood strikes were the leading edge of a communist conspiracy to subvert the United States government.[32]

In August of 1947, Dunne was called to testify before the House Committee on Education and Labor in order to clarify his role in the labor unrest that had engulfed Hollywood since the end of the war. Although cleared of any wrongdoing or communist activities, the Jesuits soon reassigned Dunne out of Los Angeles to Phoenix, largely owing to the controversy surrounding his prolabor politics. It was the beginning of a great deal of change in Los Angeles, as the grip of the more militant strand of Catholic anticommunism began to gather strength as the 1940s drew to a close.

In 1948, Joseph Cantwell retired as archbishop of Los Angeles and was replaced by James Francis McIntyre, who had served as Cardinal Spellman's chancellor in New York. McIntyre was deeply conservative, both theologically and politically, and committed to the stridently anticommunist politics of his mentor. One of McIntyre's first acts as archbishop was to officially dissolve the Catholic Interracial Council (CIC-LA), a move that has been widely interpreted to reveal the new archbishop's insensitivity to racial issues. However, even in this instance, issues of race, labor, and politics collide. In 1946, the CIC-LA had given their annual award to Los Angeles CIO chief Slim Connelly, a noted communist and dedicated Catholic who had done much to organize Los Angeles' growing industrial labor force throughout the 1940s. The move had infuriated many in the archdiocese, including Father Tom McCarthy, the editor of the archdiocesan newspaper, *The Tidings*. McCarthy wrote an angry letter to LaFarge in New York denouncing the CIC-LA's recognition of such a controversial figure who could be found, McCarthy noted, "at many questionable meetings around the city." Undoubtedly, McIntyre took McCarthy's concerns into account when he dissolved the CIC-LA, another victim of the early Cold War.[33]

Conclusion: Dunne v. Blanshard

In exile in Phoenix, Dunne worked in the local Jesuit parish, waiting for his opportunity to reconnect with the political scene in Los Angeles. In 1949, he was inspired to write a response to Paul Blanchard's book *American Freedom and Catholic Power*, which indicted the Catholic Church as inherently un-American, antidemocratic and authoritarian—charges that carried particular gravity as the United States struggled for global dominance against the Soviet Union. Blanchard's book was a best-seller and reignited the long-running debate in American history over the ability of the Catholic Church to embrace democratic values, even as it revived the equally venerable tradition of American anti-Catholicism.

In 1950, Harvard Law School invited Blanchard and Dunne to Cambridge to debate their respective positions at a public forum. In the political funhouse that was the early Cold War, the liberal Blanchard in many ways stood to the political right of Dunne on any number of issues. Yet it was Dunne who was called upon to defend his commitment to democracy. During the debate, Blanchard recapitulated the major arguments from his book, citing undue Catholic influence in everything from medicine to education that did not admit of democratic participation. In particular, Blanchard singled out Catholic opposition to birth control and the liberalization of divorce laws, as well as the Catholic hierarchy's penchant for censorship.[34] It was a familiar litany that might have been heard, with slightly different particulars, in the nineteenth century as well as the mid-twentieth century.

Despite his own struggles with the Catholic hierarchy, Dunne responded as a forthright Catholic apologist, demonstrating both his doctorate in political science and his extensive philosophical training by parsing Blanchard's statements like a latter-day scholastic theologian. He defended in particular Catholic political action through the National Catholic Welfare

Conference, as well as traditional Catholic conceptions of the relationship of church and state. Moreover, Dunne also argued that Blanchard had made the mistake of conflating the moral and the political. For Catholics, Dunne claimed, some things are simply right or wrong, beyond the wrangling of politics. Perhaps, in the end, Dunne's progressive politics of the 1940s were ultimately more about his burning sense of justice and morality than they were about a political platform. The issues he chose to focus on—from the Short case to the CSU strike—strongly suggest this was the case.

In his response to Blanchard, Dunne was once again the missionary, proclaiming the faith to an often-indifferent audience, as laughter occasionally greeted his serious responses on that night in Cambridge in 1950. The moment strikingly captures, however, Catholic politics of the Cold War that were very much in flux. Ultimately, Dunne was far from what would later be known as a liberal Catholic during the great transformations unleashed in the Catholic Church by the Second Vatican Council. Instead, he was a rather traditional figure who tried to forge a different path through the thickets of Cold War politics from that of many of his contemporaries in the Church. Dunne's vision of racial justice, labor activism, and a more capacious anticommunism would not come to define the mainstream of Catholic Cold War politics as did the darker visions of Spellman, McIntyre, and McCarthy.

Postscript

In 1953, the National Catholic Welfare Conference, speaking in the name of the Roman Catholic Bishops of the United States, issued a statement outlining its social teaching in a document entitled, "The Dignity of Man." It began with a traditional appeal to Catholic doctrine, with its distinctive blend of philosophical and theological reasoning, arguing for the inherent dignity of all human beings predicated on their relationship with God, the "mode of [human] existence," and the "nobility of [human] destiny."[35] Despite beginning with this series of intellectualized abstractions, the document soon turned to its primary focus: the economy, labor, and education as fundamental areas of American life in which dignity must be protected. While arguing in favor of private property, the bishops also noted that all economic activity must serve the common good. This instruction was in keeping with the longer history of Catholic social teaching, which began in 1893 with Pope Leo XIII's encyclical, *Rerum Novarum*, which set out a vision of economic activity rooted in strongly communitarian values as a check on the excesses of nineteenth-century capitalism.

Inextricably connected with the bishops' notion that the economy was meant to serve the common good of all people was the idea that human labor possessed dignity in its own right and that labor unions represented the best means for the dignity of the working class to be recognized and assured. The Catholic Church had similarly developed its teaching on labor and labor unions through the various social encyclicals, beginning with those of Leo XII and continuing throughout the twentieth century's various papacies. In 1953, the American bishops were therefore attempting to apply what was already an established Catholic position on the economy and labor to the changing circumstances of the postwar world, most notably the emergence of the capitalist West and Soviet-dominated Eastern Bloc as rivals for ideological supremacy. "The worker is not a hand, as individualistic capitalism contends; not a stomach to be fed by commissars, as communism thinks; but a person," the bishops wrote, worrying that the bipolar postwar world left little room for the Catholic vision of society.[36]

The bishops concluded their 1953 statement with both a plea for and a compelling defense of the centrality of dignity as an organizing principle of all human society, and therefore of the American political order as well. "We must . . . expend every effort to see that this dignity is . . . nurtured by society, guarded by the state, stabilized by private ownership and exercised through creative activity," the bishops argued, but in their view, they were not merely offering a lesson in Catholic political theory. Rather, the American bishops, a group that included the archbishop of Los Angeles, Cardinal McIntyre, warned Catholics and non-Catholics alike that a failure to recognize human dignity would result in "increasing chaos" and a world potentially destroyed, if not by moral decay, then by nuclear annihilation.[37]

As the second half of the twentieth century unfolded, this Catholic concept of dignity would continue to evolve, with Jesuits and religious other activists at the forefront of advocating for the dignity of immigrants, racial minorities, and a plethora of other marginalized groups. By the 1980s, Los

Angeles-based Jesuits such as Greg Boyle and Michael Kennedy became potent voices for the human rights and dignity of refugees from war-torn Latin America, and later, for gang members and prisoners. The twenty-first-century advent of the Black Lives Matter movement has also prompted American Jesuits to a reevaluation of their individual and institutional contributions to racial justice and the perpetuation of injustice. In many ways, Dunne's activism in Cold War Los Angeles provides a "usable past" as the United States and the Catholic Church face another reckoning with race—another trial by fire.

Notes

1.   This essay is adapted from Chapter 1 of my larger work, *The Politics of Dignity: Religion and the Making of Global Los Angeles* (Chicago: University of Chicago Press, forthcoming).

2.   See Mike Davis, *City of Quartz: Excavating the Future in Los Angeles* (New York: Verso, 1990), 397ff.

3.   Paul Blanshard, *American Freedom and Catholic Power* (Boston, MA: Beacon press, 1949). The book originally appeared as a series of articles in *The Nation* magazine.

4.   This account is largely adapted from George Dunne's autobiography, *King's Pawn: The Memoirs of George H. Dunne, S. J.* (Chicago: Loyola University Press, 1990), 33ff.

5.   See Frank Dikotter, *The Age of Openness: China before Mao* (Berkeley: University of California Press, 2008), 48.

6.   For a historical overview of Catholic social thought from a European perspective, see Joe Holland, *Modern Catholic Social Teaching: The Popes Confront the Industrial Age, 1740–1958* (New York: Paulist Press, 2003).

7.   See Harlan Beckley, *Passion for Justice: Retrieving the Legacies of Walter Rauschenbusch, John A. Ryan, and Reinhold Niebuhr* (Louisville, KY: John Knox Press, 1992).

8.   One of the best accounts of these missionaries is George Dunne's own *Generation of Giants: The Story of the Jesuits in China in the Last Decades of the Ming Dynasty* (Notre Dame, IN: University of Notre Dame Press, 1962).

9.   See James T. Fisher, *The Catholic Counterculture in America: 1933–1962* (Chapel Hill: University of North Carolina Press, 1989).

10.   See Dunne, 75ff.

11.   George H. Dunne, "The Sin of Segregation," *Commonweal* (Sept. 21, 1945): 542–45.

12.   See John T. McGreevy, *Parish Boundaries: The Catholic Encounter with Race in the Twentieth-Century Urban North* (Chicago: University of Chicago Press, 1996).

13. See David W. Southern, *John LaFarge and the Limits of Catholic Interracialism, 1911–1963* (Baton Rouge, LA: LSU Press, 1996).

14. This case, and Marshall's role in it, has recently received a good deal of scholarly attention. See Mark Brilliant, *The Color of America Has Changed: How Racial Diversity Shaped Civil Rights Reform in California, 1941–1978* (New York: Oxford University Press, 2010); Peggy Pascoe, *What Comes Naturally: Miscegenation Law and the Making of Race in America* (New York: Oxford University Press, 2009); and Fay Botham, *Almighty God Created the Races: Christianity, Interracial Marriage, and American Law* (Chapel Hill: University of North Carolina Press, 2009).

15. Dan Marshall, letter to John Lafarge, S.J., dated 10/4/1948, Papers of John LaFarge, S.J., Box 29, Folder 13, Georgetown University Archives.

16. George H. Dunne, "Socialism or socialism?" *Commonweal* (November 23, 1945): 134–39.

17. See Patrick H. McNamara, *A Catholic Cold War: Edmund A. Walsh, S. J. and the Politics of American Anticommunism* (New York: Fordham University Press, 2005).

18. See *King's Pawn*, 82–83.

19. Ibid., 86

20. This approach is suggested by the articles in the recent collection, Shelton Stromquist, ed., *Labor's Cold War: Local Politics in a Global Context* (Urbana: University of Illinois Press, 2008).

21. See, for example, Scott Kurashige, *The Shifting Grounds of Race: Black and Japanese Americans in the Making of Multiethnic Los Angeles* (Princeton: Princeton University Press, 2008).

22. Shana Bernstein, *Bridges of Reform: Interracial Civil Rights Activism in Twentieth-Century Los Angeles* (New York: Oxford University Press, 2011).

23. Josh Sides, *L. A. City Limits: African American Los Angeles from the Great Depression to the Present* (Berkeley: University of California Press, 2003).

24. George H. Dunne, "The Short Case," *Commonweal* (March 1, 1946): 494–97.

25. Fay Botham, *Almighty God Created the Races: Christianity, Interracial Marriage, and American Law* (Chapel Hill: University of North Carolina Press, 2009), 16ff.

26. The follow-up article is George H. Dunne, "No Accident!" *Commonweal* (May 24, 1946): 134–38.

27. See Dunne, 132ff.

28. Langston Hughes, "Trial by Fire," *Chicago Defender* (May 22, 1948): 14.

29. "Trial by Fire: Priest Writes Play to Wage War Against the Sin of Racism," *Ebony* (June 1, 1947): 31–35.

30. See Steven Rosswurm, *The FBI and the Catholic Church, 1935–1962* (Amherst: University of Massachusetts Press, 2009), 123ff.

31. See Gerald Horne, *Class Struggle in Hollywood, 1930–1950* (Austin: University of Texas Press, 2001) for a book-length account of the strikes, including Dunne's role.

32. Dunne, 152ff.

33. Based on a letter from Rev. Thomas J. McCarthy to John LaFarge, S,J., dated

8/28/1946, in Papers of John LaFarge, S.J., Box 29, Folder 13, Georgetown University Archives.

34.   The transcript of the forum has been preserved as a short book, *The Catholic Church and Politics: A Transcript of a Discussion of a Vital Issue* (Cambridge, MA: Harvard Law School Forum, Inc., 1950).

35.   Special to *The New York Times*, "Text of Statement by Catholic Bishops in U. S. on 'Dignity of Man,'" *New York Times*, November 22, 1953.

36.   Ibid.

37.   Ibid.

Epilogue

JOHN T. MCGREEVY

AMONG THE MANY VIRTUES of this set of essays is their collective ability to provide a long view. Historians are splitters by professional inclination. We divvy the world into medieval, early modern (try explaining that to a layperson) and modern, and within those chronological framings make fine distinctions based on subject and national origin. One much disputed line between early modern and modern is often drawn at what Robert Palmer long ago called the Age of Democratic Revolution. The French Revolution was Palmer's pivot point, but scholars now spy the modern in new forms of popular sovereignty and republican government on both sides of the Atlantic.[1]

The history of the Society of Jesus or Jesuits rests on a different division. The Old Society begins with Ignatius and his companions in Paris in 1534, runs through the extraordinary expansion of the Society around the world in the sixteenth and seventeenth centuries, and culminates in the suppressions beginning in Portugal and Portuguese colonies in the 1750s and the general suppression ordered by Clement XIV in 1773. Twenty-three thousand Jesuits from Rome to Madrid to Mexico City became diocesan priests or abandoned the priesthood altogether. Governments confiscated libraries, property, church buildings, and, in Amsterdam, paintings by Peter Paul Rubens.[2]

The New Society, founded in 1814, included some doughty veterans from the Old Society. It also included a handful of younger men trained in the few places where papal edicts had little effect such as the Russian Empire under Catherine the Great. But like so many of their Catholic contemporaries in the aftermath of the French Revolution, Jesuits in the New Society understood themselves as working against a corrupt modernity, not with it. Jesuits in the Old Society routinely worked at the frontiers of science and culture. They composed operas for Catholic monarchs and Indigenous peoples in South America, mapped the Orinoco River, and diagnosed the origins of syphilis.[3]

Jesuits in the New Society took a more cautious view than their predecessors. They fostered loyalty to the papacy (and helped draft the declaration of papal infallibility in 1870), cultivated ultramontane devotions such as the Sacred Heart and revived Thomistic or Scholastic philosophy as a challenge to a modern philosophical lineage stretching from Descartes to Kant. One Irish Jesuit scanned the room at a gathering of the world's Jesuits in 1829 and admitted that "the Society can no longer boast of so many brilliant men as she had in the age when Scholasticism flourished." He nonetheless insisted that Scholasticism "has always been the Theology of the Society and the weapon with which our forefathers conquered the enemies of the Catholic Truth."[4] At the same meeting, the assembled Jesuits cautioned "against the dangers of novelty, especially in any matters that in some way touch upon religion."[5]

Given this history, how can we understand the Jesuits and race? The conventional understanding of race rests on a contemporary scholarly resistance against any idea of the natural. "Race" before the modern era is, by definition, anachronistic and requires ironic quotation marks. In this view, the premodern world included differentiation based on religion or culture, but the modern notion of "race" emerged as a corollary of Darwinian biology and eugenics. Anti-Judaism for Martin Luther differs from anti-Semitism for Adolf Hitler.

A few of the authors in this collection reference historian David Nirenberg on this topic. They do not linger on his claim that ideas of race extend back into the medieval period.[6] Yet these essays suggest it might. One privilege of studying the Jesuits, after all, despite the break between the Old and New Societies, is the ability to examine a vast chronological sweep. The East India company is no more. Neither is the French monarchy. But the Jesuits still live and work under rules composed in the sixteenth century, and their spiritual development is centered on exercises arranged by Ignatius himself.

Nirenberg specializes in the history of late medieval Spain, also Ignatius's birthplace. The diversity of the Iberian Peninsula during this period, with Jews, Muslims, and Christians jostling up against one another has made it a laboratory for testing the limits of religious pluralism. Ignatius welcomed Jewish converts to Catholicism as members of the Society of Jesus, and at least one of his successors as father general of the Jesuits was a "New Christian" of Jewish heritage. Nonetheless, in 1593, the Society under pressure from a monarchy eager to eradicate the Jewish presence in Spain, banned entrants "who are descended from parents who are recent Christians."[7] A highlight of Emanuele Colombo's lucid essay is a close reading of a text by Antonio Possevino, a contemporary of Ignatius who defended the presence of New Christians among the Jesuits. To oppose them meant saying that "baptism was less than baptism." The twelve apostles, Possevino explained, were Jewish. As were his seventy-two disciples.

Distinctions based on lineage risked blunting the missionary efforts of the Society. If "New Christians" or Jews (or Muslims) were to be banned, what about pagans in Africa and Asia or Protestants in Europe? Several essays in this volume explore variations on this theme, particularly how ideas of civilizational superiority morphed over time into justifications for slavery based on race. Through a compelling reading of challenging Portuguese sources, Liam Brockey demonstrates how in Macau and Japan in the 1590s Jesuits relied upon unfree labor, probably indentured servants for the most part, as was typical and expected of colonial elites. Erin Rowe expertly shows us Jesuit complicity in forms of slavery in sixteenth-century Seville, but also the startling, and even moving, conviction, among Jesuit scholars that black bodies would remain black in the afterlife. Moving across the Atlantic to Chile, Andrew Redden challenges the imposition of modern racial hierarchies on his subjects, but he also convincingly shows how ideas about the superiority of European civilization could be imposed on Mapuche Indians. Susan Deeds decodes how optimistic programs of Jesuit evangelization of Native peoples in northwestern Mexico evolved into despair as disease and migration diminished Indigenous communities. Michelle Molina scrutinizes the instructions of a Jesuit administrator in colonial Mexico. In his detailed instructions for "servants and slaves," she uncovers a civilizational and at times racial hierarchy, and how the same instructions might provide the tools for servants and enslaved people to undermine it.

The continuities across the early modern and modern periods are significant. Before the suppression, Jesuits were among the largest landowners in Latin America and among the owners of the largest number of enslaved people. After the refounding of the Society, Jesuits in Maryland continued to own enslaved people. They famously sold 272 men and women in 1838 to aid a Georgetown University on the brink of insolvency and broke up dozens of families in the process. No Jesuits in Europe or North America took a leading role in the movement to abolish slavery, which was led by the same Protestants and secular liberals ultramontane Jesuits most mistrusted. One of the few Jesuits to support abolition, the Austrian Francis Weninger perhaps did so because he witnessed the horror of a New Orleans slave auction. But he also saw in the wartime Republican party "bigoted Puritans" eager to destroy Catholicism.[8]

Jesuit prejudice toward Jews also endured. Distinguishing between a religious anti-Judaism and a racial anti-Semitism in the modern period is perhaps a mistaken quest. The saturation of Jesuit edited *Civiltà Cattolica* with anti-Judaic and anti-Semitic essays in the late nineteenth century is easy to demonstrate.[9] In Central Europe, especially, Jesuits combined an enthusiasm for *Rerum Novarum*, the 1891 encyclical seen as the touchstone for Catholic social thought, with anti-Semitic bromides. To question modern capitalism often meant indulging in stereotypes about Jewish control of capitalism. The Polish Jesuit Marian Morawski and the Hungarian Jesuit Bela Bangha separately argued for the desirability of reducing Jewish influence.[10]

By the 1930s, Jews seemed to some Jesuits as, paradoxically, embedded in both capitalist and communist modernity. "Only from this perspective," wrote the German-Polish Jesuit Erich Przywara, could Christians understand traps set by "bolshevist as well as capitalist Jews, the West-Judaism of America and the East-Judaism of Russia."[11] Gustav Gundlach, perhaps the most important Jesuit social theorist of the early twentieth century, agreed. He rejected laws targeting Jews and reminded Catholics that Jews remained a "chosen people within the divine and Christian economy of salvation." But he also warned of the "truly harmful influence of the Jewish segment of the population in the areas of economy, politics, theater, cinema, the press, science and art." He thought it worrisome that Jews managed to "operate within the camp of world plutocracy" as well as "international Bolshevism."[12] An Austrian Jesuit opposed the Nazis in the 1930s, but he echoed sixteenth-century debates in Spain when he wondered whether even baptism could cure Jews of defects carried in their genes. The sacrament might not overcome "biological substance."[13]

How a powerful Jesuit anti-racism emerged out of this often-racist milieu is a story as yet only superficially told. In this volume, James O'Toole eloquently traces the halting efforts to integrate Jesuit institutions in the United States with African American Catholics. In Europe, at the same moment, many of those Catholics who first challenged anti-Semitism within the Catholic community were Jewish converts. Some of these men and women influenced Augustin Bea, a German Jesuit, Hebrew Bible scholar, and confessor to Pius XII, who as a cardinal helped draft the paragraphs describing the Jews as "brothers"—no longer enemies—in *Nostra Aetate*, one of the key documents of the Second Vatican Council.[14]

More broadly, personal experience with oppressed racial groups in missionary work catalyzed a shock of recognition. One of Gustav Gundlach's collaborators on a never released encyclical condemning racism, commissioned by Pius XI before his death, was John LaFarge, an American Jesuit.[15] LaFarge began his career in southern Maryland working with African American Catholics descended from enslaved people, a few from enslaved people once owned by Jesuits. He founded the Catholic Interracial Council movement. LaFarge's caution could be off-putting to bolder contemporaries—into the early 1940s he cautioned against racial intermarriage as a matter of prudence—but his insistence on racial equality as a basic human right was pathbreaking. One of LaFarge's American contemporaries, George Dunne, S.J., became interested in Matteo Ricci and his ability to introduce Catholicism into Chinese civilization in the sixteenth century. At the same moment, and not coincidentally, Dunne declared racial segregation a sin in 1945 and aided in the dismantling of California's restrictions on interracial marriage a few years later.[16]

As in the sixteenth and seventeenth centuries, racism in the mid-twentieth-century Church became seen as an obstacle to successful evangelization. The missionary field's leading figure became the Belgian Jesuit and Louvain professor Pierre Charles, S.J., who had begun holding seminars on planting Indigenous churches, not simply converting souls. Charles taught thousands of students, many of them future missionaries, and became a consultant to the Vatican. Catholic scholars influenced by Charles developed parallel programs in missiology at the Catholic University of Nijmegen and other Catholic universities, most notably in Rome.

Even as he trained future missionaries not to assume that European civilization was superior to that of the Indigenous peoples they hoped to convert, Charles battled racism within his own church and contemporary Europe. He authored one of the first, and only, Catholic attacks on the anti-Semitic Protocols of Zion and denounced the "political passion, as opposed to scientific reasoning, that underwrote such spurious texts. "It is difficult to understand," he explained, "how a circumspect observer could accept doctrine other than that of the substantial equality of all races."[17]

After the Second World War, and the Shoah, Jesuits quietly abandoned any restrictions on Jewish converts joining the Society.[18] As European colonial empires collapsed, more Jesuits urged their colleagues to distinguish conversion to Christianity from conversion to Western mores. In 1946, a Jesuit General Congregation could still refer in rote fashion to "missions among the infidels." One decade later another Jesuit General Congregation insisted on striving to "understand [the] culture, history and religious teachings" of Indigenous peoples.[19] A Belgian Jesuit coined a verb— "inculturate"—that became talismanic for successive generations of Catholic missionaries, signaling a turn away from soul by soul conversion to embedding Catholicism into local societies.[20]

Pushing this change forward were Catholics from the Global South. African Catholic students studying in Rome and Paris in the 1950s— including notables such as Senegal's future President, Leopold Senghor— founded journals and organized themselves to advocate for both political and theological decolonization.[21] The first Filipino leader of the Jesuits in the Philippines was Horacio de la Costa. De la Costa had been interned by the Japanese during World War II and had obtained a PhD in history from Harvard before returning to Manila. And as early as 1952 he insisted that

Catholicism should not be viewed as a Western import, but instead belonged "fully as much to Asia as to Europe."[22]

In the wake of the Second Vatican Council, the German Jesuit and theologian Karl Rahner posited the idea of a "world Church in a fully official way." In the nineteenth century the Church "exported a European religion as a commodity it did not really want to change . . . together with the rest of the culture and civilization it considered superior." The Council was different. The primary practical achievement of the council, after all, had been requiring the translation of the liturgy into the vernacular. "The victory of the vernacular in the church liturgy," Rahner argued, "signals unmistakably the coming-to-be of a world Church whose individual churches exist with a certain independence in their respective cultural spheres, inculturated, and no longer a European export."[23]

In the 1970s, Jesuits from the global South, including Latin America, South Asia, and the Philippines, where Horacio de la Costa was a key interlocutor, reflected on theological insights they might bring to the wider church. Pedro Arrupe, the Jesuit father general in the immediate postconciliar era, spent most of his career as a missionary in Japan and survived the dropping of the atomic bomb on Hiroshima. Visiting the Philippines, he explained that he could no longer distinguish between "mission" and "non-mission" territories. Filipino Jesuits must "answer the needs of the Philippines in the theological language and thought of the Philippines."[24] In the mid-twentieth century the largest single group of Jesuits lived in the United States. In the mid-twenty-first century, the largest single group of Jesuits comes from South Asia.

A more multicultural Society of Jesus will mean yet another reassessment of how Jesuits understand race. The outcome of that reassessment is uncertain, and African, Latin American, and South Asian Jesuits may approach these questions differently than scholars based in Western universities. But it does seem that the Jesuits and the wider Catholic Church are in an unusually fluid moment, with the erosion of the racial categories established in the early modern era and strengthened up through the mid-twentieth century. Assessing both the origins of these hierarchies and their evolution may be the most valuable contribution our contributors make. They goad future scholars to better understand how such hierarchies deform our contemporary church and world.

Notes

1.   R. R. Palmer, *The Age of the Democratic Revolution: A Political History of Europe and America, 1760–1800* (Princeton: Princeton University Press, [1959] 2014); Hilda Sabato, *Republics of the New World: The Revolutionary Political Experiment in 19th Century Latin America* (Princeton: Princeton University Press, 2018).

2.   Joep Van Gennip, "'Contulit Hos Virtus, Expulit Invidia': The Suppression of the Jesuits of the Flemish-Belgian Province," in *The Survival of the Jesuits in the Low Countries 1773–1850*, ed. Leo Kenis and Marc Lindeijer, S.J. (Leuven: Leuven University Press, 2019), 95.

3.   Chad M. Gasta, "Opera and Spanish Jesuit Evangelization in the New World," *Gestos* 22 (2007): 85–106; Margaret R. Ewalt, *Peripheral Wonders: Nature, Knowledge, and Enlightenment in Eighteenth Century Orinoco* (Lewisburg, PA: Rowman and Littlefield, 2008), 113; Charles E. Ronan, *Francisco Javier Clavijero, S.J., 1731–1787* (Chicago: Loyola University Press, 1977), 133.

4.   John T. McGreevy, *American Jesuits and the World: How an Embattled Religious Order Made Modern Catholicism Global* (Princeton: Princeton University Press, 2016), 16.

5.   General Congregation 21, Decree 14 [1829] in *For Matters of Greater Moment: The First Thirty Jesuit General Congregations. A Brief History and a Translation of the Decrees*, ed. John W. Padberg, S.J., Martín D. O'Keefe, S.J., and John L. McCarthy, S.J. (St. Louis, MO: Institute of Jesuit Sources, 1994), 440.

6.   David Nirenberg, "Was There Race Before Modernity?: The Example of Jewish Blood in Late Medieval Spain," in *Neighboring Faiths: Christianity, Islam and Judaism in the Middle Ages and Today*, ed. David Nirenberg (Chicago: University of Chicago Press, 2014), 169–90.

7.   Fifth General Congregation [1581], Decree 52 in *For Matters of Greater Moment*, 204.

8.   John T. McGreevy, *Catholicism and American Freedom: A History* (New York: W. W. Norton, 2003), 78.

9.   David I. Kertzer, *The Popes Against the Jews: The Vatican's Role in the Rise of Modern Anti-Semitism* (New York: Knopf, 2001), 135–46.

10.   Balázs Trencsényi, Maciej Janowski, Monika Baar, Maria Falina, and Michal Kopecek, *A History of Modern Political Thought in East Central Europe. Volume I: Negotiating Modernity in the "Long Nineteenth Century"* (Oxford: Oxford University Press, 2016), 552–53; Paul A. Hanebrink, *In Defense of Christian Hungary: Religion, Nationalism, and AntiSemitism, 1890–1944*, (Ithaca, NY: Cornell University Pres, 2006), 56.

11.   Aaron Pidel, S.J., "Erich Przywara, S. J. and 'Catholic Fascism': A Response to Paul Silas Peterson," *Journal for the History of Modern Theology/Zeitschrift für Neuere Theologiegeschichte* 23 (2016): 27–55.

12.   Gustav Gundlach, S.J., "Anti-Semitism," [1930] reprinted in Georges Passelecq and Bernhard Suchecky, *The Hidden Encyclical of Pius XI*, trans. Steven Rendall (New York: Harcourt Brace, 1997), 47–49

13. John Connelly, *From Enemy to Brother: The Revolution in Catholic Teaching on the Jews* (Cambridge: Harvard University Press, 2012), 23–24.

14. On the never released encyclical, *The Hidden Encyclical of Pius XI*.

15. Connelly, *From Enemy to Brother*, 213–16; 242–58.

16. John LaFarge, S.J., *Interracial Justice* (New York: America Press, 1937); David W. Southern, "But Think of the Kids: Catholic Interracialists and the Great Taboo of Race Mixing," *U. S. Catholic Historian* 16 (1998): 67–93; George Dunne, "The Sin of Segregation," *Commonweal* 42 (September 21, 1945): 542–45.

17. Jean Piroote, "La 'science des mission,' à Louvain: Le rôle des milieu louvanistes dans les développements de la missiologie et la rencontre des religions," in *L'Afrique et la mission: Terrains anciens, questions nouvelles avec Claude Prudhomme*, ed. Oissila Saaidia et Laurick Zerbini (Paris: Karthala, 2015), 198; Connelly, 54.

18. Twenty Ninth General Congregation [1946] Decree 8 in *For Matters of Greater Moment*, 625.

19. General Congregation 29, Decree 5 [1946] and General Congregation 30, Decree 54 [1957] in *For Matters of Greater Moment*, 624, 675.

20. J. Masson, "L'Église ouverte sur le monde," *Nouvelle Revue Théologique* 84 (1962): 1032–43, esp. 1038.

21. Elizabeth A. Foster, *African Catholic: Decolonization and the Transformation of the Church* (Cambridge, MA: Harvard University Press, 2019).

22. Horacio de la Costa, *The Jesuits in the Philippines, 1581–1768* (Cambridge, MA: Harvard University Press, 1961); Horacio de la Costa, S.J., "Riding the Whirlwind," *Social Order* 2 (1952), 247.

23. Karl Rahner, S.J., "Towards a Fundamental Theological Interpretation of Vatican II," *Theological Studies* 40 (1979): 716–27.

24. Provincials of the Society of Jesus, "The Jesuits in Latin America," [1968] in *Liberation Theology: A Documentary History*, ed. Alfred T. Hennelly (Maryknoll, NY: Orbis Books, 1990), 77–83; Horacio de la Costa, S.J., "The Missionary Apostolate in East and Southeast Asia," [1972] in Horacio de la Costa, S.J., *Selected Homilies and Religious Reflections*, ed. Robert M. Paterno, (Manila: Philippine Province of the Society of Jesus and Ateneo de Manila, 2002), 252–71; Pedro Arrupe, "Talk to the Jesuits of the Philippines," [September 19, 1971] in Arrupe, *Jesuit General in the Philippines*, (Manila: Philippine Province of the Society of Jesus and Ateneo de Manila University, 1972), 142; "Report on the Dialogue with the Father General," [September 19, 1971] in Arrupe, *Jesuit General in the Philippines*, 153.

Contributors

Liam Matthew Brockey is a professor of history at Michigan State University. He is the author of *The Visitor: André Palmeiro and the Jesuits in Asia* (Harvard University Press, 2014) and *Journey to the East: The Jesuit Mission to China, 1579–1724* (Harvard University Press, 2007; paperback 2008).

Emanuele Colombo is a professor of Catholic studies at Depaul University. His publications include *In viaggio. Gesuiti candidati alle missioni tra Antica e Nuova Compagnia* (Il Sole 24 Ore, 2014) (co-author with Marina Massimi), *Convertire i musulmani. L'esperienza di un gesuita spagnolo del Seicento* (Bruno Mondadori, 2007), and *Un gesuita inquieto: Carlo Antonio Casnedi (1643–1725) e il suo tempo* (Rubbettino, 2006).

Susan M. Deeds is a professor emerita at Northern Arizona University. She is the author of *Defiance and Deference in Colonial Mexico: Indians under Spanish Rule in Nueva Vizcaya* (University of Texas Press, 2003) and co-author (with Michael C. Meyer and William L. Sherman) of *The Course of Mexican History*, 6th–11th eds. (Oxford University Press, 1998–2018).

Sean Dempsey, S.J., is an assistant professor of history at Loyola Marymount University, where he teaches broadly in modern US history. His research is focused on the intersection of religion and politics in American cities after 1945. He is currently completing work on his first book, *The Politics of Dignity: Religion and the Making of Global Los Angeles*, under contract with the University of Chicago Press.

John T. McGreevy is the Francis A. McAnaney professor of history at the University of Notre Dame. His publications include *Parish Boundaries: The*

Catholic Encounter with Race in the Twentieth Century Urban North (University of Chicago Press, 1996), *Catholicism and American Freedom: A History* (W. W. Norton, 2003), and *American Jesuits and the World: How an Embattled Religious Order Made Modern Catholicism Global* (Princeton University Press, 2016).

Nathaniel Millett is an associate professor of history at Saint Louis University. He is the author of *Maroons of Prospect Bluff and their Quest for Freedom in the Atlantic World* (University Press of Florida, 2013).

J. Michelle Molina is an associate professor of history at Northwestern University. She is the author of *To Overcome Oneself: The Jesuit Ethic and the Spirit of Expansion* (University of California Press, 2013).

James M. O'Toole is a professor and the Clough Millennium chair in history at Boston College. His publications include *The Faithful: A History of Catholics in America* (Harvard University Press, 2008), *Passing for White: Race, Religion, and the Healy Family, 1820–1920* (University of Massachusetts Press, 2003), and *Militant and Triumphant: William Henry O'Connell and the Catholic Church in Boston, 1859–1944* (University of Notre Dame Press, 1992).

Charles H. Parker is a professor of history at Saint Louis University. His publications include *Global Calvinism: Conversion and Commerce in the Dutch Empire, 1600–1800* (Yale University Press, forthcoming), *Global Interactions in the Early Modern Age, 1400–1800* (Cambridge University Press, 2010), and *Faith on the Margins: Catholics and Catholicism in the Dutch Golden Age* (Harvard University Press, 2008).

Andrew Redden is a senior lecturer in Latin American history at the University of Liverpool. He is the author of *The Collapse of Time: The Martyrdom of Diego Ortiz (1571) by Antonio de la Calancha [1638]* (De Gruyter, 2016) and *Diabolism in Colonial Peru, 1560–1750* (Pickering & Chatto, 2008).

Erin Rowe is an associate professor of history at Johns Hopkins University. She is the author of *Black Saints in Early Modern Global Catholicism* (Cambridge University Press, 2019) and *Saint and Nation: Santiago, Teresa of Avila, and Plural Identities in Early Modern Spain* (Pennsylvania State University Press, 2011).

Index

Abernathy, Ralph, 228
abolitionism, 8, 264
Acaxees, 166, 176
Acevedo y Fonseca, Gaspar de Zúñiga, 99, 101, 126n9
Acosta, José de, 5, 40, 98; on calendar systems, 123; on China and Japan, 123–24; civilization hierarchy of, 125; on Indigenous people, 120–22; on migration, 121; on New World, 120–21; on oral tradition, 122; on Peru, 124; on pictographs, 124; salvific ethnology of, 114–24, 125
Acquaviva, Claudio, 23, 28–30, 99–101; letter to Possevino, 46n43; Possevino appeal to, 32–33, 36
Adam and Eve: descendants of, 65, 116, 118; sin of, 59, 119; whiteness of, 66
African Americans, 18; eugenics movement and, 9; in Jesuit schools, 216–20, 227; Jesuits refusing to educate, 14; recruiting students, 231; service to community, 214, 229; at SLU, 185; World War II veterans, 217
afterlife, 2; body in, 62, 64; Roa on, 63–64
Agassiz, Louis, 13
Age of Democratic Revolution, 261
Akbari, Suzanne, 11
Alarcón, Garcia Girón de, 31
Alliance of Theatrical and Stage Employees (IATSE), 252–53
Almeida, Luís de, 6, 81

alumbrado movement, 24
Álvarez, Jorge, 56
An American Dilemma (Myrdal), 217
American Freedom and Catholic Power (Blanshard), 239, 254
Anchieta, José de, 38
Andalusia, 24, 53; Jesuits, slavery in, 54–58; Roa in, 54–56
anticommunism, 239, 241, 248–49, 253
anti-Judaism, 262, 264
anti-Semitism, 58, 262, 264, 266
apartheid, 9–10
Apostles of Empire (McShea), 4
Araoz, Antonio de, 25–26
Aristotle, 8
Arrupe, Pedro, 14–15, 231; on American Negro, 214, 216; on racism, 213–14
Ásia Extrema (Gouvea), 86–87
Association of Black Collegians, 197
Atlantis, 121
Augustine of Hippo, 63–64
Avila, Alonso de, 55
Avila, Juan de, 24
Aztecas, 5, 120, 165

Bangha, Bela, 264
Bannon, John Francis, 200–201
baptism, 34; correct baptism, 57–58; forced baptism, 55, 57–58; *Instrucción que han de guardar los hermanos administradores de haciendas del campo* on, 152–53; Jesuit method, 58, 59; for protection against disease, 169

CPSIA information can be obtained
at www.ICGtesting.com
Printed in the USA
LVHW102156300622
722395LV00035B/60

9 780826 363671